"*Counseling the Hard*
counseling. Friends of biblical counseling will find
stretched to grow at every point. Critics of biblical counseling will see long-standing caricatures dissolve. True wisdom comes exquisitely balanced. This book breathes forth the fragrance of such wisdom. I hope all readers share something of my bottom-line response: Father of all mercies, make my life and my counseling embody more love and more truth, more of all good gifts and worthy skills."

—***David Powlison,*** faculty member and counselor, Christian Counseling & Educational Foundation (CCEF); editor, *The Journal of Biblical Counseling*

"*Counseling the Hard Cases* is an excellent example of how to do biblical counseling that is both true to God's Word and practically relevant to the complex issues behind the fallen human heart. I commend all these competent counselors for giving us tremendous insight into helping people gain much hope and help for their spiritual lives. I especially appreciated the contributor's singular commitment to the sufficiency and superiority of Scripture in counseling. May this book be greatly used by counselors, for their counselees, and in the teaching of counseling."

—***Lance Quinn,*** pastor, Grace Advance, Grace Community Church, Sun Valley, California

"While many books have *argued* for the sufficiency of Scripture, few have *demonstrated* sufficiency by showing what it looks like in real-life problems. That's why *Counseling the Hard Cases* will be a valuable resource for both counselors and pastors—it will show that God's Word is fully adequate to address life's hardest problems."

—***Deepak Reju,*** pastor of biblical counseling and families, Capitol Hill Baptist Church, Washington, DC

"'Well, Dr. Mack, that's all very nice, but what do you do when people have really serious problems?' With one brief statement the woman interviewing me communicated her view about the insufficiency of Scripture in providing help for people who have what she and others would consider hard and complex counseling cases. Regrettably, that woman's perspective represents the opinion of many, both Christian and non-Christian. I wish I could have directed her to a book with examples of people receiving help by the skillful and accurate use of Scripture, but, at the time I met her, *Counseling the Hard Cases* had not yet been written. I'm glad it is now available, and I predict that it will be mightily used by our Lord in the strengthening of people's faith in and use of God's all-sufficient and superior Word."

—***Wayne Mack,*** biblical counselor, author, and trainer ministering in South Africa

Counseling the Hard Cases

True Stories Illustrating the Sufficiency of God's Resources in Scripture

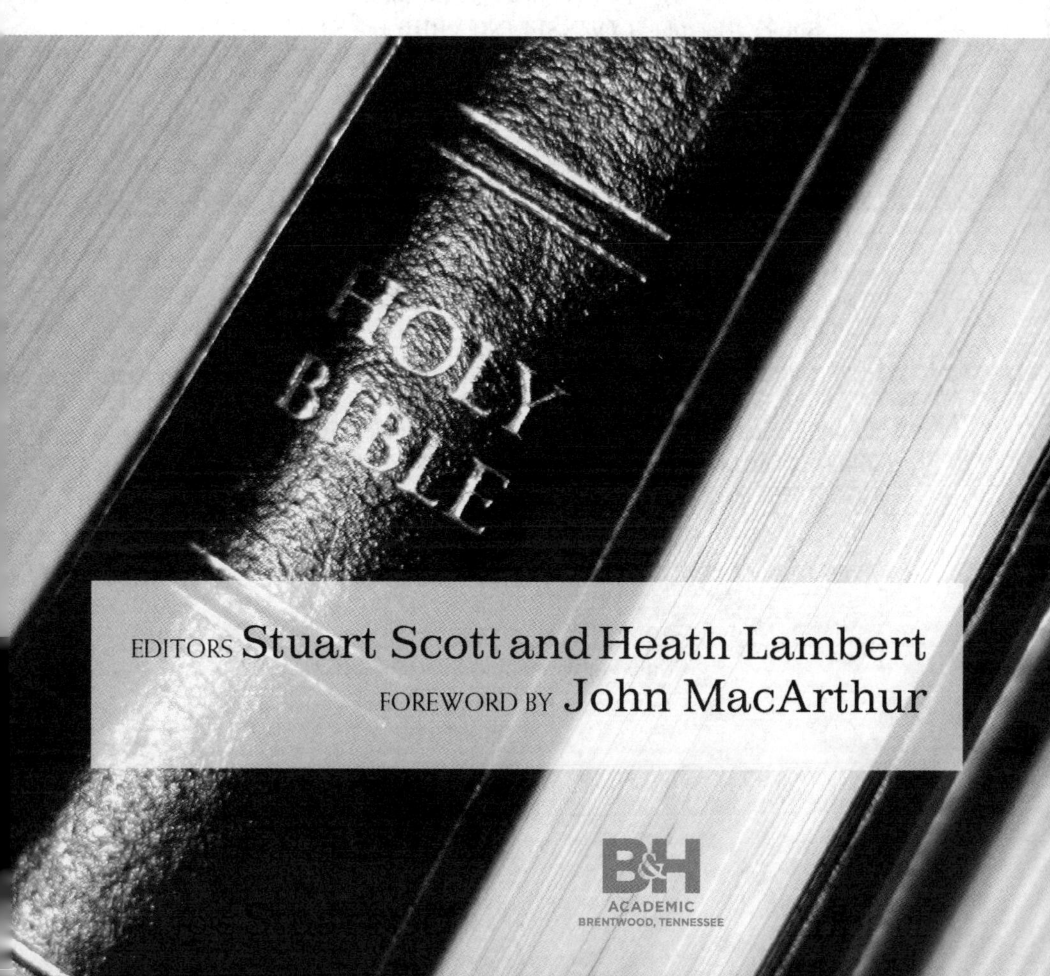

EDITORS Stuart Scott and Heath Lambert
FOREWORD BY John MacArthur

B&H
ACADEMIC
BRENTWOOD, TENNESSEE

Counseling the Hard Cases: True Stories Illustrating the Sufficiency of God's Resources in Scripture

ISBN: 978-1-4336-8579-8

Published by B&H Publishing Group
Brentwood, Tennessee

(Previously published 2012 in hard cover,
ISBN: 978-1-4336-7222-4, now O.P.)

Dewey Decimal Classification: 253.5
Subject Heading: COUNSELING \ BIBLE—STUDY AND TEACHING \ SPIRITUAL HEALING

Printed in the United States of America

15 16 17 18 19 20 • 28 27 26 25 24

To all those counselees who humbly sought help,
received God's grace to change,
and are now being used by Christ to counsel others.
May God bless you.

Contents

FOREWORD

THE BIBLICAL COUNSELING MOVEMENT HAS long been caricatured by its various critics as shallow, superficial, and largely ineffective for the greater challenges men and women face in this life. Those critics might cite instances of people giving bad or even hurtful advice while *claiming* to be doing biblical counseling. But authentic biblical counseling is simply biblical wisdom, properly applied by spiritually mature counselors. How could that be hurtful?

When godly people, armed with the confidence that God's Word is entirely sufficient, prayerfully and skillfully, gently but firmly come alongside those who are confused, lost, hurting, or otherwise struggling with some personal or spiritual dilemma, the Lord is sovereignly disposed to use his Word through such counsel in ways that please him. His Word is the one thing that never returns void (Isa 55:11).

This is why I am happy to commend to you this book: *Counseling the Hard Cases: True Stories Illustrating the Sufficiency of God's Resources in Scripture.* Its contributors are unified in their commitment to Scripture as the sufficient mode *and* method of counseling. That is the very commitment I have sought to maintain for all my years as pastor-teacher here at Grace

Community Church. It is likewise the shared commitment of our faculty in training our students at The Master's College and Seminary. Each one of us would say with settled conviction: "Your testimonies are my delight; they are my counselors" (Ps 119:24 ESV).

If you want to read firsthand examples of caring, wise, and biblically sound counsel being applied to those who are struggling with the perplexities of living in a fallen world, then read on. The approach to counseling modeled here comes from experienced men and women who believe that God's Word is totally adequate to handle anything and everything the world, the flesh, and the Devil may throw at the believer. These seasoned counselors are—as I am—thoroughly convinced that no manmade method of counseling is equal to the 66 books of the Bible in depth, power, or enduring efficacy.

The sufficiency and authority of Scripture has been the central theme of my ministry for more than half a century, and I am profoundly grateful that one of the fundamental principles on which the biblical counseling movement is based is a commitment to that same principle. In the words of Ps 19:7–11 (ESV):

> The law of the Lord is perfect, reviving the soul; the testimony of the Lord is sure, making wise the simple; the precepts of the Lord are right, rejoicing the heart; the commandment of the Lord is pure, enlightening the eyes; the fear of the Lord is clean, enduring forever; the rules of the Lord are true, and righteous altogether. More to be desired are they than gold, even much fine gold; sweeter also than honey and drippings of the honeycomb. Moreover, by them is your servant warned; in keeping them there is great reward.

May you profit from this book as you read from competent counselors who take God's Word seriously. Allow the insights they've gained from Scripture to shape your own approach to helping people who are hurting.

John MacArthur, pastor-teacher
Grace Community Church, Sun Valley, California
President, The Master's College and Seminary

Preface

THIS IS A BOOK OF stories about real people—all of whom have sought counseling during crisis moments in their lives. In this book you'll meet "Ashley," "Tony," "Brian," "Sarah," "Clark," "Mariana," and others—real people with faces, addresses, lives, and people who love them. Each suffers from significant emotional and spiritual problems. They received some of the most serious diagnoses it is possible to receive in this world: anorexia, bipolar, postpartum depression, and dissociative identity disorder. They struggled with homosexuality, worry, and rage. They sought help from secular, medical, and religious professionals before finally coming to biblical counselors for help. This is not only a book about people with problems; it is also a book about how God uses his Word to guide his people to become instruments of grace in the lives of those with very serious problems, bringing restoration, hope, peace, and healing to them.

These stories are important. They are powerful accounts that testify to the effectiveness of God's Son, God's Word, and God's church in helping people with some of the hardest counseling conundrums. Large groups of Christians are not yet aware that God has given his people reliable and significant resources sufficient to help people with any problems that require counseling.

These stories must be told because we long for all Christians to know the Scriptures and the power of God (Matt 22:29).

Our Audience

We offer this book with several different groups of people in mind. First, we write for ministers of the gospel struggling on the front lines of the kingdom of God. Daily you encounter people who are struggling in significant and profound ways. You are involved in the weary task of sitting with people and trying to help them anchor their lives to Scripture while pointing them to the Redeemer found therein. We want to encourage you in your labors. Our prayer is that this book will be effective to show you that Jesus Christ always has sufficient power to help, no matter how severe the difficulty.

Second, we write for students of biblical counseling. Many thousands of students are enrolled all across the country in undergraduate courses, master's degrees, and doctoral programs focused on biblical counseling. More Christians are being equipped by their local churches and various other training programs to help address and minister to the onslaught of problems faced in the modern context of ministry. We are grateful for your labors in preparing for gospel ministry. We pray that this book will strengthen you in the Scriptures. The Word of God is indeed adequate to help even the most troubled.

Finally, we write to those who disagree with us about the sufficiency of Scripture in the counseling process. Whether you consider yourself an integrationist, a Christian counselor, or a Christian psychologist, differences of opinion regarding the sufficiency of God's Word to administer an effective counseling ministry may divide us. Though the issues behind that disagreement are important and significant, we are united by something much more profound—the blood of Jesus Christ. In light of that union, it is regrettable when the exchanges between our various groups are not loving and productive. We want to confess plainly in this book that you are our brothers and sisters in Christ, and we love you. We hope you will not sense that we are bashing anyone or that we think we have nothing to learn from those with whom we disagree. Instead, we hope you will see that the contributors of this book are men and women who are passionate about Christ and his perfect Word. We long for the most troubled people to find counselors who will point them to our matchless Savior, the only source for true and lasting healing.

We will build some fences in this book, but that is not a bad thing. Fences keep things organized, and you can always talk over them and build strong relationships despite the divide. We hope many conversations and relationships will continue to develop among our various movements. We offer this book to you—our coheirs in Christ—in humility and love, with many prayers that God might be pleased to give you some glimpse of the profundities of Scripture that you may not yet fully appreciate.

A Few Words About Reading This Book

Whether you are a minister of the gospel, a student of counseling, or an advocate of a different counseling position, a few things will be helpful for you to understand as you read. First, our contributors are active counselors who describe actual people with real problems. They have endeavored to stay as true to the actual events as possible. Because of the personal nature of the issues, however, it is important to preserve the confidentially of all those who sought help. We have protected their personal information in three different ways. Some case studies in this book change the identifying information of the person discussed. The details of the problem are the same, but the personal information has been altered so that the counselee remains anonymous. Other case studies are composites. In these case studies the counselor has helped a number of different people with the same problem and has chosen to show their approach to the issue by blending the stories of several different counselees. Finally, some contributors have obtained explicit permission from those they helped to share their stories without anonymity.

Second, this is a book of stories that describe how the various contributors proceeded through counseling with people in their individual situations. It is not a methodology that describes how you should proceed with every counselee experiencing a similar problem. Of course there will be commonalities and overlap, but it is essential to affirm that in God's world no two situations are exactly the same. Though the chapters provide methodological guidance for how you might move forward in comparable situations, please do not assume that what is appropriate in one context is always appropriate in another.

Acknowledgments

A project like this is always a collaborative effort, and so we have many people to thank. First, we are thankful to all of the contributors to this book. They each have very busy ministries and took the time to share their experiences. We appreciate their work on this project and their labor for the kingdom of Jesus in their other ministries. We have been encouraged in our walks with Christ as we have seen their ministries pictured in the chapters of this book.

Second, we are also grateful for the team at B&H Publishers. In particular, we are thankful for Jim Baird and Chris Cowan. Many of the contributors to this volume as well as both editors experienced family and medical emergencies during the work on this book. Such emergencies were often serious and made it difficult to reach deadlines. We were encouraged by the grace and flexibility of Jim and Chris in the midst of such circumstances. Working with them was always a joy.

Third, in our work of editing, we received a great deal of help. Many different people assisted in a number of ways, but it is important to mention the work of three people in particular. Joshua Clutterham took several days out of his busy schedule to help us do some massive work on a few chapters. David Powlison took an entire day to review the first chapter and provide helpful feedback. Finally, David "Gunner" Gundersen served as our editorial assistant for this book. Gunner carefully read each chapter, made helpful stylistic changes, and made sure each chapter was formatted correctly. We *never* could have finished this book if it were not for his incredible efforts.

Finally, we are thankful for you and your commitment to read this book. It is with great delight that we present to you *Counseling the Hard Cases: True Stories Illustrating the Sufficiency of God's Resources in Scripture.* As you read the stories of these men and women, we pray that your life will be gripped by the Savior who gripped them. May the same Word that strengthened them strengthen you.

Stuart Scott & Heath Lambert
Summer 2011
Louisville, Kentucky

Chapter 1

Introduction: The Sufficiency of Scripture, the Biblical Counseling Movement, and the Purpose of This Book

Heath Lambert

THIS BOOK IS A COLLECTION of true accounts about real people. The men and women featured here received hope, peace, joy, and dramatic change in their lives from Jesus Christ as they met with him in the pages of his Word, the Bible. These stories recount the details of how these people came to seek biblical counseling for problems they were experiencing in their lives, how caring Christians assisted them and oriented them toward Jesus, and how they encountered the rich and transforming presence of Christ through his Word in the community of the church.

The problems recounted in these stories are not trivial. The people in the following pages struggled with some of the most difficult and complex problems that any human can encounter in this life. They struggled with pain and difficulty for weeks, months, and even years, seeking help from many sources. Our contributors engaged them in relationship, walked with them through difficulty, and watched as Jesus used the ministry of counseling to bring life, comfort, and transformation.

These counselors-turned-storytellers ministered out of the shared conviction that God has given his people adequate resources to do the work of conversational ministry. They believe that God has given his people a Savior, a Bible, and a church—all of which equip his people to tackle the kinds of problems that surface in counseling—even when those problems are extremely challenging. They believe that God equips his people to counsel the hard cases.

If you are familiar with the counseling conversations taking place among Christians over the last several decades, you know that this is an audacious assertion. The church has been engaged in an ongoing debate over the resources necessary for counseling. Most do not agree with the conviction that Christians have sufficient resources to inform counseling conversations. The contributors of our book believe, however, that God has given his church all the graces necessary to do counseling. God's inerrant, authoritative, and sufficient Word reveals a church, calls all Christians to ministry in that church, identifies the Spirit as the empowering force for that ministry, points in the direction of prayer as the dynamic means of encountering God, and demonstrates that all these belong to Christians because of the finished work of Christ. Because of this strong disagreement over sufficiency, we want to frame the counseling context of these stories before telling them. The scenarios did not arise in a vacuum, and they must be retold in the context of the much larger Christian conversation about counseling resources. That conversation has been dominated by questions about the sufficiency of Scripture.

Counseling Debates and the Sufficiency of Scripture

Is Scripture sufficient to inform all the possible counseling situations in this fallen world? The implications of such a question are massive. If Scripture is an overflowing source of wisdom for all counseling, then the pressing task for Christians is to be busy mining the text of Scripture for an understanding of the manifold problems people experience and for the wisdom to help them. If Scripture, though valuable and useful, is ultimately inadequate as a source of wisdom for all counseling, then the urgent work is to look to the corpus of secular psychology for those truths that supply the Bible's lack. The debate revolves around the relationship between an understanding of hard problems, the nature of counseling, the contents of Scripture, and the role of secular psychology. How we answer the question about the sufficiency of Scripture ultimately describes our understanding of the content of Scripture and defines the kind of literature counselors should use to help them in their work—whether theological or psychological in nature. Christians have disagreed about this question. The rhetoric has been bitter at times.[1] Of course, all such disagreements are a result of our fallen nature and are also regrettable (Phil 2:2; 1 Pet 3:8). Yet, as unfortunate as such disagreements have been, they have revealed some honest and important issues. That is to say that when we talk about these matters, we are talking about the resources and methods we use to minister to people and whether those people are ultimately helped. Such issues are far from inconsequential.

The debate began in the late 1960s with the work of Jay Adams. By the time Adams began to write about counseling, it had been over a century since a Christian had written a book explaining how to use the Bible as *the* source of wisdom to help people with their counseling-related problems.[2] It is not possible here to address all of the manifold factors that led to this situation.[3] The point to understand is that by the middle of the twentieth century most Christians did not believe that the Bible was a book that was pointedly relevant for the kinds of conversations that happen when counseling someone with hard problems. Instead, mainline

---

[1] See Gary Collins, "An Integration Response," in *Psychology & Christianity: Four Views*, ed. Eric L. Johnson and Stanton L. Jones (Downers Grove: InterVarsity, 2000), 232; Mark R. McMinn and Timothy R. Phillips, "Introduction: Psychology, Theology & Care for the Soul," in *Care for the Soul*, ed. Mark R. McMinn and Timothy R. Phillips (Downers Grove: InterVarsity, 2001), 12–13.

[2] Ichabod Spencer, *A Pastor's Sketches* (Vestavia Hills, AL: Solid Ground, 2001).

[3] For more information, however, see Heath Lambert, *The Biblical Counseling Movement After Adams* (Wheaton: Crossway, 2011).

Protestant pastors began to mix their liberal theology with secular psychological principles to create what became known as "clinical pastoral care." Later, so-called integrationists sought to do the same thing but replaced liberal theology with conservative theology. The evangelical commitments of the integration movement were an improvement. It led to less optimism and naiveté concerning the worldview commitments of secular psychologists, but the outcome was the same. Christians—whether liberal or conservative—continued to believe that the Christian counseling resources found in the Bible were weak while secular resources for counseling found in the modern psychological corpus were strong.[4]

By the middle of the twentieth century, the Christian effort to help people with their problems had basically become a conversation about how much and what kind of secular psychology to add to the inadequacies of Scripture to offer *real* help. This conversation turned into a debate with the groundbreaking ministry of Adams. His central contribution to Christian counseling was a bold and controversial claim that the task of counseling was a theological enterprise that should be primarily informed by a commitment to God's Word. He further argued that any attempt by the discipline of psychology to address counseling-related issues must be judged according to biblical standards rather than secular ones. In his first book on counseling, Adams stated:

> All concepts, terms and methods used in counseling need to be re-examined biblically. Not one thing can be accepted from the past (or the present) without biblical warrant. . . . I have been engrossed in the project of

---

[4] For more information tracing the development of mainline Protestantism to the integration movement, see E. Brooks Holifield, *A History of Pastoral Care in America* (Nashville: Abingdon, 1983); Donald Capps, *Biblical Approaches to Pastoral Counseling* (Philadelphia: Westminster, 1981); Harry Emerson Fosdick, *The Living of These Days* (New York: Harper & Row, 1956), 214–15, 280; Seward Hiltner and Lowell Colston, *The Context of Pastoral Counseling* (Nashville: Abingdon, 1961); Andrew Abbott, *The System of Professions: An Essay on the Division of Expert Labor* (Chicago: University of Chicago, 1988); Howard Clinebell, *Basic Types of Pastoral Counseling* (Nashville: Abingdon, 1966); Anton T. Boisen, *The Exploration of the Inner World: A Study of Mental Disorder and Religious Experience* (New York: Harper & Row, 1954).

> developing biblical counseling and have uncovered what I consider to be a number of important scriptural principles. It is amazing to discover how much the Bible has to say about counseling, and how fresh the biblical approach is. The complete trustworthiness of Scripture in dealing with people has been demonstrated. There have been dramatic results. . . . Not only have people's immediate problems been resolved, but there have also been solutions to all sorts of long-term problems as well. . . . The conclusions in the book are not based upon scientific findings. My method is presuppositional. I avowedly accept the inerrant Bible as the standard of all faith and practice. The Scriptures, therefore, are the basis, and contain the criteria by which I have sought to make every judgment.[5]

With these words the biblical counseling movement was launched, and the debate about the sufficiency of Scripture for counseling followed hard in its wake.

Since the 1950s a number of different groups have articulated different counseling theories. There have been many different views of how the Christian faith relates to psychology.[6] Each position possesses critical distinctions that create boundaries between the other views. Basically, three groups have emerged: One group is secular psychology, which believes that the Bible is completely irrelevant to counseling. Another group is biblical counseling, which believes that the Bible is sufficient for counseling. A third group takes their cures from the first and believes that the Bible is relevant to counseling but insufficient for it. In this

---

[5] Jay Adams, *Competent to Counsel* (Grand Rapids: Zondervan, 1970), xviii–xxi. In the very next line Adams clearly stated that his commitment to Scripture did not mean that he believed his own interpretation of Scripture to be infallible. He further qualified his strong assertions by saying that he did not reject science but rather welcomed it as "[a] useful adjunct for the purposes of illustrating, filling in generalizations with specifics, and challenging wrong human interpretations of Scripture, thereby forcing the student to restudy the Scriptures. However, in the area of psychiatry, science largely has given way to humanistic philosophy and gross speculation."

[6] Eric L. Johnson, ed., *Psychology and Christianity: Five Views*, 2nd ed. (Downers Grove: IVP Academic, 2010), 29–38.

chapter I refer to this large, complex third group of evangelicals as Christian counselors.[7] There are other issues in play, but the chief disagreement remains the perennial question of the adequacy of the contents of Scripture to inform counseling comprehensively.[8]

The Sufficiency of Scripture

Since this debate began, Adams, together with his heirs in the biblical counseling movement, have defended Scripture's sufficiency against Christian counselors who advocate an insufficiency position concerning Scripture's relationship to counseling.[9] The biblical counseling view of sufficiency is not simplistic as critics have charged: How can you believe that all information about

---

[7] Within this large group of Christian counselors, I include the integration movement, the Christian psychology movement, and the transformational psychology position.

[8] In the pages that follow I talk over the sufficiency fence with two neighbors in counseling. I interact with Eric Johnson, *Foundation for Soul Care: A Christian Psychology Proposal* (Downers Grove: IVP Academic, 2007) and Stan Jones, "An Integration View" in *Psychology and Christianity: Five Views*, ed. Eric Johnson, 2nd ed. (Downers Grove: IVP Academic, 2010), 101–26. I also make a few references to Stan Jones and Richard Butman of *Modern Psychotherapies: A Comprehensive Christian Appraisal* (Downers Grove: InterVarsity, 1991). Johnson identifies himself as a Christian psychologist, whereas Jones and Butman refer to themselves as integrationists. The two groups are alike in that neither affirms the sufficiency of Scripture for counseling. They are also alike in that each advances strong arguments against the sufficiency of Scripture for counseling—many of which have not received an adequate response at this point. I appreciate and have learned much from each man. In fact, Johnson taught some of my doctoral courses, and I consider him a friend. I hope that my words about the positions of all three are both truthful and loving (Eph 4:15).

[9] Though many in Adams's biblical counseling movement have advanced, developed, and refined some elements of his model, every biblical counselor has followed him in a commitment to the sufficiency of Scripture. Some have charged that many in the biblical counseling movement have disagreed about whether the Scriptures are adequate for counseling. But the truth is that the biblical counseling movement has been united in an unshakable commitment to the sufficiency of Scripture in helping people with their counseling-related problems. For just one example, see the statement on Scripture's sufficiency from the Biblical Counseling Coalition (BCC) at http://biblicalcounselingcoalition.org/about/confessional-statement. This BCC statement was approved by a diverse group of biblical counselors from almost every institution in the country committed to biblical counseling—including most of the contributors to this volume. That so many could sign such a robust statement stands as a testimony to the unity of the movement on this issue.

people is in the Bible? How can you reduce counseling to quoting Bible verses? Biblical counselors have never articulated such simplistic caricatures created by critics. Instead, they have stated their position in dynamic and nuanced terms. Biblical counselors have advanced their belief that Scripture is an ample source of wisdom for counseling ministry in two principal ways. First, biblical counselors have affirmed sufficiency by redefining secular psychology's diagnosis of the problems people face. Second, biblical counselors have affirmed Scripture's sufficiency by paying careful attention to the content of the Bible. Each of these is engaged in turn.

Redefining Secular Psychological Diagnoses

Modern psychologies have a secular, anthropocentric starting point. This has pervasive effects beginning with diagnostic categories. From the very beginning, psychologists have sought to help people with their life problems apart from any awareness of God, Christ, sin, the purposes of God in suffering, and Holy Scripture.[10] Secular psychology proceeds on the assumption that people can be understood, and their problems ameliorated, in a thoroughly man-centered way. Of course, there is nothing shocking about this. Christians do not expect unregenerate people to behave and think like regenerate people (1 Cor 2:14–16). What is shocking is that Christians themselves so often look to their theories about people, their understandings of their problems, and their efforts at assistance as the central resource for helping others. Too often Christians fail to consider that God has revealed his own competing understanding of what is wrong with people, along with startlingly different prescriptions for what people need and how to help.

When Adams founded the biblical counseling movement, he was concerned that the church had imported secular diagnostic categories and had ignored the way problems are explained in the pages of Scripture. He argued:

---

[10] Sigmund Freud, *The Question of Lay Analysis* (New York: Norton and Company, 1950). Cf. Freud, *Psychoanalysis and Faith* (New York: Basic Books, 1964), 104.

> Organic malfunctions affecting the brain that are caused by brain damage, tumors, gene inheritance, glandular or chemical disorders, validly may be termed mental illnesses. But at the same time a vast number of other human problems have been classified as mental illnesses for which there is no evidence that they have been engendered by disease or illness at all. As a description of many of these problems, the term mental illness is nothing more than a figure of speech, and in most cases a poor one at that. . . . [The problem with the "mentally ill"] is autogenic; it is in themselves. The fundamental bent of fallen human nature is away from God. Man is born in sin, goes astray "from his mother's womb speaking lies" (Psalm 58:3), and will therefore naturally (by nature) attempt various sinful dodges in an attempt to avoid facing up to his sin. He will fall into varying styles of sin according to the short term successes or failures of the particular sinful responses which he makes to life's problems. Apart from organically generated difficulties, the "mentally ill" are really people with unsolved personal problems.[11]

Adams articulated the fundamental critique of secular psychology: their understanding of people's problems is oriented away from God. When psychologists diagnose persons with difficulties they see medical problems, developmental difficulties, and dysfunctional behaviors. They do not see the operations of sin. They do not see guilty people who create difficulties for themselves and exacerbate existing problems by their moral failures before God. They do not see innocent people who are menaced by those who transgress against them. They do not see God the Savior of sinners as the refuge for the afflicted. In missing these categories, secularists miss reality (Rom 1:18–23).

Secular psychologists cannot truly understand the problems people have because people's problems are deeply theological. Secularists suppress the truth in unrighteousness and so miss the

---

[11] Adams, *Competent to Counsel*, 28–29.

godward dimension at the root of all problems that lead to counseling. None of this means that advocates for sufficiency have nothing to learn from science or from secular efforts at helping people. Biblical counselors can learn much, and they have been saying this from the beginning.[12] In fact, biblical counselors have consistently stated that the *observations* of secular psychology can often fill in gaps for—and provoke biblical counselors to more careful biblical reflection about—all manner of issues. The secular interpretations of those observations (as well as the efforts at ministry) by psychologists are what biblical counselors have objected to since they are contaminated by an atheistic worldview. For biblical counselors, secular psychology—although able to observe many things—is unable to interpret the significance behind their observations.

It is difficult to overstate the importance of this argument. Christian counselors, believing that Scripture is ultimately insufficient for counseling, argue that secular approaches to counseling address more issues and deal more profoundly with them than the biblical authors do.[13] They fail to understand that all problems in living—emotional, mental, relational, behavioral—have a spiritual core. This is a powerful argument for the adequacy of Scripture's counseling resources. It claims that a biblical understanding of the problems people have, which is rooted in life lived before a sovereign God, has been hijacked by humanistic thinkers and thus secularized. This argument turns the debate on its head: the real concern is not with the sufficiency of Scripture but with the sufficiency of psychology. When problems are understood in the light of Christ's light, it is psychology—not Scripture—that is truly insufficient to help people.

---

[12] Adams, *Competent to Counsel*, xxi; Jay Adams, *What About Nouthetic Counseling?* (Grand Rapids: Zondervan, 1976), 31; Wayne A. Mack, "What Is Biblical Counseling?" in *Totally Sufficient*, ed. Ed Hindson and Howard Eyrich (Ross-Shire, Great Britain: Christian Focus, 2004), 51; David Powlison, "Questions at the Crossroads: The Care of Souls & Modern Psychotherapies," in *Care for the Soul*, ed. Mark R. McMinn and Timothy R. Phillips (Downers Grove: InterVarsity, 2001), 14–15.

[13] Jones, "An Integration View," 108–15.

Paying Careful Attention to the Contents of Scripture

Redefining secular psychological diagnoses into theological categories is not the only way biblical counselors have advanced an understanding of the sufficiency of Scripture. Careful investigation into the contents of Scripture has also marked the mission. Biblical counselors have shown how a correct understanding of the contents of Scripture leads to a conclusion that the Bible is sufficient for counseling ministry. Over the years biblical counselors have used a number of different arguments about the canon of Scripture to advance their belief in the sufficiency of God's Word. These arguments fall reasonably into four categories.

Biblical texts. First, biblical counselors have argued for the sufficiency of Scripture for counseling by highlighting specific biblical texts. It is impossible to highlight every passage that directly bears on the nature of Scripture's sufficiency for counseling. It is only necessary to focus on two classic passages. One text that biblical counselors have turned to time and again is 2 Tim 3:14–17, where Paul wrote to Timothy:

> But as for you, continue in what you have learned and firmly believed. You know those who taught you, and you know that from childhood you have known the sacred Scriptures, which are able to give you wisdom for salvation through faith in Christ Jesus. All Scripture is inspired by God and is profitable for teaching, for rebuking, for correcting, for training in righteousness, so that the man of God may be complete, equipped for every good work.

This passage has been used by many biblical counselors to support their claim that Scripture is sufficient to provide the wisdom necessary to solve problems requiring counseling. Christian counselors have argued, however, that this text merely shows that Scripture is sufficient to make us wise for salvation, not that it is adequate to address the many different counseling-related problems we might face.[14] David Powlison responded:

---

[14] Johnson, *Foundations*, 180–86; Jones and Butman, *Modern Psychotherapies*, 26–27.

> Scripture proclaims itself as that which makes us "wise unto salvation." This is a comprehensive description of transforming human life from all that ails us. This same passage goes on to speak of the Spirit's words as purposing to *teach* us. The utter simplicity and unsearchable complexity of Scripture enlightens us about God, about ourselves, about good and evil, true and false, grace and judgment, about the world that surrounds us with its many forms of suffering and beguilement, with its opportunities to shed light into darkness. Through such teaching, riveted to particular people in particular situations, God exposes in specific detail what is wrong with human life. No deeper or truer or better analysis of the human condition can be concocted.[15]

Powlison understands salvation here in maximalist terms. Counseling theorists who find the Scriptures insufficient seem to understand "salvation" here in minimalistic terms. In 2 Timothy, salvation is not a limiting term but rather a mammoth expression referring to all of the problems from which Jesus intends to redeem his people. Will there be dissociative identity disorder in heaven? No. How about obsessive-compulsive disorder? No. Postpartum depression? Not a chance. Indeed, none of the difficulties in living mentioned in this book will exist in heaven. Why? Because these problems will finally be eradicated by the precious blood of Jesus and the life-giving Spirit in God's great work of salvation.[16]

The full salvation that Jesus brings is not instantaneous. It grows slowly over time. This is why the rest of the 2 Timothy passage is vitally important. Salvation happens in a process—the believer is "*train[ed]* in righteousness." We grow up. The

---

[15] David Powlison, "Is the Adonis Complex in *Your* Bible?" *The Journal of Biblical Counseling* 22, no. 2 (2004): 43.

[16] Neither will there be difficulties that are obviously physical in nature. That is a different matter, however, because the Bible addresses spiritual and physical issues in an asymmetrical way. "Even though our outer person is being destroyed, our inner person is being renewed day by day" (2 Cor 4:16). The Bible indicates with the hope that is in Christ, it is possible for our spiritual problems (our difficulties requiring a counseling solution) to recede. The Bible never indicates this to be the case with regard to our physical problems.

Scriptures are critical to help us grow. The Scriptures impart instruction (teaching). The Bible makes us aware of our problems (reproof). The Scriptures are profitable for pointing in the direction of positive change (correction).

If you pay attention to these categories, you can see how they are the elements of any halfway decent counseling theory—religious or secular. All counseling theories possess some apprehension of what is wrong with people (a "diagnosis" or version of reproof); what should be right (a goal of healthy humanness—a version of correction); some process of communicating that understanding; and some theory of what the change process might look like ("teaching" and "training"). All counseling theories take this form even though the contents are radically divergent. Scripture takes this form. To say that the Bible is profitable for these things is tantamount to saying that Scripture is profitable for counseling. A person only misses this connection when he misconstrues problems in living by employing secular categories and demanding that Scripture speak in those same categories.

Another passage often highlighted by biblical counselors is 2 Pet 1:3–4:

> His divine power has given us everything required for life and godliness through the knowledge of him who called us by his own glory and goodness. By these he has given us very great and precious promises, so that through them you may share in the divine nature, escaping the corruption that is in the world because of evil desires.

Ed Bulkley described this passage as one that clearly affirms the sufficiency of Scripture for counseling:

> A necessary presupposition of biblical counseling is that God has indeed provided *every* essential truth the believer needs for a happy, fulfilling life in Christ Jesus. It is the belief that God has not left us lacking in *any* sense. The apostle Peter states it emphatically. . . . Note the word *everything*. God has provided absolutely *everything* man needs for physical and spiritual life. This is a primary

> consideration. If Peter is correct, then God has given us all the information we need to function successfully in this life. *Every* essential truth, *every* essential principle, *every* essential technique for solving human problems has been delivered in God's Word.[17]

Biblical counselors believe that Christians possess everything necessary to help people with their nonmedical problems (2 Pet 1:3–4). Peter does not teach that Christians have access to everything there is to know about everything but that we have access to everything *necessary*. We possess everything *essential*. We have *Christ*. God's Word provides Christians with what we need for the counseling ministry.

This granting of all essential things flows from the faithfulness of God in Christ. That is to say that God has provided these essentials *in Christ*. The Bible is sufficient because Christ is sufficient, and God shows us in his Word how to encounter him in all of life's complexities. Biblical counselors trust they have what they need for counseling because they believe the promise of these resources in the faithfulness of God in Christ.

Many committed Christians are not convinced, however. They love God and the Bible, but they do not see the sufficiency of Scripture for counseling as one of the glories of this passage. Those who deny the sufficiency of Scripture for counseling question the biblical counselor's interpretation of this passage in two ways.

Some argue that applying this passage to counseling is illegitimate because it does not specifically mention the Bible. "It has to be pointed out that Scripture is not mentioned here," wrote Eric Johnson.[18] The argument is that Peter does not identify Scripture as the source of all things needful but rather God himself as the source.[19] After all, the text does say, "*His divine power* has given us everything required for life and godliness."

---

[17] Ed Bulkley, *Why Christians Can't Trust Psychology* (Eugene, OR: Harvest House, 1993), 268.

[18] Johnson, *Foundations*, 118; cf. 19.

[19] "We must remember that it is God, not the Bible itself, who is declared to be all-sufficient, to provide all that pertains unto life" (Jones and Butman, *Modern Psychotherapies*, 26).

This point is certainly correct—as far as it goes. God gives Christians the power to live lives fully pleasing to him, but how do we have access to such divine power? Peter explained that this power comes through the knowledge of Christ manifested in his precious and great promises. The word "Scripture" is not used here, but no faithful Christian interpretation of Peter's words could conclude that a person has access to this knowledge of Jesus Christ and his promises *apart from Scripture*. It is gloriously correct: sufficiency rests on Christ and not on the Bible. When critics use this to neutralize sufficiency, however, it proves little. The same text that teaches this principle simultaneously drives Christians to the pages of Scripture to grasp the promised divine resources. They are correct in what they affirm but mistaken in what they deny.

A second criticism against the biblical sufficiency view of 2 Pet 1:3–4 is that the Bible, rather obviously, does not include the reams of information that come on the table during counseling. Stan Jones wrote, "There are many topics to which Scripture does not speak—how neurons work, how the brain synthesizes mathematical or emotional information, the types of memory, or the best way to conceptualize personality traits."[20]

Once again this objection is accurate—as far as it goes. The Bible certainly does not tell us everything we come to know or might want to know.[21] Such an argument, however, has never been made by biblical counselors. The carefully developed view of the biblical counseling movement is not that the Scriptures provide Christians with all of the information we *desire* but rather with the understanding we *need* to do *counseling ministry*.

I have counseled people who were "down in the dumps" and people who were extremely depressed. I have counseled couples who wanted a marriage "tune-up" and couples on the brink of divorce. I have counseled cutters, worriers, wife abusers, drunks, heroin addicts, and people just wanting to die. Never were any of the categories mentioned by Jones (knowledge of how neurons work, information about how the brain synthesizes information, types of

---

[20] Jones, "An Integration View," 116.

[21] Jones and Butman, *Modern Psychotherapies*, 27.

memory, or conceptualizations about personality traits) pivotal in whether the counseling succeeded or failed. What is pivotal in such situations is access to the power of God through his Word—access that has enabled me to unpack powerful themes of redemption. What helped such strugglers? What turned on the lights? What gave them hope? What guided them? *Psalms, Romans, 1 Corinthians, John's Gospel.* Anyone who has relied on God's Word as the sufficient source of wisdom for counseling could give the same testimony.

Other texts could be mentioned, but this sampling provides ample evidence that a biblical counselor's conviction about the sufficiency of Scripture grows out of an understanding of explicit texts in the Bible.

The form of Scripture. The Bible presents a diverse assortment of communication styles. God reveals himself to us in the pages of his Word in a dynamic package of history, parables, proverbs, poetry, prophecy, song, letters, and apocalyptic literature. Beyond the many different genres, God displays other kinds of diversity in his communication in Scripture. Sometimes the Bible speaks in generalities—"All those who want to live a godly life in Christ Jesus will be persecuted" (2 Tim 3:12). At other times it speaks specifically—"I urge Euodia and I urge Syntyche to agree in the Lord" (Phil 4:2). The Bible uses hyperbole—"Hezekiah trusted in the LORD God of Israel; not one of the kings of Judah was like him" (2 Kgs 18:5). The Bible uses scientific accuracy—"The cloud covered it for six days. On the seventh day He called to Moses from the cloud" (Exod 24:16). Sometimes the Bible describes God anthropomorphically—"The LORD's hand is not too short to save, and His ear is not too deaf to hear" (Isa 59:1). At other times God is described with more theological precision—"God is spirit" (John 4:24). The Bible employs different genres and literary methods to communicate all that God wants his people to know.

Such an understanding of Scripture is important because the counseling approach of Christian counselors commonly argues for Scripture's *in*sufficiency by pointing out that the Bible's instruction is unscientific. Eric Johnson wrote:

> The extreme sufficiency position would seem to entail that the Bible is adequate as a scientific text, that it is scientifically sufficient, having the same level of precision, specificity and comprehensiveness regarding psychological and soul-care topics that one finds in good contemporary psychological textbooks and journal articles, and that is obviously not the case.[22]

Biblical counselors have not argued that the Bible is adequate as a scientific text. They have argued that the Bible is adequate *as it is*. The demand that the Bible be scientific in order to be sufficient originates with the various *in*sufficiency positions. Such views betray a fundamental dissatisfaction with the form of Scripture, and those who express this dissatisfaction reveal their partiality to scientific modes of discourse. Of course, there is nothing wrong with a scientific style of communication, but when a preference for that kind of communication leads to disappointment with the text that the Lord has actually given, it becomes a problem.[23]

Biblical counselors, on the other hand, have rejoiced in the many and varied forms found in the Bible, believing that such a

---

[22] Johnson, *Foundations*, 122. In this quotation Johnson did not intend to make a reference to the biblical counseling movement in general but to a subgroup within the movement he refers to as Traditional Biblical Counseling (TBC). Johnson argued that TBC has a more strict understanding of sufficiency than others in the biblical counseling movement. I have shown elsewhere, however (see Lambert, *The Biblical Counseling Movement After Adams*), that no such distinction can be made within the movement. The beliefs that Johnson criticized as unique to so-called TBC are actually the same sufficiency beliefs of the biblical counseling movement as a whole. For more discussion on the Bible as a scientific text, see Johnson, *Foundations*, 182–89. In these pages Johnson explained the differences between the biblical text and scientific texts. He explained how it is inappropriate for biblical counselors to demand that the Bible function as a scientific text. The problem with his argument is that biblical counselors do not make such a demand. Their conviction is that the Scriptures are sufficient for counseling without being scientific in nature. Johnson's argument misunderstands the convictions of the biblical counseling movement and is therefore irrelevant to their arguments.

[23] None of this is meant to indicate that counseling approaches such as integration and Christian psychology place no value on the Bible. Most of these people have great love and regard for the Scriptures. What is being addressed here is their level of respect for the form of Scripture with regard to counseling over and against a more scientific mode of literature.

colorful format was given purposefully by God as a vibrant and instructive revelation for his people. Ed Welch commented on this element of biblical sufficiency:

> Given the degree to which God has revealed himself and ourselves, we can assume that the Bible's counsel speaks with great breadth, addressing the gamut of problems in living. It is certainly able to speak to the common problems we all encounter, such as relationship conflicts, financial pressures, our responses to physical health or illness, parenting questions, and loneliness. But it also speaks to distinctly modern problems such as depression, anxiety, mania, schizophrenia and attention deficit disorder, just to name a few. Of course, the Bible doesn't speak to each of these problems as would an encyclopedia. It doesn't offer techniques for change that look like they came out of a cookbook. But through prayerful meditation on Scripture and a willingness to receive theological guidance from each other, we find that the biblical teaching on creation, the fall, and redemption provide specific, useful insight into all the issues of life.[24]

Welch's strong statement about sufficiency comes in the context of appreciating the style of revelation given in Scripture. Disappointment with the form in which God has communicated his truth grows out of a prior fascination with a scientific manner of discourse employed by psychology to communicate its diverse understandings of people and its various approaches to help. Those fascinated by that mode of communication are typically frustrated when they come to Scripture and find it less formal, scientific, and encyclopedic.

In the face of such frustration and disappointment, it is important to remember that while scientific discourse is one good way to communicate many things, it is not the only way—or even the best way. One of the reasons this is true is because God has

---

[24] Ed Welch, "What *Is* Biblical Counseling, Anyway," *The Journal of Biblical Counseling* 16, no. 1 (1997): 3.

chosen to communicate with humans in all of the ways mentioned above—from narrative to apocalyptic. God's choice to communicate through a spectrum of genres makes the issue here larger than sufficiency. His chosen form of infallible communication (the Bible) makes this an issue of biblical authority as well. A belief in the authority of God's Word mandates our submission to that authority in whatever form it takes. In a corollary way, such authority also forbids discouragement that Scripture has not been given in some other mode that we might prefer, whether scientific or encyclopedic or otherwise.

In fact, God knew exactly what he was doing in communicating his truth through his chosen styles. The dynamic forms of Scripture make the Bible much more interesting to read. Why is it that far more people sit in their living rooms and read the Bible than will ever read *The Journal of Psychology*? God's style of communication in Scripture speaks to people in ways that are deeply powerful, emotional, wise, and compelling. His words are accessible to a broad spectrum of people. No matter how insightful a scientific text may be, it will never have the power to affect the soul in the way God's more colloquial manner of speech does. In addition to these powerful characteristics, the form and style of the Bible in no way undermine its power to communicate authoritatively. Texts do not need to be scientific to be authoritative, profound, precise, and relevant for counseling. Such a sense of authority, profundity, precision, and relevance is only lost to those who come to the text with an *a priori* belief that unscientific forms of discourse are inherently less valuable. We must embrace it as an article of faith, trusting in our God of steadfast love, that his way of communicating with us is superior to other modes we might prefer.

God's language for problems. A third major element biblical counselors have emphasized in the debate over the sufficiency of Scripture has to do with terminology. Biblical counselors want to appreciate the language God uses to describe people's problems. The previous section considers the canonical form of Scripture. This section zeros in on the language God uses to describe people's individual problems.

In the *Diagnostic and Statistical Manual of Mental Disorders*,[25] secular professionals applied secular labels to life problems. These labels sound official and scientific: agoraphobia, borderline personality disorder, oppositional defiant disorder, and the like. Though they have a technical ring, these labels describe behaviors repeatedly observed by many others. The Bible describes the same kinds of problems, but it uses different language: fear, pride, cravings, disobedient to parents, and things like these. The Bible's concrete language is closer to the actual observations. Differences in nomenclature do not amount to denials of observations.[26]

What happens when Christian counselors begin with the nomenclature used by secular psychologists?[27] They feel frustrated when they come to Scripture. The Bible does not address problems they learned in their interaction with the secular psychologies. They are unable to see the Bible's relevance. Biblical counselors, on the other hand, start with the Bible and desire to use the sort of language God uses—concrete, vivid, oriented to issues of good and evil, true and false, right verses wrong.

The divergence of language reveals different starting points. For example, the term *bulimia* does not appear in Scripture, but this does not preclude God from talking about a problem like this in different language. The Bible regularly uses the categories of sinful desire, works of the flesh, and lusts of the flesh. The "bulimic" vacillates between sinful cravings for thinness and sinful cravings for the comforts of food. The bulimic's gluttony and self-induced vomiting describe the oscillation. When understood in this light, the Bible's language is far more profound than the secular label. The Bible makes sense of both poles of bulimic behavior (bingeing and purging) and connects the extremes of behavior to life lived before the face of God.

---

[25] *Diagnostic and Statistical Manual of Mental Disorders: DSM-IV* (Washington, DC: American Psychiatric Association, 1994).

[26] E.g., David Powlison, "Is the Adonis Complex in *Your* Bible?" *The Journal of Biblical Counseling* 22, no. 2 (2004): 42–58; Marshall and Mary Asher, *The Christian's Guide to Psychological Problems* (Bemidji, MN: Focus, 2004).

[27] Jones, "An Integration View," 110.

Those not embracing the sufficiency of Scripture for conversational ministry are perplexed by biblical counselors who steer away from language considered profound by secular psychology and are frustrated by the use of other language for problems that they consider to be relatively beside the point. For biblical counselors who start with the language of Scripture, however, secular classifications are not profound but present an understanding that runs contrary to God's revelation that emphasizes the spiritual nature of people's problems.

Comprehensive, not exhaustive. Fourth and finally, biblical counselors have argued for the sufficiency of Scripture for counseling by arguing that Scripture includes comprehensive resources for counseling rather than exhaustive ones. Those who disagree frequently object that the content of Scripture is limited. Stan Jones and Richard Butman, whose work is often credited as a strong argument against the sufficiency of Scripture, explained this point:

> While the Bible provides the most important and ultimate answers as well as the starting points for knowledge of the human condition, it is not an all-sufficient guide for the discipline of counseling. The Bible is inspired and precious, but it is also a revelation of limited scope, the main concern of which is religious in its presentation of God's redemptive plan for his people and the great doctrines of the faith. The Bible doesn't claim to reveal everything which human beings might want to know.[28]

Their point is happily conceded. Indeed, the Bible's revelation is limited in scope. The Bible does not reveal everything human beings desire to know, nor does it claim to do so. In fact, biblical counselors have never argued that the Bible is exhaustive in its contents. They agree that the Scriptures are limited. The real question that must be answered is what those limitations are.

---

[28] Jones and Butman, *Modern Psychotherapies*, 27. For a similar argument, see Johnson, *Foundations*, 119, 184.

Biblical counselors *have* argued that Scripture is comprehensive. Scripture does not contain every last bit of information that can be known. Scripture contains all things that bring the counseling task into focus like a pair of glasses.[29] Scripture is relevant to the counseling task like a compass that reorients every problem. The grace of Christ is a master key that allows access to even the most difficult issues of life. Jones and Butman miss this reorienting and refocusing effect of God's Word when they reduce the Bible's comprehensive contents down to "God's redemptive plan and the great doctrines of the faith." These 10 words are employed to reduce the contents of the Christian faith and show the irrelevance of Scripture to the counseling problems people face. They are meant to make Scripture seem so high-flying that it never touches down in the lives of people. Such a distillation mocks the contents of the Bible and rips the vitality out of biblical categories.

Biblical counselors also refer to those 10 words as a summary of the contents of Scripture. They take the summary, however, and run in the opposite direction. For biblical counselors those 10 words summarize the teachings of Scripture in all their beauty, profundity, glory, richness, depth, detail, truth, and power. Those 10 words summarize 10 million glorious details in Scripture. They refer to God's understanding of what is wrong with us, what he thinks should be right with us, and how he intends to redeem us and repair us through the precious blood of Jesus.

When these 10 words are used to describe the limitations of Scripture and the inadequacy of God's resources for conversational ministry, biblical counselors cry "Foul!" In these 10 words biblical counselors see dozens of years of ministry, hundreds of books and articles, thousands of counselees, and tens of thousands of hours of careful counseling conversation. In these 10 words millions of people have found relief from the pain of childhood abuse,

---

[29] John Calvin, *Institutes of the Christian Religion*, Library of Christian Classics, vols. 20–21, ed. John T. McNeill, trans. Ford Lewis Battles (Philadelphia: Westminster, 1960), I.6.I. Calvin's analogy has been applied to counseling by David Powlison, *Seeing with New Eyes: Counseling and the Human Condition Through the Lens of Scripture* (Phillipsburg, NJ: P&R, 2003), 9–16.

strength to overcome sin, light in the midst of the darkest despair, and hope to endure unrelenting pressures. These 10 words are the comprehensive keys which unlock the problems that bind humanity. They are not a summary statement describing the limitations of Scripture. They encapsulate God's antidote that can defeat the precise details of sin and despair in all their twisted forms.

Earlier David Powlison was quoted as saying that salvation is a "comprehensive description of transforming human life from all that ails us." This is what he said about the power of Scripture to address all of our life problems in a comprehensive way:

> Our Father teaches us the common themes threading through all of life. Wisdom. A feel for how life breaks, a skilled engagement. *Kyrie eleison*, Lord, have mercy. Teach us this skill of skills. It's to die for, and to live for. In the economy of our God's instruction, things that He said and did with desert shepherds in the ancient Middle East proved directly instructive and encouraging to urban Greco-Romans one or two thousand years later (Rom 15:4; 1 Cor 10:11) and prove the same for us today, yet another couple thousand years along. Wildly different circumstances are not fatal to significance and relevance. There is no temptation that is not common to all (1 Cor 10:13), yet no situations or persons are identical. The merciful Father comforted Paul in *his* troubles, making him able to comfort those facing *any* trouble (2 Cor 1:4), including you in *your* troubles, so that you also can help those in any trouble. This dynamic of the living and omni-adaptable Word creates one of the many deep joys of Christian faith. It also makes you game to tackle any problem however unfamiliar, dark, and contorted.[30]

Powlison went on to explain how the Bible gives master categories and explanations which are sufficient to help us understand and help people with any problem that can be faced and counseled in this life.

---

[30] Powlison, "Is the Adonis Complex in *Your* Bible?" 43. Cf. Powlison, "Critiquing Modern Integrationists," *The Journal of Biblical Counseling* 11, no. 3 (1993): 24–34, 26–27, 30.

These master categories—these large-scale interpretive themes—ensure Scripture's sufficiency for counseling. No single theory—or any collection of them—can ever reach the impossible standard of being exhaustive. No counseling theorist—not Freud, Adler, Jung, Maslow, or anyone else—has ever created an exhaustive counseling theory. They created theories that were system constituting. Their theories were general in nature and limited in scope. Details got filled in as their theories were worked out over time. Scripture has enduring and all-encompassing relevance—it is sufficient—precisely because it is not exhaustive but rather comprehensive.

Every counseling system is, essentially, a worldview which presents its own understanding about how life works best and how best to help someone make changes in his life consistent with that worldview. Biblical counselors believe—at the level of worldview—that Scripture holds its own against any of the other dozens (hundreds? thousands?) of worldviews out there. They further believe that since the biblical worldview comes from God, it is superior to all others. The worldview that comes from God is superior because it is true. The book you are reading is an exercise in proving that the large, dynamic, adaptable, comprehensive, God-breathed worldview presented in the pages of Scripture is precisely what makes the Bible sufficient to engage the particulars of numerous and complex problems.

Our Purpose

These arguments about the categories of secular psychology's diagnosis of problems and the contents of Scripture summarize the views that biblical counselors have held and developed for almost a half century about the sufficient wisdom contained in the Scripture for hardships that require counseling. These arguments form the context for the stories in this book. These arguments have persuaded our contributing authors (and many others) that Scripture is comprehensively sufficient to do ministry with people experiencing profound difficulties in their lives.

The reason for this book, however, is to avoid making that argument in the abstract. Anyone who teaches biblical counseling knows what it's like to be discussing the sufficiency of Scripture and to see a hand go up: "But what about the hard cases? What about schizophrenia, sexual abuse, eating disorders, bipolar? When you say that the Bible is sufficient, do you really mean that it's sufficient for *those problems*?" These questions arise because the problems are real and the arguments can seem abstract. It is one thing to hear that God's categories in the Bible rightly identify and engage all the different problems people face. It is another thing to show how that looks when encountering a complex, secularly defined problem like dissociative identity disorder.

That gap is precisely where this book is meant to fit. This is not a book of arguments. It is a book of stories. It is a book about counselors and their relationships with people who have struggled in profound ways. It is a book about how those counselors used God's words in Scripture as the sufficient source of wisdom to help people. Each one of the counselees in this book had a severe problem with a secular diagnosis, a problem that God was pleased to change by the power of his Son Jesus and through the personal ministry of the Word of God. Taken together, these stories constitute a powerful argument that the Scriptures are indeed sufficient for the kind of effective counseling those outside the biblical counseling movement claim we cannot do. These stories are offered with a prayer that they will encourage you with the understanding that the perpetually relevant truths in God's Word are sufficient to make the man of God complete and equipped for every good work (2 Tim 3:17).

Chapter 2

"Mariana" and Surviving Sexual Abuse

Laura Hendrickson

Mariana's Story

MARIANA[1] WAS A 45-YEAR-OLD MARRIED woman with a history of severe sexual abuse in childhood who had received psychotherapy for dissociative identity disorder (DID) for 20 years. She had also been diagnosed with bipolar disorder when her pastor referred her to the Institute for Biblical Counseling and Discipleship (IBCD).[2] Although Mariana was still taking an antidepressant and two mood-stabilizing medicines, she had stopped her psychotherapy for DID and had been counseled by her pastor for two years prior to coming to IBCD. Mariana was the third of six children born into an intact middle-class family. Her parents told the family repeatedly that Mariana was not her father's biological daughter but that she was the product of the rape of her mother by Mariana's paternal grandfather. Mariana also was told that her mother refused to bring her home from the hospital after her birth. Her Aunt Sophia, her father's sister-in-law, took her home and named her. Mariana was returned

[1] For the sake of privacy, all names used in this case study are pseudonyms.
[2] See www.ibcd.org.

to her parents' home while still an infant, but her mother never accepted her.

Mariana's father, an alcoholic, molested her for the first time when she was four years old. This abuse continued regularly over the next few years while her father continued his sexual relationship with his wife, who gave birth to other children. After a vicious fight between her parents when she was about seven, Mariana was given by her mother to her father to service him sexually. From this point on, Mariana and her father shared a bedroom while her mother slept with Mariana's sisters. The family moved frequently from town to town to conceal the dark secret.

Mariana's mother physically and verbally abused her. Mariana was neglected, stripped naked, and then beaten, locked in closets, and deprived of food. At Christmas she would receive no gifts. Her mother told her that she was evil, that God hated her, and she forbade her to pray or read a Bible. However, Aunt Sophia was sometimes able to take her to church. Mariana recalls loving Jesus from early childhood and experiencing his presence and comfort while being molested and abused. But because her mother taught her that God required perfection and punished harshly for disobedience, she internalized a legalistic worldview ruled by a harsh deity void of grace. Aunt Sophia moved with her children back to her native South America when Mariana was about 10, taking with her the only loving relationship Mariana would experience until her marriage.

In her adolescent years Mariana started cutting, turned to anorexic and bulimic behaviors, and struggled with depression. She eventually ran away from home to attend college, but she found it difficult as she struggled with an intense sense of shame and unworthiness. She habitually stayed awake all night to avoid having nightmares in a room with others and avoided showering or dressing in anyone's presence.

While in college Mariana met her future husband, Leon, and began living with him. He suggested that she would not be so fearful and ashamed if they were married. She agreed although she feared that he would hurt her as her father did. In spite of her fears, the two were married. Soon they decided to have children.

Mariana called her mother in desperation when her firstborn daughter was four months old, asking how to make her child stop crying. Her mother exclaimed incredulously, "She's four months old and still crying? Put a pillow over her face until she stops. You'll only have to do it a few times, and she'll learn." This triggered an overwhelming flood of memories of childhood abuse. At this time Mariana began to fear that her husband would hurt their daughter, and she became verbally abusive toward him. She decided to address her own history of abuse with her parents, but her attempts over the next few years were unsuccessful. She cut off contact with them. When our counseling relationship began, Mariana had not spoken with her parents in 20 years.

In God's providence a Christian couple named Julie and Pete came into Mariana and Leon's lives. This couple built a strong relationship with Mariana and Leon and shared the gospel with them. Mariana and Leon both believed and entered, for the first time, a vital relationship with Christ. Julie was burdened to help Mariana with her emotional problems, so she brought her to their church's deliverance ministry where they tried healing services and exorcism.

Mariana also saw multiple licensed professional Christian counselors. One of them told Leon that she was a pathological liar who could never be an adequate wife and mother because her own mother was "psychotic." This female professional encouraged Leon to divorce Mariana, seek custody of the children, and keep them away from their mother. Others hypnotized Mariana and told her that she had multiple personalities, an idea she had not considered prior to counseling.

Mariana began experiencing flashbacks, vivid reexperiences of earlier abuse. Nightmares were constant. She engaged in self-mutilation, attempted suicide, and was repeatedly hospitalized. Over time Leon became concerned that her helpers, although licensed counselors, might not be competent. He insisted that she see a psychiatrist through their health maintenance organization (HMO).

Mariana spent the next several years under the care of Dr. Ergenbreit, who diagnosed her with DID (dissociative identity disorder was then known as multiple personality disorder). He hypnotized her, placed her on psychotropic medicines, and held psychotherapy sessions to talk with the various personalities he identified. Mariana's life became even more chaotic. She required hospitalization and numerous extra therapy sessions to help her deal with her increasingly turbulent emotions. Dr. Ergenbreit told her that he could not perform all the therapy she needed, so he referred her to another Christian therapist who also hypnotized her. While seeing this therapist, Mariana began "remembering" things that she's now quite sure never happened, such as murdering two children born from her relationship with her father and being the subject of bizarre satanic rituals.

Soon she transitioned to Dr. Freeman, a Christian psychologist who had published a book on multiple personalities and satanic ritual abuse. She met with him as often as three times a week for about eight years. His treatment was a collage of late twentieth-century therapeutic fads. He hypnotized her and led her through "healing of the memories" where she was encouraged to recall every detail of her abuse while visualizing Jesus as present to comfort her. She describes the vivid process initiated by Dr. Freeman as 10 times more painful than the initial abuse. His "overlay" of Jesus onto her memories never rang true to her. Ironically, she shared with Dr. Freeman that she *had* experienced Jesus' comforting presence during her abuse as a child. He told her that was not really Jesus but an effect of her disorder.

Although Mariana was instructed to suppress her other personalities except during therapy, she began experiencing numerous episodes in everyday life where "they took over," something that had never happened before the therapy began. Over time these alter egos became more and more distinct from Mariana herself, each having its own name, likes and dislikes, tone of voice, style of dress, and even handwriting. She was ultimately diagnosed with 35 personalities, and Dr. Freeman created a chart describing their characteristics and relationship to one another.

Mariana was encouraged to let "them" emerge in therapy so each one could talk to Dr. Freeman (often repeatedly) about the traumas they experienced. Two or three of them were sometimes asked to discuss an event together since many of them supposedly had overlapping memories. This approach resulted in Mariana's painfully reliving each memory many hundreds of times. Not surprisingly, she descended into yet more emotional deterioration marked by wild mood swings and constant crises. She had been assured that she would get worse before she got better, so she continued with the therapy.

Eventually Dr. Ergenbreit, who had performed hypnosis sessions and monitored Mariana's antidepressant treatments for several years, left her HMO. Her care was assigned to Dr. Zimmer, who later diagnosed her with bipolar disorder and prescribed additional medications. As Dr. Zimmer learned more about Dr. Freeman's treatment, he tried to persuade Mariana to stop seeing him. In turn Dr. Freeman believed that Mariana's medicines were interfering with his psychotherapy, and he urged her to stop seeing Dr. Zimmer. Mariana continued to see both of them because the medicines blunted her emotions, and she maintained hope that her therapy would eventually bring a long-awaited cure.

Either her husband, Leon, or her friend, Julie, attended every session Mariana had with Dr. Freeman. Leon was asked to give his wife the freedom to work full-time on her traumas by relieving her of her household responsibilities, and he did so. Rather than helping her, however, this loss of responsibility produced even more deterioration in Mariana's emotions and behavior. Ultimately she was unable to enter her own kitchen without experiencing flashbacks of abuse by her mother, and she was unable to shower without reexperiencing her father's rapes. She stayed out of the kitchen and stopped bathing.

Dr. Freeman next told her that she needed to experience having a happy childhood with a good mother, so with Leon's concurrence Mariana left him and their three children to move in with

Julie and Pete. Together this new "family" reenacted Mariana's childhood, starting from infancy, with Julie as her "good mother." Mariana recalls tea parties, playing dress-up, and calling Julie "Mommy."

Four months later Leon was no longer on board. He gave Mariana an ultimatum: Either she came home or their marriage was over. She returned home, but the turbulence continued. She struggled with her roles as wife and mother, never took up her household responsibilities again, and continued to have numerous flashbacks and emotional crises.

After she attempted suicide again and was confined to a psychiatric hospital for six weeks, her pastor visited her and offered biblical hope that she could change. He urged her to give up her therapy with Dr. Freeman, and she followed his advice. This pastor counseled Mariana for two years, telling her that her problem was not that she had a mental illness but that she had made sinful, selfish choices. He held a family meeting and emphasized to Leon and their children that Mariana was not sick but sinful. As a result the family became angry toward Mariana, and she became angry with God, languishing in guilt and shame. It seemed that all avenues of help had been fully exhausted, and Mariana lost hope. As the counseling stalemated, her pastor referred her to IBCD, where she met with two different female counselors prior to meeting with me.

Counseling Mariana

During the course of our formal counseling relationship, Mariana and I met together 58 times. This number of sessions is not typical and would become overbearing in other, simpler cases. The innumerable thorny strands, however, woven through Mariana's story were embedded in her heart and wrapped around her soul; the wounds, inflicted both by others and by herself, were jagged and deep. Patiently cutting through this web with God's Word and carefully applying the balm of his promises would require significant time and substantial patience from both of us. After our conversations I was convinced that Mariana was a believer, but she never received any instruction on how to live out her life as a Christian in a way that glorified Christ. It was a privilege to take the long road with her and help her in this regard.

Because of our abundance of conversations together, the counseling process is best shared by arranging the material chronologically and thematically instead of describing each individual meeting. Each major issue was discussed many times in counseling as new information emerged or new challenges arose.

Getting to the Truth

At our first session, Mariana told me that she had a problem with lying. She had been labeled a liar since childhood. She confessed that she was not even sure that everything she told me about her past had actually happened. Although she had always remembered having been molested and abused, some of her memories emerged as the result of hypnosis and other interventions.

Because she had been accused of lying by previous counselors, I wondered whether Mariana raised this subject at our first session to see how I would respond. I decided that since love thinks the best (1 Cor 13:7), I would presume that Mariana was telling me the truth in the absence of contrary evidence. I informed her that memories recovered under hypnosis are often unreliable or completely false but that the truth would probably become clearer to her as we worked together. I emphasized that I viewed my role as coming alongside her as a sister in the Lord, not as an omniscient counselor who could discern truth from falsehood. Although I could not tell her whether she had believed lies about her past, I could help her address the lying she knew she was doing in the present.

Many survivors of abuse are habitual liars because they were raised in families where dishonesty was a normal part of life. They have learned to use deceit to protect themselves. I asked Mariana why she thought she lied. "Because I don't know what's true anymore," was her poignant response. Mariana also wondered whether this type of deception was really lying since she believed what she was saying at the moment she said it.

I told her that although her lying had become so natural that it seemed almost automatic, it really was still lying. Since Christ calls us to walk in the truth, breaking this habit was not optional for her. Mariana had to acknowledge that such deceit is sinful (Prov 28:13). This would mean taking responsibility for her deceptions and confessing her sin—agreeing with God that she truly had a choice about whether to lie.

This truth was the first expression of a theme we returned to repeatedly: Even though a sinful behavior may be practiced for so long that it feels involuntary, if we acknowledge it as a sin, repent of it, and ask for grace, the Lord will enable us to cast it away and clothe ourselves with the corresponding virtue (Eph 4:22–32). I balanced this principle with the complementary truth that her gracious Savior understood how difficult it would be to break a habit that had dominated her since childhood. He would be patient with her and would give her as much grace as she needed (1 Cor 10:13).

Making the Cross Central to Her Life Story

Like most abuse survivors, Mariana struggled with guilt and shame. As a coping mechanism, she had come to see her lying as an involuntary symptom of her mental illness. This perspective helped her endure the shame she felt for her many failures because seeing her lying as involuntary meant that her deceptions were not her fault. Such a self-deceiving perspective did not give Mariana the clear conscience she was longing for.

I told Mariana that her real problem was not mental illness but an inadequate understanding of what Christ had accomplished on her behalf through his sinless life and substitutionary death. She did not have to continue struggling with guilt over her failures because she had already been declared not guilty through Christ's atoning sacrifice. She needed the truths expounded in Romans 6–8, truths which provide freedom from the guilt of sin and offer a divine source of power for battling ongoing temptation.

The worldview Mariana had learned from her previous counselors had done just the opposite—it defined her by the trauma she had experienced, reinforced her victimhood, and limited her perception of her power to change. Cutting hard against the grain of past counsel she had received, I told her that to understand the events of her life she needed to place Christ's death at the center of her story.

Drawing a time line to represent her life, I added a cross on the line, corresponding to the time she came to faith. I pointed out that when God forgave her and raised her to new life in Christ, her earthly life had divided into two parts—the old life and the new (Rom 6:2–11). Formerly she was powerless to stop sinning because she was enslaved to sin and loved her sin, but now she did not have to sin any more (Rom 6:12–14). God's Word said that she had a choice.

Jerry Bridges's book *The Gospel for Real Life*[3] amplifies this theme as it richly illustrates how the redemption and restoration found in Jesus Christ intersect with everyday life. I asked Mariana to read this book with me so that she could soak herself in the truth that she was completely forgiven and cleansed. We worked through this book together for our first 20 sessions, utilizing the discussion questions to apply the book's principles directly to Mariana's own struggles. At the same time Mariana was intensively studying and meditating on Romans 6–8 in order to marinate her mind in the realities that she had been declared righteous by faith. She once was dead but is now alive. Her life had not been tweaked but transformed. She could now present herself to the Lord for obedience through his powerful grace.

Learning to Trust

By the mercy of God, Mariana began to respond vigorously—though somewhat legalistically—to my counsel. She contacted Julie, her "good mother" during her 20 years of psychotherapy, and confessed numerous lies. She also told Julie that she would not be continuing the "mother-daughter" relationship with her because she did not want to continue relating to Julie as a sick little girl.

---

[3] Jerry Bridges, *The Gospel for Real Life* (Colorado Springs: NavPress, 2003).

I had not yet broached the topic of Mariana's simulated relationship with Julie. Breaking it off had been Mariana's own idea, but I did not argue with her. I would not have advised making a radical break like this so early in counseling, but since she had already taken the step, I tried to help her deal with the feelings engendered by cutting the cord with Julie.

Although she had acted boldly, Mariana soon was expressing fear that God was "stripping" her by removing some of her supports such as her make-believe relationship with Julie. If jettisoning relationships that had previously brought her comfort was the path of restoration, Mariana feared that she would be left with nothing. I encouraged her to trust the gentle Savior who will not break a bruised reed or put out a smoldering wick (Isa 42:3). I also pointed out that abuse survivors struggling with shame often feel that they are stripped, naked, and exposed. Reminding her that God does not strip us when we turn from our sin at salvation, the exact opposite truth—that he clothes us with Christ's righteousness (Rev 7:13–17)—brought some helpful correction here to her thoughts and emotions. I offered Ezek 16:1–13 as an additional picture of how God clothes the unwanted and the unlovely (though I strongly cautioned Mariana not to read any further than v. 13 since the overall chapter was addressed to apostate Israel and not to faithful Christians).[4] This became the first iteration of another major theme in counseling: Those who trust in Christ will not be put to shame (Rom 5:3–5; 10:11).

From a different angle I emphasized to Mariana that she had never needed a human "good mother" to help her recover from the evil that was done to her because God is her Father who had loved her and adopted her (Rom 8:15–17). Despite growing up in an abusive and unloving family, her restoration and stability in the present were not dependent on simulating a new earthly family.

---

[4] Ezekiel 16 employs powerful metaphors about nakedness, shame, and prostitution to illustrate Israel's apostasy from her covenant God. I did not want Mariana to read the rest of the chapter and mistakenly identify herself with the disturbing and humiliating picture of apostate Israel.

The fatherly care of her gentle and gracious God would be enough for her.

I also cautioned Mariana that she could not sanctify herself. Rather, she needed to trust Christ to sanctify her in his own time (1 Thess 5:23–24). Mariana objected that she did not like the idea of surrendering control to the Lord; and although control became an issue that we returned to repeatedly over the coming weeks and months, I decided not to address it too strongly at this early stage in our relationship. Instead, I encouraged Mariana simply to tell Jesus how she felt and trust that he would give her the grace she needed.

Trust can be quite difficult to learn, especially for someone with Mariana's devastating past and long-standing patterns. Soon after we began talking about the issue of control, Mariana called me in hysterics, complaining of fear and uncontrollable mood swings. She told me that she was afraid I would lock her in the closet naked, something her mother used to do to her. It sounded like she was starting to view me as her new "mother," so I reminded her of her recent decision to give up her simulated "good mother" Julie. As much as I wanted to reassure Mariana at that moment that I would never hurt her, I deliberately pointed her to the Lord rather than to my own reliability as her source of safety. I reminded her that she could apply the principles she was learning in counseling to what was troubling her as she looked to the Lord in prayer. I ended the conversation fairly quickly and prayed with her that she would look to him as her loving heavenly Father when she was afraid.

Mariana later wrote me a poem about this incident. She explained to me that she had fallen apart emotionally because she was overwhelmed by the hope that my counsel had engendered in her. Tellingly, she also referred to herself in the poem as "we." The poem said that "everyone" had wanted to tell his or her stories to me, and this thought overwhelmed her. We talked about the feeling that there were many people inside of her, and I reminded her that although this was a powerful metaphor that captured her emotional pain, the Bible tells us always and everywhere that we are one person, not many personalities in one body.[5] I continued to address my counsel solely to her as a whole person and never asked her to manifest any of her "alters." Over time she abandoned the use of this metaphor to describe her internal state. Today Mariana says that she never had multiple personalities until they were "discovered" through hypnosis.

Confronting Seemingly Involuntary Phenomena

Mariana told me she understood that she did not have a mental illness, but she wondered why she was experiencing seemingly involuntary phenomena. As she began to fall asleep, she felt a spinning and falling sensation, saw flashing lights, re-experienced abuse, and became hysterical. This typically lasted several hours every Saturday night and required Leon's intensive involvement to calm her down. She mentioned that her father had often raped her on Saturday night. This was also when her mother often abused her.

I wondered whether Mariana feared losing control as she surrendered herself to sleep (the desire to remain in control is common among survivors of abuse). This fear of losing control made sense to Mariana. I reminded her that Christ is always in control and he takes care of her even while she is sleeping (Ps 4:8). She would need to remind herself of this truth when she began to feel afraid. Even though these fearful sensations seemed to originate outside of her, they always occurred at a predictable time on Saturdays, so it seemed unlikely that these were truly random, involuntary events. Regardless of their source, Mariana's challenge and calling were the same. God was summoning her to look to Christ in faith and to seek the calmness that comes from trusting him rather than surrendering to her emotions.

Mariana added that Leon would usually read Psalm 23 to her during these distressful times. These readings had a calming

---

[5] I am indebted to biblical counselor Ed Welch for his understanding of multiple personalities as a metaphor rather than as an objective reality (see Edward Welch, "Insight into Multiple Personality Disorder," *The Journal of Biblical Counseling* 14, no. 1 [1995]: 18–26).

effect, but only after a couple hours of hysteria. I encouraged her that she could actually decide to calm down more quickly and to ask Leon to turn to the Bible first rather than bringing it out as a last resort. These seemingly involuntary experiences became less overwhelming and continued to end more quickly as Mariana and Leon adjusted their responses. After a few weeks, Mariana no longer experienced the terrible sensations. She admits that remnants of this behavior can still emerge today under severe stress (which is not surprising), but she is now able to deal with them on her own.

Shame, Fear of Man, and Pride

In a subsequent session Mariana visibly shook with fear as she demanded to discuss a subject of her own choosing. I had not observed this combination of fear and aggression previously. Rather than immediately asking her what she wanted to talk about, I asked her why she was shaking. She answered that she was afraid and ashamed. Her fear reminded me of the time when she was afraid I would lock her in the closet naked. I wondered whether she was experiencing a similar fear now. She replied that she was. Although she told me she did not believe that I would hurt her, she did admit (when I asked) that she had been visualizing me doing bad things to her prior to the session.

I encouraged her not to visualize or believe things she knew were untrue. I also told her that she could respond to frightening images like these by speaking truth to herself and telling herself that they were not real. Mariana had never considered talking down these false imaginations. Her previous psychotherapist had always received her metaphorical fears as reality, and she had never before been encouraged to reorient herself to actual reality when they occurred.

I reminded her that the Bible teaches that her ultimate aim is to glorify God, not to protect herself from hurt or humiliation. I encouraged her to identify the times she feared being shamed and to ask herself whose glory she was worried about—God's or her own? I pointed out that even if I should say something cruel or painful to her, I would be the one sinning, not her. The shame would belong to me.

Once again Mariana was being called to trust in the one true God who is loving, gracious, and compassionate (Exod 34:6). No human being deserves ultimate trust because only God is trustworthy. If Mariana placed her trust in him, she would be safe in God's care in spite of any threats. I told her that I could not promise her that I would not fail her in some way in the future since I am a sinful, fallible human being. I could promise her that if she placed her trust in the Lord, he would keep her under his care (Prov 29:25).

Finally, I explained how pride is linked to shame. Although Mariana often felt ashamed when she thought about herself, she could also be harsh, superior, and self-righteous toward the failures of others. I described how her shame and her pride were mirror images of each other, both springing from the same fountain in the heart (Prov 4:23). When we are relying on our own righteousness, we will always struggle with either pride or shame. When we feel that we have done well, we will grow proud. When we recognize that we have failed, we will fear exposure and will be ashamed.

Mariana endured relentless experiences of shame throughout her childhood. Her father had stripped her and used her physically while her mother had stripped her and exposed her emotionally (by shaming her before others). Most people who have experienced similar treatment are eager to prove that they are not as bad as they have been told. Clinging to Christ in faith was the only ultimate remedy for Mariana's shame. God's full acceptance of her on the basis of Jesus' forgiveness and cleansing was the only reality powerful enough to undercut and eradicate the shame she felt from her past abuse and her own former sins.

Mariana was still sinful by nature. Apart from Christ her destiny would have been an eternity in hell. To find emotional peace, she needed to stop struggling to persuade herself and everyone else that she was good enough. Instead she needed to trust the One who had already made her good enough through Christ. To supplement these vital points, I asked her to read through Ed Welch's *When People Are Big and God Is Small*,[6] which explains how the enslaving desire to please others arises from a selfishly warped perspective in which the approval of others is weighty and threatening while our great Creator, Redeemer, and Judge stands small and shriveled in the background. I also asked her to meditate on the verses from Romans 6–8 that we had previously discussed for many weeks, journaling her responses as she struggled to master these concepts.

Dealing with Painful Memories

We next addressed the flashbacks Mariana experienced when she entered the kitchen or took a shower. Psychologists use this common term to describe overpowering memories that cause a survivor to feel as though she is actually back in the abusive situation causing her to lose partial or complete contact with reality. Mariana believed her flashbacks occurred randomly and involuntarily and she was powerless to stop them. She described them as an alternate reality entered involuntarily, a place where the real world no longer existed. After further questioning, however, it became clear that entering the kitchen or taking a shower often triggered painful memories. Understandably, Mariana responded to these memories with extreme distress and, ultimately, ended up cowering in a corner, screaming. These episodes required her husband's heroic intervention to reorient her. The flashbacks could not be completely involuntary and random because they never occurred when her children were present. Normally, they occurred when Leon was available to comfort her.

I reminded Mariana that because her psychotherapists both tolerated and expected unrestrained behavior during flashbacks, Mariana had practiced relinquishing control of herself and her emotions for quite some time. To the contrary, the apostle Paul, despite being imprisoned and alone himself, still exemplified persistent joy (Phil 4:4) as he encouraged the believers in Philippi to

[6] Edward Welch, *When People Are Big and God Is Small: Overcoming Peer Pressure, Codependency, and Fear of Man* (Phillipsburg, NJ: P&R, 1997).

dwell on things that are true, honorable, just, pure, lovely, commendable, morally excellent, and praiseworthy (Phil 4:8). Even though Mariana felt as though these experiences were beyond her control, the Bible teaches that she had far more control than she thought. Her emotional responses were not irresistible as she had come to believe. By the power of the Spirit, she could begin to express the fruit of the Spirit, such as self-control (Gal 5:22–23). I explained to Mariana that she could choose to look toward Christ in faith and remember that she did not have to yield to these temptations which were calling for her to abandon herself to an emotional reaction to her memories. Over time this habit would lose its power over her as she stopped yielding to it, just as any other habit does. I also shared with Mariana that I had experienced times of fear as well, though those moments had not led to hysterics. I told her that I am learning to look to the Lord in faith when I am afraid (Ps 56:3–4) and she could learn to do the same. Sharing openly about how God empowered me to trust him in the midst of my weakness gave Mariana hope.

However unpleasant her experiences, there was also a reward associated with them. Mariana received Leon's full support and special attention while she was hysterical, revealing that she had learned to give up control of her emotions in a way that demanded her husband's care. I suggested that she ask Leon to help her remember that she did not have to yield to her emotions when she became upset. I also urged her to listen to him the first time he spoke rather than having hysterics for a couple of hours and calming down gradually. She agreed to try this approach. They began praying together when these experiences began.

These outbursts were more resistant than the Saturday evening hysterics. Over time they became less frequent. Practically, I asked Mariana to focus on journaling potential triggers to these episodes, contemplating what she could have done differently after they ended, and applying the scriptural principles we discussed to her times of emotional upheaval. By the time we finished our counseling, her emotional patterns were showing substantial growth. She was only losing control occasionally and only in response to the most overwhelming situations, and she would usually recover quickly.

Identifying and Modifying Potential Triggers

As we worked together to bring these behaviors back under Mariana's conscious control, I also tried to help her discover what was provoking them. Her journaling assignments helped us recognize her patterns of response as they came upon her. It became clear that although certain locations were definitely connected with the memories that triggered her outbursts, these memories were not simply the product of environmental exposure. What was going on in her heart was even more important.

I learned that after a disagreement with Leon, Mariana would stew in anger and bitterness and would not speak further with him about the issue. She would begin to feel guilty and ashamed of her reaction and feared losing her relationship with him. This in turn would lead to self-deprecating thoughts, self-punishment, and ultimately despair. At this point a memory would arise, and she would have a flashback. The flashback produced an emotional release that reversed her negative feelings and brought Leon to her side to lovingly care for her. Once it was over, she felt much better. She also felt vindicated from the self-condemnation that had precipitated the attack because her breakdown had proven to her that she was not an angry person. Rather, the flashback reminded her that she was a victim of the anger and predation of others.

These breakdowns provided a way out of her emotional pain, but they also engendered constant chaos in the family (see Prov 14:12; 16:25). I reminded Mariana that God calls us not to suppress the truth in fear or shout the truth in anger but rather to speak the truth in love (Eph 4:15, 25–27). I encouraged her to practice speaking loving truth rather than suppressing her anger and bitterness until they erupted into rage or were transmuted into a flashback.

I also cautioned her that as she practiced this new behavior, she would inevitably fail at times. When she began stewing in anger, she needed to repent immediately and speak the truth to

Leon in love. If she began to have a flashback, she could remind herself that she did not have to be mastered by her feelings.

I encouraged Mariana to see herself simultaneously as a sinner and one who is sinned against, pointing out that every single one of us shares in these dual identities. We do not have to deny our own sinful anger because we have a Savior who has already paid for our sins and credited us with his own righteousness. We can agree with what the gospel says about our sinfulness without becoming overwhelmed by guilt and shame. Further, we do not have to prove that we are victims rather than victimizers out of a desperate effort to persuade ourselves that we are righteous. We have Christ's righteousness already. We can rest in this.

Perfectionism Versus Progressive Sanctification

As Mariana's behavior began to improve, Leon asked when she would be well enough to take up her household responsibilities. By this he meant cooking, cleaning, and listening to him instead of just talking about her own feelings. This was the first time I became aware that a fundamental part of Mariana's psychotherapy had been the expectation that Leon would take care of all the housework along with functioning as a sort of 24-7 co-therapist. He lived in hope that one day this unbalanced marital situation would end.

I told Mariana that she needed to begin resuming her responsibilities immediately because the way she was living stood against God's clear design for a married woman (Titus 2:3–5; cf. 2 Thess 3:10–12). The excessive time available for introspection likely was contributing to her emotional instability. I also encouraged her to consider returning to college to finish her degree. She wrestled with whether she should do this so we studied the Proverbs 31 woman to discover the many different roles a believing woman might embrace to enhance her family's enjoyment and security. Mariana ultimately did return to college and later studied biblical counseling as well.

As she began struggling to do the housework, I discovered that Mariana's reluctance to do these chores was related to her shame. Because her mother had abused her and called her "dirty" when she did not clean perfectly, Mariana still felt ashamed when she "failed" to meet her mother's standard in adulthood. For years she had alternated between exhausting herself trying to clean the kitchen perfectly and giving up because her efforts led to a sense of failure. These unpleasant responses caused her to avoid housework, and they even instigated flashbacks when she entered rooms especially associated with her shame, like the kitchen.

I also learned that Mariana had not shopped alone in years. She said she "couldn't go anywhere" because she feared losing control of herself in public. To keep her calm, Leon either shopped for her or accompanied her when she went to the store. She also neglected cooking because she was avoiding the kitchen, and she slept much of the day while Leon was at work. All of these patterns kept Leon at her side, minimizing the amount of time she spent alone without him. Naturally, Leon longed for her to get up with him in the morning, make him breakfast, and see him off to work.

I set up an escalating exposure plan calling for Mariana to rise early, make breakfast, and go to the grocery store daily after seeing Leon off to work. She was to pray for grace before entering, pick up one or two items, and leave quickly. Even if she grew uncomfortable, she was to continue shopping instead of leaving in fear. Once she arrived home each day, she was to do some cleaning. The cleaning was limited at first, particularly in the kitchen and bathroom where her memories were most poignant. Finally, she was to make a quick dinner. Mariana's confidence grew as she discovered that she was able to tolerate short exposure to the places and activities she dreaded. As she followed through, the exposures were lengthened until she shopped for everything and accomplished all the housework herself without experiencing distress.

A few weeks after beginning this program, Mariana nearly dropped out of counseling because she felt like a failure after becoming overwhelmed at Walmart. She had been able to talk herself out of the panic and had completed her shopping, but she was deeply ashamed that she had not fulfilled her assignment perfectly. I asked her about the rest of her week, and she told me that she had made breakfast for Leon and grocery shopped every day. I reframed her story as a victorious week, explaining that concentrating on this one struggle had caused her to cast the whole week as an overwhelming failure when the opposite was true. This kind of all-or-nothing thinking is common in abuse survivors. For Mariana, it triggered shame and flashbacks.

I emphasized the progressive nature of sanctification. Her journey was a step-by-step walk in which she would work out the Christian life daily as God energized her to accomplish his will (Phil 2:12–13). She needed to join Paul in framing the Christian life as warfare (Eph 6:10–18), recognizing that no warrior wins all his battles. This is why we must "walk by faith, not by sight" (2 Cor 5:7). She could rest in his performance (2 Cor 5:21), a theme I returned to repeatedly in subsequent sessions.

As flashbacks and other sensations began to decrease, Mariana began to recognize that she used her constant emotional crises to keep her husband close to her and to control the rest of her family. This realization provided fresh motivation to break her reactionary habits. She began to feel more pain over the suffering she had caused her own family than over the suffering her parents had caused her. She also began to shift her emphasis from seeking freedom from pain to seeking holiness, a mind-set which an earlier biblical counselor had emphasized but that Mariana had not understood until this phase of our time together.

Occasional setbacks continued to occur, but these now offered opportunities to identify the ways in which she allowed herself to avoid doing difficult things. One day she described her habitual choice of losing control of her emotions "like wrapping myself in a warm blanket." The habit felt comforting because of its familiarity. In response we returned to Romans 6 and applied Paul's teaching about the believer's death to sin to Mariana's personal challenge of dying to the attractive yet deadly habits of her thought life.

Psychotropic Medicines

As we continued to work on the various habits and sensations woven through Mariana's life, she was being weaned off her many psychotropic medicines. She started this process without discussing it with me in advance. Once I learned that she was already in the process of being weaned off her medicines, we spent several sessions discussing the role of medication and other physical interventions as they related to her emotional responses.

One drug after another was decreased in dosage and then set aside entirely. She found that her thinking became clearer, making it easier for her to identify unbiblical thought patterns and correct them. She concluded that being on high doses of several medicines had not controlled her emotional outbursts. They actually made it harder for her to recognize and battle the thoughts that precipitated them before a major episode occurred. She weaned herself of all her medications and participated in the remainder of her counseling without any of them being reinstated.[7]

New Memories, Fresh Forgiveness, Fresh Repentance

After we had met together for a number of months, Mariana learned that her father had passed away two months previously. She had not been informed. This opened a long period of struggle with competing feelings of love and anger toward him. She grieved that she would never hear her father ask for her forgiveness. She also grieved to think that he was certainly in hell since he had died without Christ. His death revived many painful memories that would need to be discussed, and Mariana feared that she would be driven mad by her feelings. She found herself sorely tempted to retreat back into childlike behaviors due to the stress, a process she referred to as "making myself little." I reassured her that she

---

[7] For more information on this topic, see Laura Hendrickson and Elyse Fitzpatrick, *Will Medicine Stop the Pain? Finding God's Healing for Depression, Anxiety, and other Troubling Emotions* (Chicago: Moody, 2006). Also see Dan Wickert's more extensive discussion of medication in this book in "'Mary' and Paralyzing Fear," 111.

was capable of dealing with her feelings as an adult in Christ's power, and she was faithful to battle her threatening emotions.

However, in the next few months, a flood of new recollections about her father's sexual abuse emerged. Some of these were difficult to acknowledge. Mariana realized that once molestation had become a regular part of her life, she had responded sexually to her father and had even initiated sexual relations at times. She had done this in order to gain control of his abuse, which she perceived to be inevitable. This newfound acknowledgment produced great shame. Mariana also remembered thinking of him in a romantic way and begging him to rescue her from her mother by running away with her. To make matters worse, she also recalled sexually abusing two younger sisters several times when she was 10 years old. Victims of sexual abuse sometimes engage in abuse themselves because it makes them feel powerful and in control of others. Even as a child Mariana discovered that the sense of control was not worth the guilt she felt over mistreating her sisters, so she stopped on her own without her sin being discovered by others. The fact that Mariana had asked both sisters for forgiveness some years prior to beginning counseling did not eliminate her shame.

These were very challenging issues to discuss. I sought to comfort Mariana by reminding her that it was understandable for her to respond sexually to her father due to their long-standing forced relationship. God had created her as a sexual being, and it was not primarily her fault that she had learned to respond with pleasure under repeated stimulation. Her initial experience of pleasure was not sinful for her; the sin belonged to her father who initiated her into this perverted experience. With this in mind, we explored what responsibility she bore for the ways she may have engaged in the sexual relationship once she understood it was wrong, balancing this with the fact that her participation was coerced rather than consensual.

We used a similar balance of principles to address the sexual abuse of her siblings. I recognized that this response to her abuse was understandable in such a twisted situation. Yet it was still sinful. Understanding that reactions like these were not unique to her when it came to the hearts and bodies of sexual abuse survivors helped Mariana see that she was not irredeemable or freakishly evil, as she had feared. Her temptation was "common to humanity" (1 Cor 10:13), and Christ had already paid the penalty for her sins.

It was challenging for me to speak the truth in love into this difficult issue because in highlighting her responsibility for her own sins I ran the risk of sounding like Mariana's harsh, judgmental mother who had blamed her for her own victimization. I encouraged Mariana to accept responsibility for her own sin while simultaneously insisting that she was not responsible for the sins that had been committed against her. This distinction was difficult for Mariana to make because the two issues had been linked in her mind. I emphasized again that the more we acknowledge our own sins, the more we realize that no one is purely a victim. We may have been grievously sinned against, but we have all responded in sinful ways. No matter what has been done to us, we all need forgiveness for our own sins. Failing to acknowledge this about ourselves only makes us hypocrites like the unforgiving servant (Matt 18:23–33).

When Mariana was able to recognize that she bore some responsibility for her sin without accepting the "dirty" and "evil" judgments of her mother, a great burden was lifted from her heart; she embraced Christ's forgiveness eagerly. This victory opened the way for several weeks of discussion dealing with struggles that Mariana continued to have in her sexual relationship with her husband. As we examined right and wrong in the sexual realm through the lens of Scripture, Mariana found a great deal of release from guilt and shame.

Mariana experienced another sense of release and liberation two years after her father's death when she spoke with her older sister for the first time in 20 years. Her sister was able to verify many of her memories. This objective voice helped Mariana answer some of her relentless questions about which memories were real and which were the results of suggestion and previous psychotherapies. She had spent many years often wondering whether she was "just making it all up." Through her sister she learned that she had not experienced satanic ritual abuse and she did not murder the children she bore to her father. The real story was that her father's incestuous children did not survive their premature births, possibly because Mariana was induced early by her parents. Mariana also learned that she had indeed been abused in the ways documented in her history. Putting this question to rest gave her a sense of peace and the ability to move forward.

After making this fresh family connection, Mariana carefully considered the possibility of confronting her mother about the abuse and giving her the opportunity to ask for forgiveness. By this time Mariana understood the gospel well enough that she was willing to extend forgiveness freely, but both of us were concerned about the potential for a serious setback if Mariana reopened her heart to her mother's influence. In any case her mother was now suffering from dementia and was less likely to respond well to a confrontation than she might have in the past. We jointly decided to table the subject for the time being, but Mariana left counseling understanding that I was happy to help her tackle the issue in the future if the circumstances and timing were right.

Where Was God?

Mariana and I had discussed a myriad of issues during our time together, and there were several more angles yet to be addressed. One immense question now demanded our focus: "Where was God when I was abused?" How could God be all-knowing, all-powerful, and all-good in light of Mariana's dark experiences? Such understandably common questions haunt the minds of abuse survivors.

A key passage I highlighted during these discussions was Exod 34:5–7 where God reveals himself to Moses with a description of his full-orbed character—compassionate, gracious, patient, and loving, and also just, wrathful, and full of vengeance for his enemies. I highlighted God's compassion, mercy, and justice in the Psalms as well, asking Mariana to spend this season of counseling praying various psalms of lament that echoed her personal experience.[8]

The lament psalms are blended expressions of grief and trust as suffering believers cry out in anguish asking God some of the most honest and direct questions found in Scripture. They are beloved by believers of every generation because they reflect the sincere questioning of sufferers and resound with the unique emotions that accompany the darkest experiences of life. However, the psalms of lament are also interwoven with a strong thread of faith as the psalmists cling to the belief that God's steadfast love and unwavering justice will reconcile all of our pain and puzzlement in the end.

As for Mariana, she found it helpful when I joined her in expressing gratitude for Jesus' presence and comfort during her childhood abuse. She came to trust his character to work all things for good (Rom 8:28) even when she did not understand the details herself. The Holy Spirit ultimately did his greatest work in her heart as she listened to God's Word preached by a pastor who had suffered deeply. This pastor exhorted his listeners to take refuge in God's sovereignty and goodness and to entrust their dark experiences to his providential and good design for their lives. Mariana still says that she was fundamentally changed by her experience listening to this pastor and contemplating these truths, and she found peace and resolution regarding God's role in her suffering.

Marriage and Family Issues

Several months passed, and the personal impact of her father's death lessened. As Mariana's emotions settled down, marital and family issues began to emerge. Because she had been disturbed for so long, the dynamic of her family had been substantially shaped by her struggles. Once she began functioning better, other

---

[8] I am indebted to biblical counselor David Powlison for the idea of using lament psalms with abuse victims (see David Powlison, *Recovering from Child Abuse: Healing and Hope for Victims* [Greensboro, NC: New Growth Press, 2008], 11–15). Some examples of lament psalms are Psalms 6; 22; 55.

family members began feeling safe enough to express their own long-suppressed emotions. Mariana and Leon began receiving marital counseling with a male IBCD counselor, and some of their adult children participated when necessary. I continued to support Mariana with individual sessions, as this period of counseling was challenging for her.

Mariana continued to feel safest when she was in control, but this produced friction in her marriage as Leon came to understand that God had called him to lead his family. He saw that yielding to Mariana was not really helping her grow (Eph 5:22–24). As they worked together to overcome old patterns and adjust their marriage to a biblical standard, both made many mistakes.

Leon initially became somewhat authoritarian as he attempted to lead his family, and Mariana alternated between challenging him angrily and taking refuge in hypersubmissive behavior, fearing that she might lose him. I continued to emphasize that Mariana should speak the truth in love (Eph 4:15) and gently correct Leon when he sinned rather than manipulating, raging, or suppressing her feelings (Eph 4:14–15, 25–27). She must make a gracious appeal when she disagreed with a decision (1 Sam 25:18–35).

At one point Mariana became concerned that Leon was engaging in unrepentant sin. She believed that submission required that she comply in silence with his choices for their family. I did not have firsthand information about this problem from Leon, so I did not confront it directly. It was, however, a good opportunity to encourage Mariana not to assent in silence to choices that she understood from Scripture as wrong (Acts 4:18–20; 5:27–29). I also encouraged her to bring her concerns to their marital counselor because biblical love does not passively accept a brother's continuing in sin without correcting him (Luke 17:3; Gal 6:1–3; Col 3:16; Heb 3:13). We addressed a wife's responsibility when she believes her husband is doing wrong, using the examples of Ananias and Sapphira (Acts 5:1–11) and Abraham and Sarah (1 Pet 3:1–7).

This balance of principles was difficult for Mariana to understand and even more difficult to put into practice because it was hard for her to confront lovingly when she was carried away by her emotions. She also struggled to respond appropriately to Leon's biblical rebukes. During this period I had her supplement her meditation with assigned Scripture verses and her intentional practicing of new behaviors at home with readings in the book, *Helper by Design* by Elyse Fitzpatrick.[9] I wanted her to saturate her mind with the wise biblical nuances that informed her role as a woman, nuances that would help her navigate this new marital balance.

As Leon and Mariana began to develop new interpersonal skills, both their marriage counselor and I encouraged them to seek oversight from their home church. An associate pastor was identified who agreed to meet with them, and the marriage counseling at IBCD ended. I began tapering the frequency of my meetings with Mariana.

A few months later, after the family enjoyed a three-week extended family Christmas in peace, Mariana agreed that she was ready to stop meeting with me. We spent a few weeks remembering what she had learned throughout our time together and reminiscing about how far she had come. At our final meeting Mariana understood that if she had difficulties in the future she could return for additional help.

Conclusion: Life After Counseling and Lessons Learned

I heard from Mariana from time to time over the next few years. She and Leon continued to face challenges in their marriage, and their relationships with their three adult children remained difficult. They had occasional, as-needed family counseling sessions at IBCD or with pastors at their local church. Over time, however, their family life calmed down. Mariana has now grown in her faith for several years without any psychotropic medications or personal counseling. The family has not required outside help in some time.

---

[9] Elyse Fitzpatrick, *Helper by Design: God's Perfect Plan for Women in Marriage* (Chicago: Moody, 2003).

Leon took an entrepreneurial position and hired Mariana as his assistant. Their ability to function as marriage partners greatly improved as they worked together for nearly two years. She proved to be a capable helper for Leon, enhancing his earning ability significantly. They also trained as biblical counselors and began counseling couples together through their church's counseling ministry. They are both currently working on their counseling certification through the National Association of Nouthetic Counselors (NANC).[10]

Mariana reports that her daughter told her recently, "You aren't even the same person you were before you began counseling." Her older son recently married and gave Mariana and Leon their first grandson. Although her relationship with this son was once severely damaged, she now describes it as close and cordial. Her relationship with her younger son has been the hardest to restore, but she reports that recently a full reconciliation occurred in this relationship.

Mariana tells me that her life was permanently changed by my illustration of her life as a time line divided into old and new by the power of Christ's death and resurrection. Prior to counseling, Mariana saw herself as permanently damaged by her terrible experiences in childhood—powerless to be anything other than a helpless victim. Seeing herself as clothed with Christ's righteousness and risen to new life gave her hope that she could change the patterns of the past by relying on his power.

There are two opposite temptations that counselors face as they seek to work with a counselee who has a troubled past. One is to view conversations about the past as intrinsically healing; the other is to ignore the influence of the past. Psychotherapists, following Freud and his intellectual heirs, believe that rehearsing

---

[10] The National Association of Nouthetic Counselors (NANC) was founded in 1975 as "a fellowship of Christian pastors and laymen banded together to promote excellence in biblical counseling." The word "nouthetic" derives from the Greek verb *noutheteō* which means "to admonish." See *www.nanc.org* for more information including training and certification opportunities.

the injuries of the past with accompanying emotional discharge[11] enables a counselee to master overwhelming trauma. However, this approach did not produce healing in Mariana. Rather, it enabled an intensification of her emotional responses that, in turn, multiplied her interpersonal chaos.

While the psychotherapy Mariana describes obviously presents a legitimate target for criticism, it is important to remember that her former psychotherapists were advising her at a time when there was a virtual mania for recovered memories. Numerous books on this subject were being published, many troubled women were convinced they had multiple personalities, and most therapists believed in the existence of satanic, ritual abuse. It is not as productive as it may seem to critique this extreme example of a therapeutic fad since few people continue to practice it.

It is more valuable to focus on the biblical incongruity with the psychotherapeutic belief (still held today) that trauma must be reexperienced repeatedly in therapy so that the victim can "master" it. No scriptural principles suggest that repeated emotional indulgence produces healing. Rather, the opposite is suggested by the murderous outcome of Cain's flaring bitterness (Gen 4:1–8) and Absalom's simmering anger (2 Sam 13:20–29), to cite just two examples. Instead, Phil 4:8 commands us to dwell on what is true, honorable, just, pure, lovely, commendable, morally excellent, and praiseworthy.

Does this mean biblical counselors should ignore the influence of the past in their counseling? Mariana saw Christian counselors who encouraged her to forget what is behind her and reach forward to what is ahead of her (Phil 3:13). She was accused of making up her history of abuse, pushed to forgive before being given the opportunity to tell her whole story, and discouraged from discussing painful subjects. Much of this previous counseling focused on identifying and forsaking known patterns of sin, such as the lying that she mentioned at our first session.

---

[11] This "emotional discharge" is known in psychotherapeutic terms as *abreaction*.

These essential angles were an important aspect of my counsel to Mariana as well, and they formed a portion of every session we had together. Correction was offered from an empathetic perspective that formed slowly as I gradually learned all that she had endured. Because she knew that I grasped the enormity of what she had been through, she came to feel safe with me. It was essential for her to be sure that I was not secretly judging her as irredeemably "evil" as her mother had said for years. Because she knew that I understood how she had become the woman she was and that I did not condemn her for it, she was finally able to share her deepest secrets, such as the molestation of her sisters and her sexual response to her father. If she had not felt free to share these things, she might have left counseling still unsure whether she was truly counted righteous in Christ.

Christian women who have been abused in childhood often confuse the exhortations and commands in Scripture with the harsh judgments of their abusers. They feel condemned by the passages intended to comfort them. For this reason it is crucially important to build a firm foundation on the indicatives of Scripture (what God has done for believers and what is already true of believers) while simultaneously addressing failures to live in accordance with biblical imperatives (what Christians are to do in Christ).[12] As I worked with Mariana to break down her destructive emotional habits, I constantly returned to the foundation of her possessing Christ's righteousness. To make any substantial and lasting progress, she had to learn to rest in this reality instead of her own performance. As this truth became more deeply embedded in Mariana's thinking, the perfectionism, guilt, and shame that stemmed from her failure to meet her mother's standard of righteousness gradually lost its power over her emotions.

Another important factor in Mariana's improvement was coming to believe the scriptural teaching that even disturbed

---

[12] I am indebted to biblical counselors Elyse Fitzpatrick and Dennis Johnson for emphasizing scriptural indicatives as well as imperatives in counseling. See Elyse Fitzpatrick and Dennis Johnson, *Counsel from the Cross: Connecting Broken People to the Love of Christ* (Wheaton: Crossway, 2009).

women like her could change. First Corinthians 6:11 concludes a list of life-dominating sins with the frank statement, "Some of you used to be like this. But you were washed, you were sanctified, you were justified in the name of the Lord Jesus Christ and by the Spirit of our God." Mariana had participated in 20 years of Christian psychotherapy which had emphasized the truth of God's love for her without adequately confronting her sin or unpacking Scripture's expectation that true repentance would result in a changed life. A balanced biblical counseling approach addresses both of these truths.

At the same time we must be careful not to impart a "just-do-it" theology when confronting a counselee with the scriptural expectation that repentance will lead to change. Mariana came to counseling persuaded that her uncontrolled reactions to her overwhelming emotions were inevitable. She had already received Christian counseling that emphasized her need to stop reacting the way she was, to no avail. She truly wanted to change and had come to believe that Scripture testified that she had the power to change, but she still was not changing. This was one reason she kept returning to the supposed involuntary nature of the various phenomena she experienced.

Working with someone who has practiced surrendering herself to her emotions for years requires much patience. In this type of situation, the counselor must be willing gently to repeat core teachings as often as necessary. Concluding that counselees with severe disturbances are not really trying can have destructive results in their lives. More than one counselor, both spiritual and psychotherapeutic, had basically called Mariana a liar and a drama queen. She certainly could be both at times, but she was also a human being made in the image of God as well as a struggling believer who deserved to be respected as such even if she sometimes had difficulty conforming her behavior to the Bible's standard.

This underscores the need to be realistic about the investment of time required of counselors who endeavor to help seriously disturbed abuse survivors. Although many such people respond well to a short-term course of counseling, deep-seated, chronic problems like Mariana's require unbending patience, sincere love, generous time, proven trustworthiness, and a sturdy reliance on the power of the Holy Spirit ministered through God's Word and prayer. Cases of severe sexual abuse can be like icebergs: vast and jagged portions of the story hidden beneath the surface emerge only gradually. May God provide abundant grace to all those he calls to this challenging ministry.

Chapter 3

"Brian" and Obsessive-Compulsive Disorder

Steve Viars

A Normal-Town Biblical Counselor

The Lord has given me the privilege of serving as a pastor in Lafayette, Indiana, for nearly 25 years. Our county population hovers around 165,000, and our city is home to Purdue University. In many ways we are a typical mid-sized Midwestern town. We have an interesting mixture of engineers and farmers, radicals and soccer moms, athletes and couch potatoes. Lafayette is large enough to have a television station but small enough that there is rarely anything exciting on the news.

I became interested in biblical counseling as a seminary student when I took a training course that literally changed my life. The principles of the sufficiency of Scripture and progressive sanctification opened my eyes to the many ways God wanted to change me as a young married man. I learned a gospel-centered approach to soul care that was focused on the person and work of Christ. The training program included actual case observations where I was able to watch trained counselors read God's sufficient Word and effectively apply it to the hearts and lives of troubled people. It was thrilling to see men and women fall in love with

Christ as they learned how his redemptive plan dovetailed with their own complex circumstances.

I later did doctoral work in biblical counseling because I wanted to keep learning more. I wanted to enhance my own trajectory of personal growth while becoming better prepared to counsel with Scripture others in their times of need.

A Church-Based Counseling Ministry

In 1977 our church launched a biblical counseling center to serve our community. We wanted to glorify God in our town by offering counseling services based on God's sufficient Word. We also wanted to provide a place where other pastors, missionaries, and key lay leaders could receive training that would prepare them to offer similar ministries wherever God placed them. Decades later we offer 80–120 hours of biblical counseling each week to members of our community—all free of charge. We have found this to be a marvelous way to shine the light of Christ in our town by sharing his love with people in need. Through the years scores of men and women have been won to Christ through this ministry, and many Christians have found answers and direction for how to grow and change though applying God's Word to their lives.

As might be expected, our counselors encounter many garden-variety problems. We help many men and women who are struggling with problems in their marriages or with their children. We frequently minister to those wrestling with depression and anger. Many people come for help with financial problems, difficulties at work, trouble with extended family members, and many other common life issues. A fair amount of what we do is somewhat routine.

However, even in a garden-variety town like Lafayette, counseling occasionally brings a shock. It's like the way one of my friends describes his surgical practice: "98 percent mundane and 2 percent sheer terror." On plenty of occasions when counselees have begun to tell their stories, I have been startled by the personal complexities and situational conundrums that spring up in this "normal" town.

People who struggle with behaviors that fall under the secular label of "Obsessive-Compulsive Disorder" (OCD) have sometimes presented me with just this kind of deep and tangled complexity. I have often had the privilege of working with people diagnosed with this "disorder."

The Many Faces of OCD

Not long ago I saw a man whose job involved emptying mail from postal sacks. His task seemed simple enough, but he had a problem: he constantly worried that he might have left an item at the bottom of the sack. After emptying a bag, he would begin processing the items only to find himself wondering whether he had completely emptied the sack. He would pick up the bag and look inside again. After confirming (again) that the sack was indeed empty, he would go back to processing the items. Soon his thoughts would be drawn back to the sack. His boss was not amused when he walked in one day and found the man with the empty sack on his head.

I also counseled a woman who constantly stared at her administrative errors. She worked in an office and believed that if she was careful enough, she would never make a mistake. If she accidentally copied something upside down on the copier, she would bring the wasted piece of paper back to her desk and go through a ritual of mental flagellation. Her boss would come in and find her in a coma-like state. His patience, understandably, was growing thin.

I will never forget the man who arrived with his face covered with small cuts and scrapes. I wondered if he had been in a car accident or had been attacked by a rabid animal. I would have never anticipated his story: his injuries were inflicted with his own razor while he tried to shave every vestige of whisker from his face. I later learned that he viewed facial hair as unsanitary and unattractive, but he could never get his face clean enough to meet his self-imposed standard of hygiene.

I once ministered to another man diagnosed as OCD who believed he needed to completely empty his intestines of all waste.

He would stay in the bathroom for hours at a time, often all day or all night. He had stopped trying to work long before I met him, and his wife told horror stories of having to clean up the bathroom after her husband emerged—exhausted after long hours in the bathroom.

Brian, OCD, and Odd-Numbered Streets

Then there was a young man named Brian.[1] I was surprised when, during our first evening together, Brian admitted that he was unable to drive his car on odd-numbered streets. I was amazed at his tale of developing elaborate strategies to guarantee that he would never drive his car on anything but even-numbered roadways. I was exhausted listening to his story as I contemplated the obsessive lifestyle he had developed. I was also stirred to a silent prayer of thanks that our church is located at the intersection of State Road 26 and County Road 550.

Brian was in his early twenties when he contacted our counseling center for help. At first glance Brian was a friendly and likable person. He was holding down a job and serving in his local church across town. You would not have immediately known that Brian was struggling in any unusual way.

As he began to tell his story, his eyes shifted around the room to see how I and my two training assistants were responding. He revealed each piece of the puzzle slowly, and only after he was sure he would not be ridiculed or harshly judged, did he talk about an elaborate system he had concocted to navigate his way around town without ever being on an odd-numbered street. This system required that he spend hours looking at local street maps and determining his routes. Brian lived in constant fear that he might get lost or inadvertently make a wrong turn and foil his plan.

When Brian began realizing that his habits, like a python slowly suffocating its victim, were becoming more and more restrictive, he decided to contact our center. He knew he needed

---

[1] Brian's name is changed here, but the details of his story are the same.

help and was desperate to find answers that would really help him change.

How Should We Understand OCD?

How should we understand this type of obsessive-compulsive behavior? One of the challenges with a concept like OCD is that the terminology obviously does not originate in Scripture. This is not necessarily bad, but it does require that Christians be careful in how we understand and make use of the label. In standard books like the *Diagnostic and Statistical Manual of Mental Disorders, Fourth Edition* (*DSM-IV*), secular researchers often do an excellent job of describing and organizing symptomatic behaviors. People interested in thinking biblically about life can use a book like the *DSM* to help them formulate questions that can then be taken to the Scriptures for answers. The goal should be to allow the Bible to interpret the observations we glean from a secular source like the *DSM*.

Secular observers accurately describe the behaviors common to OCD: "The essential features of OCD are recurrent obsessions or compulsions that are severe enough to be time consuming or cause marked distress or significant impairment."[2] The real people mentioned above whom I had the privilege of counseling fit this description well. These men and women reported that they spent substantial amounts of time each day on their rituals. They also acknowledged that they felt trapped in cycles that were both loathsome and familiar.

The *DSM-IV* states that obsessions are persistent ideas, thoughts, impulses, or images that are experienced as intrusive and inappropriate and that cause marked anxiety or distress. The manual further reports that the most common obsessions are things like repeated thoughts about contamination from handshaking; repeated doubts about leaving a door unlocked; a need to have things in a particular order and experiencing severe distress when they are not; aggressive or horrific impulses like hurting

---

[2] *Diagnostic and Statistical Manual of Mental Disorders: DSM-IV* (Washington, DC: American Psychiatric Association, 1994), 417.

someone; and finally, sexual imagery such as recurrent pornographic images.[3]

The *DSM-IV* goes on to define compulsions as a person's attempts to neutralize an obsession with some other thought or action. So the person worried about contamination repeatedly washes his hands. The woman concerned about whether she turned off the stove checks it repeatedly. The parent afraid of hurting his child counts backward from a thousand. These compulsions are not performed for pleasure or gratification. The goal is to reduce the anxiety produced by the obsession. The compulsions are clearly excessive and often are not connected in any realistic way with what they are designed to neutralize or prevent.

What Causes OCD?

Secular observations and research can often help organize and describe behaviors like these. However, labels and descriptions can only take us so far. At some point we need to know not only what is happening but also *why* it is happening. Theorists suggest at least four possible answers to the question of what causes OCD: circumstances from the past, pressure in the present, genetic and physical determiners, or spiritual issues of the heart.

Nurture: Are Circumstances from the Past to Blame?

Some theorists believe that OCD behavior is a natural and innocent response to certain conditions from the past. In other words, the fundamental problem is nurture or the way in which a person was raised. For example, consider a daughter who grew up in a controlling home environment where the mother placed inordinate attention on how her girls looked before leaving the house. Now this adult daughter has trouble getting to places on time because she constantly goes back for one more look in the mirror. Some would argue that such obsessive behavior is not the grown daughter's responsibility. The fault lies with the domineering behavior of the controlling mother in the past.

---

[3] Ibid., 418.

If the Word of God is going to be our guide, is there any truth to the notion that past circumstances are partially responsible for present behavior? The answer is yes—at least to a point. Scripture does not shy away from the topic of previous sins and past suffering. Adonijah's mutinous rebellion is connected to David's parental passivity (1 Kgs 1:5–6). Hophni and Phinehas blasphemed partially because their father did not stop them (1 Sam 2:12; 3:11–14). Joseph's brothers were ruled by fear because of all they put him through (Gen 50:15–21). We all have been greatly impacted by the sinful conditions of the world in which we live. While we cannot use the dark realities of our pasts to excuse behavior that displeases God in the present, counselors should always recognize the potential presence of past suffering and should acknowledge the scars left by the jagged edges of life. This recognition should engender patience and compassion toward those struggling with repetitive behaviors that are seemingly uncontrollable. The apostle Paul, a Christian leader with a violently checkered past himself, wrote: "And we exhort you, brothers: warn those who are irresponsible, comfort the discouraged, help the weak, be patient with everyone" (1 Thess 5:14).

Environment: Is Pressure in the Present at Fault?

Another possible explanation is that persons with OCD are living under tremendous stress or unreasonable expectations. Their behaviors are simply ways to cope with overwhelming external pressures. For example, perhaps the reason the woman I mentioned stared at her photocopying mistakes was that the copying machine was too difficult to operate. Her training on the machine was minimal, and the copier had many features. Her employer expected her to be productive, and she had many tasks to accomplish each day. Or maybe the man who checked and rechecked his mail sack worked under an overbearing tyrant of a boss who derided his employees whenever they made a mistake. There was no question that his particular situation was fast paced and highly controlled.

Does this potential cause of OCD have merit? In some senses, yes. Scripture clearly illustrates the powerful effect that present trials can have in a person's life. The psalmist felt afflicted, withered, restless, tearful, and thrown aside (Ps 102:4, 7, 9–10). The prophet Habakkuk "trembled" and "quivered" at the thought of the coming Babylonian invasion (Hab 3:16). The apostle Paul repeatedly pleaded with the Lord to remove his unnamed "thorn in the flesh" (2 Cor 12:7–8). Therefore, Scripture clearly instructs followers of Christ not only to rejoice with those who rejoice but also to "weep with those who weep" (Rom 12:15). Ignoring or minimizing the present suffering of the people we counsel makes us decidedly unlike our sympathetic Savior (Heb 4:15).

Scripture also summons the believer to faith, hope, and endurance—all with the promise of God's help. The psalmist chose to trust the Lord (Ps 102:12–22, 25–28). Habakkuk found his joy in God (Hab 3:17–19). Paul discovered God's strength in the midst of his weakness (2 Cor 12:9–10). Our pressures in the present may be difficult and even demoralizing, but they do not have to be determinative.

Nature: Is My Body to Blame?

Physical factors are a third possible explanation for OCD-type behavior. Researchers use the term *ego-dystonic* to refer to the intrusive and inappropriate quality of obsessions. "This refers to the individual's sense that the content of the obsession is alien, not within his or her own control, and not the kind of thought that he or she would expect to have."[4]

Are such persons correct in believing that OCD is an alien set of thoughts or behaviors for which they are not responsible today? Is the problem really one's nature? Some counselors and theorists may dismiss such ideas out of hand because they do not want to absolve people of personal responsibility. Before answering too quickly, however, certain facts should be considered. In his helpful booklet, *OCD—Freedom for the Obsessive Compulsive*, Dr. Michael Emlet points out several possible brain-based influences

[4] Ibid.

of OCD. For example, familial and genetic studies have shown that OCD occurs more often among identical twins than fraternal twins. Children with strep throat may also experience the sudden onset of OCD behaviors, and antibiotics not only relieve the strep symptoms but also alleviate the OCD. PET scans or functional MRIs of those diagnosed with OCD sometimes show an overactivity in the basal ganglia and frontal regions of the brain.[5] These findings should come as no surprise because the Bible clearly states that our physical body is a critical element of our created state (e.g., 2 Cor 5:1–4). Therefore, it is appropriate for a counselor to encourage a counselee to have a complete medical exam while continuing to try to understand his past-to-present story.

Ideas like these are not a source of concern for biblical counselors. On the contrary, those ministering the Word through counseling should be friends of good science and desire to promote the research and development of hard data in every area of human existence. Nevertheless, there will always be deficiencies in the answers the world gives regarding the question of ultimate causes. Observable changes in the brain could easily be explained as the *result* of mental-behavioral choices, just as they could be the *cause* of those same thoughts and actions. While offering some clarifying observations and useful research, the nurture, environment, and nature theories ultimately fail to go far enough because all three fail to grapple with what Scripture reveals as the fundamental issue in every counseling case.

Heart: What Does My Behavior Reveal About My Worship?

Yes, it is possible, if not likely, that a person struggling with behaviors labeled as OCD has been impacted by some aspect of his upbringing. It is equally possible that he is facing present trials or even that physical or biological issues may be contributing factors. The power of suffering in a sin-cursed world is an

---

[5] Michael R. Emlet, *OCD Freedom for the Obsessive Compulsive* (Phillipsburg, NJ: P&R, 2004), 7–8.

ever-present reality in the counseling room. Scripture, however, prods us to go deeper. Much deeper.

God created mankind in his image and entrusted each of us with a heart. The word "heart" is used over 700 times in Scripture. It refers to our inner man, the core of our being, our mission control center. The heart is the composite of thoughts, desires, emotions, and beliefs that guides our daily choices. This is why Solomon urged his son, "Guard your heart above all else, for it is the source of life" (Prov 4:23). We all use our heart to worship *something*—whether the God of heaven and earth or something else we believe will bring us comfort, joy, and satisfaction.

In counseling a person struggling with OCD, the core issue is this: What do a person's behavioral choices reveal about his functional god? Delving into past experiences, present challenges, and physical factors should always serve the purpose of determining what is occurring in the heart of the person struggling with OCD-type behaviors. The heart is the most fertile ground for biblical counseling, and gently unearthing the spiritual issues lying beneath the surface enables the power of the gospel to shine hope and help.

Counseling Brian

All of these observations, research, definitions, debates, and scriptural realities compel us to ask one crucial question: Can the truths of the Bible really help Brian learn to drive on even-numbered streets again? Is the living and active sword of God's Word really sharp enough to penetrate the knotty complexities of bizarre behavior like OCD? Can Brian really change? The answer is a resounding *yes*, and the rest of Brian's story testifies boldly to this hope.

The Importance of Loving Involvement

On a few previous occasions Brian had ventured to share his struggles with other Christians, but he had not been treated with the comfort, help, and patience urged by Paul (1 Thess 5:14). Instead, Brian's fellow believers had shamed and ridiculed him.

At other times Christians had offered shallow counsel, suggesting that he change his behavior simply by memorizing random Bible verses or forcing himself to act differently. Because of these painful experiences, Brian was a bit tentative in our initial meetings.

Recognizing Brian's apprehension, I sought to assure him that while he was struggling with certain issues, I had areas in my own life that needed attention as well. Our goal would be to go to the Lord together to "receive mercy and find grace to help us at the proper time" (Heb 4:16). It was fascinating to watch Brian warm up to the process when he knew he was going to be treated with Christian love. Within weeks he went from being shy, quiet, and evasive in his answers to being animated, lively, and thorough in describing what was occurring in his heart and life. He actually grew to enjoy the counseling sessions and reported that he looked forward to coming in each week to examine more of what God said about the process of change.

Biblical counseling must always be done in an atmosphere of relational compassion. We should emulate the apostle Paul who was able to tell the Thessalonians, "We were gentle among you, as a nursing mother nurtures her own children. We cared so much for you that we were pleased to share with you not only the gospel of God but also our own lives, because you had become dear to us" (1 Thess 2:7–8). Biblical counseling presents not just biblical content but biblical compassion. We are not just offering scriptural truth but scriptural tenderness.

The Necessity of Hope in a Redeemer

Just as Brian's earlier ventures in vulnerability had ended in disappointment, he had also grown convinced that he would be stuck in his obsessive-compulsive patterns for the rest of his life. In fact, even though he reported that he was a follower of Jesus Christ, he believed his OCD would continue to worsen until he was entirely unable to function. This is one of the common themes I have observed in every person with whom I have ever worked who exhibited OCD symptoms—profound hopelessness.

This is also one of the primary reasons I love being a biblical counselor—the Word of God is filled with hope. One of the first verses Brian and I considered together was 1 Cor 10:13: "No temptation has overtaken you except what is common to humanity. God is faithful, and he will not allow you to be tempted beyond what you are able, but with the temptation he will also provide a way of escape so that you are able to bear it."

Brian was deeply encouraged to learn that his situation was not unique. He took God at his Word that his problems were "common to humanity" and that the Lord was powerful enough to help anyone overcome the most significant challenges. Because so many of my counselees have given me permission to use their stories whenever it will help another person, I was able to tell Brian about other men and women who had overcome OCD through the power of the gospel. He turned these words over and over in his mind like a person sucking on a sweet piece of chocolate—*my situation is not hopeless.* By God's grace Brian was being empowered to marvel at the fact that God himself is "the God of hope" (Rom 15:13). God had made him, God had saved him, and God could change him.

As Brian grew in hope, he came to understand that he was not placing his confidence in a counselor, a counseling center, or a counseling system. His hope was in a Redeemer, the Lord Jesus Christ. Eventually Brian would come to understand what Elyse Fitzpatrick and Dennis Johnson so helpfully explain:

> Most of us have never really understood that Christianity is not a self-help religion meant to enable moral people to become more moral. We don't need a self-help book; we need a Savior. We don't need to get our collective act together; we need death and resurrection and the life-transforming truths of the gospel. And we don't need them just once, at the beginning of our Christian life; we need them every moment of every day.[6]

---

[6] Elyse Fitzpatrick and Dennis Johnson, *Counsel from the Cross* (Wheaton: Crossway, 2009), 30.

As Brian pondered all of this and reviewed the way he had been attempting to handle his struggles, he readily acknowledged that he had not considered the way his relationship with Christ should inform and empower his daily lifestyle. Such an understanding was groundbreaking for Brian. An entirely new set of resources was being placed on the table. My prayer for Brian was the same as the apostle Paul's desire for his friends in Rome: "Now may the God of hope fill you with all joy and peace as you believe in Him so that you may overflow with hope by the power of the Holy Spirit" (Rom 15:13).

The theme of hope became a focal point of several of Brian's initial homework assignments. I asked him to journal the times he felt hopeless in his pursuit of change, carefully describing the context in which his discouragement appeared along with recording his feelings, thoughts, desires, words, and actions. Brian also began writing passages from God's Word about hope on index cards. He reviewed his cards nightly and during stressful times throughout the day. In our counseling sessions I also asked him to share specific examples from the previous week where he had chosen to reflect on truths from God's Word about hope and how these reflections impacted his heart and his actions. Like Ruth and Naomi thousands of years earlier (Ruth 2:19–20), Brian was coming to realize that he had a Redeemer, and hope was springing up in his heart.

The Necessity of Additional Questions

Competent biblical counselors believe in spending significant amounts of time gathering additional information by asking questions that help both counselor and counselee focus on issues of both the outer and inner man. The counseling room is often illuminated by the wisdom of Prov 18:13: "The one who gives an answer before he listens—this is foolishness and disgrace for him."

This is one reason it is so valuable to do counseling ministry in the context of a local church where counseling services are offered free of charge. The conversation is not rushed by financial concerns, and we are free to take the necessary time to get to know a counselee on a deeper level. The counselee, in turn, becomes convinced that we are not simply going to toss out pat answers or shallow solutions. Many people even report that their biblical counselor was the first person that truly seemed to care enough to ask meaningful questions and patiently hear their story. So what kinds of questions should be asked to obtain a complete picture of a person's story and get to the heart of the matter?

Feelings. Biblical counselors believe in ministering the gospel to the whole person. This ministry starts by taking the time to learn what is happening in the emotional lives of those who come to us for help. This was especially important in my relationship with Brian. I explained to Brian that I wanted to understand what was going on in his mind and heart. We looked at several of the psalms of lament and talked about how godly people in the past cried out to God in a way that was honest and authentic. I told Brian that I wanted to create an environment where he could have similar conversations with me but, more importantly, with God. This notion seemed to surprise him. Somewhere along the way he had picked up the common idea that Christians were to ignore their feelings and hide their emotions. Passages such as Ps 61:1–4 framed our discussion about a more genuine way of talking with God:

> God, hear my cry; pay attention to my prayer. I call to You from the ends of the earth when my heart is without strength. Lead me to a rock that is high above me, for You have been a refuge for me, a strong tower in the face of the enemy. I will live in Your tent forever and take refuge under the shelter of Your wings.

When Brian became convinced that it was permissible to cry out to God and to me, he began to describe a lifestyle that was ruled by fear. He would do literally anything to avoid driving his car on an odd-numbered street. His heart was gripped with the fear that terrible things would happen to him the moment he disregarded his self-imposed driving rules. When I asked him if he was experiencing any other fears, it was as if a dam broke. He looked around the room as if to say, "Is it OK for me to talk about this?" When I assured him that I really wanted to know what was happening, he went on to tell me about an entire catalog of fears ranging from the concern that he would fondle a young woman in a worship service to the fear that he would lose his salvation because of what was occurring in his heart.

Brian also described feelings of shame. It took several sessions before he was willing to look me in the eye. In our initial conversations he had frequently looked down at his feet or around at different points in my office. When he began to talk about his reluctance to let people at his church really get to know him because he was afraid they would learn his secrets, he began to calm down and looked at me directly. What if someone asked him to drive them somewhere? How would he explain his bizarre rituals to a casual acquaintance who had simply asked for a ride?

Brian knew that his emotions were not the only component of his problem, but he was relieved that someone was willing to join him in lifting the lid off of what he believed was the garbage can of a confused life. I was again reminded of Solomon's wisdom:

> Two are better than one because they have a good reward for their efforts. For if either falls, his companion can lift him up; but pity the one who falls without another to lift him up. Also, if two lie down together, they can keep warm; but how can one person alone keep warm? And if someone overpowers one person, two can resist him. A cord of three strands is not easily broken. (Eccl 4:9–12)

Yes, other significant layers of Brian's life still needed to be addressed, but having someone who would allow him to be honest about his feelings was a great encouragement to Brian.

Thoughts. One of the crucial transitions in the process of biblical counseling is moving from the emotional component of the problem to other aspects of the inner and outer person. I often start with what is occurring emotionally because that is where people in crisis are living. Their emotions are consuming them. They often even report that they have an "emotional problem."

At the right time (and hopefully in the right way), I try to point out that their emotions are simply performing one of their God-given purposes: to indicate habits of thinking, desiring, speaking, worshipping, and behaving that the Lord wants them to learn to change through the power of his Word.

In one of our early sessions, I asked Brian to describe what he typically thought about before, during, and after each of his OCD episodes. At first he found it difficult to remember. He had been so focused on his bizarre behavior that he had paid no attention to the issues of the inner man that were producing his actions. This was a strategic point in the counseling process to assign a simple "journal of upsets." The journal would function like a daily schedule where Brian was asked to note every time he had an OCD episode and to describe carefully what he was doing, thinking, and wanting in each stage of the event.

The results of this exercise were fascinating. Brian recognized a major thought pattern. His fears of driving were always preceded by episodes of sexual lust. By this point in our relationship, I had developed a level of trust with Brian, so he was willing to divulge that he was locked in a significant struggle with sinful thinking about women. Ironically, this battle was especially intense during times of worship at church. He was attracted to some of the young ladies on the worship team, and he would mentally undress them while supposedly singing and praising the Lord.

These episodes produced extreme guilt. Brian believed he would lose his salvation if he didn't atone for his sins in some way. Early in the struggle he had conjured up a self-imposed punishment of counting backwards during worship services each time he lusted after a young woman. This approach only made matters worse. At some point he graduated to the notion that he could especially please God if he only drove on certain kinds of streets. We were never able to establish any kind of rational connection between Brian's guilt and his behavioral choices. Brian simply erected a new perfectionistic standard in his heart, believing that if he practiced this kind of vehicular lent, God would forgive him for his lust and still allow him to go to heaven.

This was the first time Brian had ever connected the dots between his sexual lust and his obsessions about driving. On the one hand it was hard for him to admit what was going on in his heart, but he was also encouraged that his bizarre patterns of behavior could be explained.

Desires. One key biblical passage for Brian was Jas 1:14–15: "But each person is tempted when he is drawn away and enticed by his own evil desires. Then after desire has conceived, it gives birth to sin, and when sin is fully grown, it gives birth to death." Brian was all too familiar with the concept of sexual lust. He was surprised to learn that in the Bible lust is a much broader category than he had previously understood: it includes all kinds of inordinate desire. I encouraged him to think about what he hoped to achieve from these behaviors—what lusts of the heart were producing his bizarre thoughts and actions.

The more Brian thought about this concept, the clearer the answer became. Brian wanted to pay for his own sin. He had truly convinced himself that performing certain rituals would absolve him from the guilt associated with a lustful heart. Brian wanted atonement without a substitute and righteousness without a Redeemer. He was trying to solve his problem by turning from Christ to himself. He needed to learn how to turn to Christ and rest in his finished work.

Connecting Brian to the Gospel

When Brian began to contemplate what was occurring in his heart, he was horrified. Although he had placed his faith and trust in the finished work of Christ for his salvation several years earlier, he had since convinced himself that he was earning daily righteousness by his unusual rituals. He wept when he realized that his relentless attempts to gain God's favor on his own were a rejection of the saving work of Jesus Christ. He was broken when he finally saw his self-righteousness for what it really was—a mockery of the cross.

The Importance of Confession

As he became overwhelmed by the darkness of his sin, Brian needed to embrace the bright gospel reality that "where sin multiplied, grace multiplied even more" (Rom 5:20). Brian cried out to God and confessed his sin of believing he could find atonement in his own work. With David he said, "Be gracious to me, God, according to Your faithful love; according to Your abundant compassion, blot out my rebellion. Wash away my guilt and cleanse me from my sin. For I am conscious of my rebellion, and my sin is always before me" (Ps 51:1–3).

The Necessity of Repentance

Brian was starting to understand what produced the OCD symptoms, but this was just the beginning of the process of change. Brian had taken the initial step of confession and was experiencing divine help. As Solomon explained, "The one who conceals his sins will not prosper, but whoever confesses and renounces them will find mercy" (Prov 28:13). Brian had come to understand the source of his problem and could confess it accurately. After confessing his sin, he needed to learn what it meant to forsake his lifestyle and replace it with an inner- and outer-man approach to living that honored his Lord.

The Process of Progressive Sanctification

At this point Brian did not need a rigid 15-step method for growth because Christian growth comes not through a series of steps. There is no magic formula. At the same time the Bible is filled with principles that help God's people change progressively into the image of Christ. The apostle Peter ended his last letter by saying, "But grow in the grace and knowledge of our Lord and Savior Jesus Christ. To Him be the glory both now and to the day of eternity. Amen" (2 Pet 3:18). In a similar way Paul told his friends at Philippi,

> So then, my dear friends, just as you have always obeyed, not only in my presence, but now even more in

> my absence, work out your own salvation with fear and trembling. For it is God who is working in you, enabling you both to desire and to work out His good purpose. (Phil 2:12–13)

Brian was encouraged to learn that the Bible contained practical principles to help him change from a life that was obsessive and unproductive to a life characterized by freedom, joy, direction, and controlled choices in both the inner and outer man that brought glory to God.

It was important, however, to help Brian understand that he could only make the necessary changes through the power of his resurrected Lord. The last thing we wanted to do was to replace self-centered atonement with self-centered sanctification. Brian needed to learn what it means to preach the gospel to himself every day. As Milton Vincent explained:

> God did not give us his gospel just so we could embrace it and be converted. Actually, he offers it to us every day as a gift that keeps on giving to us everything we need for life and godliness. The wise believer learns this truth early and becomes proficient in extracting available benefits from the gospel each day. We extract these benefits by being absorbed in the gospel, speaking it to ourselves when necessary, and by daring to reckon it true in all we do.[7]

Brian had a long road ahead of him. His patterns of living were established and ingrained, but understanding that he was forgiven, accepted, and empowered "in Christ" gave him confidence that he had all the resources of heaven at his disposal if he really wanted to change in God's way. Together we examined a number of Scripture passages to drive this point home:

- I am sure of this, that he who started a good work in you will carry it on to completion until the day of Christ Jesus (Phil 1:6).

---

[7] Milton Vincent, *The Gospel Primer for Christians* (Bemidji, MN: Focus, 2008), 5.

- And I no longer live, but Christ lives in me. The life I now live in the body, I live by faith in the Son of God, who loved me and gave Himself for me (Gal 2:20).
- I am the true vine, and My Father is the vineyard keeper. Every branch in Me that does not produce fruit he removes, and he prunes every branch that produces fruit so that it will produce more fruit. You are already clean because of the word I have spoken to you. Remain in Me, and I in you. Just as a branch is unable to produce fruit by itself unless it remains on the vine, so neither can you unless you remain in Me (John 15:1–4).
- What should we say then? Should we continue in sin so that grace may multiply? Absolutely not! How can we who died to sin still live in it? Or are you unaware that all of us who were baptized into Christ Jesus were baptized into His death? Therefore we were buried with Him by baptism into death, in order that, just as Christ was raised from the dead by the glory of the Father, so we too may walk in a new way of life (Rom 6:1–4).

I talked with Brian about how to use passages such as these to begin thinking about his identity in Christ. His mind had previously been consumed with his own sexual lust and his man-made attempts to pay for his own sin. He had been focusing exclusively on himself. Over time Brian learned to focus on the beauty of the finished work of Christ and the joy of being found "in Him." The result was a growing love for Jesus and a confidence that through the power of Christ working in him, he could change. It would be a process, but it was not meant to be a performance.

The Beauty of Freedom

One aspect of the gospel that was especially important for Brian to grasp was that the blood of Christ freed him from any enslavement to sinful patterns of thinking and behaving. He learned that every time he started to believe the lie that his situation was hopeless, he needed to remind himself of the rich resources he possessed in Christ. One passage that especially connected with him was Rom 6:17–18: "But thank God that, although you used to be slaves of sin, you obeyed from the heart that pattern of teaching you were transferred to, and having been liberated from sin, you became enslaved to righteousness."

I encouraged Brian to begin thanking the Lord regularly for the freedom he enjoyed in Christ, just as the believers in Rome were exhorted to "consider yourselves dead to sin but alive to God in Christ Jesus" (Rom 6:11). Hope was blooming in Brian's heart as he continued to learn how the sufficient blood of Christ, and not a man-made behavioral ritual, was the basis of his relationship with God. As Brian Borgman observed:

> The sovereign king of the entire universe is our Father. He has not only created us, but he has also recreated us in Jesus Christ and has provided everything we need. Paul tells the timid Timothy, "For God has not given us a spirit of fear, but of power and of love and of a sound mind (2 Tim 1:7 KJV)." Unbelieving, sinful fear is contrary to what God has put in us at conversion (Rom 8:15). We overcome the grip of fear by knowing what God has done for us and in us through his Son. We break fear's grip by realizing God did not give this fear to us; rather, he has given us the spirit of power, love, and self-control.[8]

The Relationship Between Gospel Indicatives and Gospel Imperatives

At this point in my relationship with Brian, we arrived at an important crossroad. We had spent much of our time together discovering who Brian was in Christ. Now it was time to discover some of the new behaviors Brian should live out in the power of Christ. Theologians speak about the importance of distinguishing between the gospel indicatives (who we are in Christ) and the gospel imperatives (how we should act as a result). The organization of Paul's letter to the Ephesians is a classic example of this

[8] Brian Borgman, *Feelings and Faith: Cultivating Godly Emotions in the Christian Life* (Wheaton: Crossway, 2009), 129.

principle. Chapters 1–3 are saturated with gospel indicatives and 4–6 are filled with gospel imperatives.

In Ephesians 1–3, Paul expounds on the gospel indicatives and gives us a beautiful and robust understanding of what it means to be a child of God. Our new identity includes earthshaking truths: we have been chosen "before the foundation of the world" (1:4); we were adopted "through Jesus Christ for Himself" (1:5); we enjoy "redemption . . . through His blood" (1:7); and we have received the "forgiveness of our trespasses, according to the riches of His grace" (1:7). This is only a sampling of the marvelous truths regarding who we are in Christ. No wonder Paul ends these three remarkable chapters with a prayer that we would comprehend our identity in Christ (Eph 3:14–21). As James MacDonald wrote, "To really be gripped by your identity in God's greatness you must wade out of the shallow waters of self-absorption into the deep waters of praising him at all times for all things. Remember, God formed you for that very purpose. Embrace your identity as a forgiven worshiper of this all-patient God."[9]

Only after comprehending the love of Christ and our marvelous position in him can we ever begin to live in a way that honors him. This is why there is a critical transition in the book at Eph 4:1: "Therefore I, the prisoner for the Lord, urge you to walk worthy of the calling you have received." Paul then described how God's children should behave in order to please him.

Many Christians are spiritually stunted because they are trying to fulfill the commands of Ephesians 4–6 (the gospel imperatives) without soaking themselves in the foundational truths regarding their identity in Ephesians 1–3 (the gospel indicatives). Counselors must also avoid falling into either side of this ditch. On one side counselors must not focus on good behaviors while excluding the gospel indicatives that empower those behaviors. On the other side counselors must consistently explain how the heavenly realities of who we are in Christ translate into real-life actions.

---

[9] James MacDonald, *Gripped by the Greatness of God* (Chicago: Moody, 2005), 166.

The primary issue in Brian's story had little to do with his driving and had everything to do with his identity. He had to learn to think biblically about his Savior and himself (Rom 12:3). That new thinking needed to produce new patterns of living.

As Brian moved from recognizing who he was in Christ to behaving rightly in Christ, he had to keep inventory of his thoughts. Self-absorbed thinking had generated Brian's bizarre efforts at self-atonement. Now Christ-centered thinking would be necessary to generate new, godly behaviors. Brian needed to learn to evaluate every thought about the Lord, himself, his past, his environment, his struggles—everything—through the lens of God's Word. Brian had been telling himself lies over and over again; he now needed Jesus to renew his mind along the lines of Phil 4:8: "Finally brothers, whatever is true, whatever is honorable, whatever is just, whatever is pure, whatever is lovely, whatever is commendable—if there is any moral excellence and if there is any praise—dwell on these things."

As the filter of Phil 4:8 began to catch his sinful thoughts, Brian had to begin putting to death (Col 3:5) any thought that was displeasing to God. Wonderfully, by the power of the Holy Spirit, Brian actually had the ability to catch and put to death (Rom 8:13) these selfish and sinful thoughts as they appeared in his mind.

One dominating thought that Brian had to begin attacking was his sexual lust. He had to learn to put to death lustful thoughts about women and replace them with biblical ways of thinking about the people the Lord placed around him. James 1:21–25 became a critical weapon in Brian's arsenal at this stage of the battle:

> Therefore, ridding yourselves of all moral filth and evil, humbly receive the implanted word, which is able to save you. But be doers of the word and not hearers only, deceiving yourselves. Because if anyone is a hearer of the word and not a doer, he is like a man looking at his own face in a mirror. For he looks at himself, goes away, and immediately forgets what kind of man he was. But the one who looks intently into the perfect law of freedom and

perseveres in it, and is not a forgetful hearer but one who does good works—this person will be blessed in what he does.

As Brian was learning to act on God's Word and put to death his lustful thoughts, he humbly allowed me to hold him accountable as he took practical steps toward developing a renewed mind through the truth and power of God's Word. Eventually this accountability was transferred to a trusted friend who would continue to discuss this area of life with Brian on a regular basis. At first it was difficult for Brian to be open about the struggles he was having in his thought life. Over timc, however, he began experiencing the joy of authenticity and the freedom that comes from "taking every thought captive to obey Christ" (2 Cor 10:5).

Yet Brian not only had to learn to kill sinful thoughts; he also had to learn to put to death the sinful desires which produced those thoughts. So together we studied Jas 1:14–15, and Brian began to ask himself questions like, "What am I wanting in this situation?" and "What desires are motivating this kind of behavior?" As Brian answered these questions, he began to recognize one fundamental desire: "I want to atone for my sinful lust by driving my car in a particular way." By the end of our time together, Brian acknowledged the bizarre nature of that desire. But we were both reminded that when we neglect to focus on the transforming truth of God's Word, we are all prone to thoughts, desires, words, and actions that are senseless and even absurd. Solomon made exactly this point in Eccl 9:3 when he observed that "the hearts of people are full of evil, and madness is in their hearts while they live." Thank God that, by his grace and through his power, even our most heinous desires and thoughts can be put to death in Christ.

The Beauty of New Life in Christ

The gospel summons us not only to put off what is wrong but also to put on what is right (Eph 4:22–24). For Brian this meant taking the focus off of himself, forfeiting any supposed righteousness he might be able to earn, and turning his gaze to the finished work of Christ and the complete righteousness that has already been accounted to every one of God's children. Second Corinthians 5:21 became a crucial focus of our discussion: "He made the One who did not know sin to be sin for us, so that we might become the righteousness of God in Him." Brian was learning to follow the path of the apostle Paul outlined in Phil 3:7–11:

> But everything that was a gain to me, I have considered to be a loss because of Christ. More than that, I also consider everything to be a loss in view of the surpassing value of knowing Christ Jesus my Lord. Because of Him I have suffered the loss of all things and consider them filth, so that I may gain Christ and be found in Him, not having a righteousness of my own from the law, but one that is through faith in Christ—the righteousness from God based on faith. My goal is to know Him and the power of His resurrection and the fellowship of His sufferings, being conformed to His death, assuming that I will somehow reach the resurrection from among the dead.

The orientation of Brian's heart was turning toward the beauty of his Savior and the joy and privilege of growing in the knowledge of him. He learned the same lesson that C. H. Spurgeon had learned many years before:

> Oh, there is, in contemplating Christ, a balm for every wound; in musing on the Father, there is a quietus for every grief; and in the influence of the Holy Ghost, there is a balsam for every sore. Would you lose your sorrow? Would you drown your cares? Then go, plunge yourself in the Godhead's deepest sea; be lost in his immensity; and you shall come forth as from a couch of rest, refreshed and invigorated. I know nothing which can so comfort the soul; so calm the swelling billows of sorrow and grief; so speak peace to the winds of trial, as a devout musing upon the subject of the Godhead.[10]

---

[10] C. H. Spurgeon, *The New Park Street Pulpit* (Grand Rapids: Baker, 1990), 1:1.

In the course of time, Brian's bizarre behaviors began to change naturally. This natural transformation should not be a surprise because Scripture teaches us to "guard your heart above all else, for it is the source of life" (Prov 4:23). Brian's heart was being restored and guarded by the gospel; as a result, new, godly behaviors were springing up. As a result, we did not have to find all sorts of creative ways to manipulate his driving habits back into normality. As Brian allowed the Lord to change his heart, the need for ritualistic behavior became unnecessary.

It was delightful to listen to Brian's reports about his joyful ability to drive anywhere in town he desired. He spoke of seeing places in our community he had never seen before. He also found driving to be a pleasant and happy experience as he rejoiced in the way God changed his heart and life. Most importantly, he found the solitude of driving to be a perfect opportunity to focus on the finished work of our Savior. Brian had become a gospel-centered motorist who could say with the apostle Paul, "Therefore, whether you eat or drink, or whatever you do [including freely and joyfully driving your car around town], do everything for God's glory" (1 Cor 10:31).

Conclusion

Working with someone like Brian was both a challenge and a privilege. Often the Lord chooses to use opportunities like this to teach the counselor foundational lessons that will impact his own life in the present as well as the way he approaches future counseling opportunities for years to come. My relationship with Brian left me reflecting on three vital realities.

The Sufficiency of Scripture

Every counselor must decide which source of truth will serve as the fundamental grid through which he will develop and practice both his counseling theory and his counseling process. The competing explanations for OCD coming from the secular world are unsatisfactory because they are based on the ever-shifting opinions of man. Only one approach can claim the authority,

"Thus says the Lord." God's Word announces its sufficiency for all matters related to life and godliness. For example, Ps 19:7 says, "The instruction of the LORD is perfect, renewing one's life; the testimony of the LORD is trustworthy, making the inexperienced wise." And 2 Tim 3:16–17 declares, "All Scripture is inspired by God and is profitable for teaching, for rebuking, for correcting, for training in righteousness, so that the man of God may be complete, equipped for every good work." Also, 2 Pet 1:3 says, "His divine power has given us everything required for life and godliness through the knowledge of him who called us by His own glory and goodness."

This does not suggest that every helpful thought about OCD has to come from the pages of Scripture, but the Word of God should be given functional control over the ultimate explanation of the core problem expressed by OCD-type behaviors. The Word of God will always bring clarity and depth to the core issues of the heart, and it will address with precision the elements necessary for a struggling person to change. Brian reminded me of this truth.

The Centrality of the Heart

Brian also reminded me of the centrality of the heart. Hard cases involving bizarre behavior can tempt the counselor to look mainly at the outer man. While biblical counselors should place appropriate attention on matters of the body, the central focus must always be the heart. The good news is that God is powerful to help his children change in their innermost being. Teaching shallow behaviorism is fruitless and unnecessary because God's Word teaches that God's power is effective at the deepest levels of who we are. "For the word of God is living and effective and sharper than any double-edged sword, penetrating as far as the separation of soul and spirit, joints and marrow. It is able to judge the ideas and thoughts of the heart" (Heb 4:12). Brian helped me reflect on the necessity of deep-level change in the heart.

The Beauty of the Gospel

It was a personal honor and privilege for me to watch Brian grow in his love for Jesus Christ. I would never trade the opportunity God gave me to help him learn how Jesus replaces idolatrous efforts at self-atonement with a passion for the cross of Christ. Paul told the Romans, "How beautiful are the feet of those who announce the gospel of good things" (Rom 10:15). Brian reminded me of how thankful I should be for the opportunity to announce to desperately struggling people how the gospel rescues and restores.

Brian's was a difficult and seemingly bizarre case. Some believers hesitate to get involved in biblical counseling because they fear cases just like this one. Truthfully, from a human perspective, some counseling cases are unbelievably difficult and seemingly impossible. The challenge of such cases should drive us deeper into the pages of God's sufficient Word, allowing his truth to build our confidence in his power to understand and help even the toughest cases. Often these "impossible" or "bizarre" ministry opportunities draw you closer to Christ as a counselor and teach you about his sufficient grace. Never forget that "the One who is in you is greater than the one who is in the world" (1 John 4:4). Let your confidence in him motivate you to handle hard cases with gospel-centered biblical counseling and watch God's power work mighty things in your counselees—and in you.

Chapter 4

"Sarah" and Postpartum Depression

Heath Lambert

It was a beautiful summer afternoon, and I was busy working on three important responsibilities I wanted to accomplish before going home. Our church was dealing with a financial issue, and our budget team had just given me some numbers to crunch before a meeting that night. A church member had been stirring up trouble with others in the congregation, requiring me to confer with fellow church leaders about a proper course of action. Last but not least, I also was hoping to make some headway on my upcoming sermon.

As I worked feverishly, my cell phone began to ring. I did not recognize the number, considered ignoring the call, but at the last minute I picked up. "Pastor Heath," began a concerned voice, "do you have a second?" I instantly recognized the voice. It was Clark, a highly involved and well-respected member of our congregation. He said that he and his wife, Sarah, needed to talk to me about something important. As I glanced at my calendar and began suggesting times the following week, Clark interrupted to say that it was urgent and they needed to talk today. Clark was not a demanding church member, and I could hear in his voice that he really needed help. After a quick prayer asking the Lord for grace to accomplish all that he had given me to do, I said I could meet them in about 15 minutes. As I rearranged the work on my desk and prayed for wisdom in the upcoming conversation, I wondered what was so urgent.

Clark and Sarah[1]

Clark and Sarah were high school sweethearts who married midway through college. Originally from New England, they had moved to the area so Clark could take a job as a computer technician at a large business in our city. Sarah found work as a receptionist at a local law office. They had been married for seven years and seemed to love their life together. Clark had studied information technology in college and enjoyed applying what he learned at his company. Sarah's position was "just a job," but she liked it that way. She loved being able to leave her work at the office and focus exclusively on her marriage and home while not on the clock. Together they earned a comfortable living and had a happy life.

Clark and Sarah were both deeply committed Christians. They had each come to faith in Christ in high school, and they had been walking with Jesus faithfully ever since. They visited the church I served as pastor shortly after I arrived. They had grown frustrated with their former church's drift toward liberalism and were enthusiastic about our commitment to expositional preaching. They quickly jumped into the life of our church. They rarely missed a service, served in numerous ministries, and displayed an obvious love for Christ.

Clark and Sarah were also deeply in love with each other and strongly committed to having a healthy and growing marriage. They were devoted to biblical principles regarding the structure of their marriage, serving each other, and resolving conflicts in a way that honored Christ. Apart from these foundational values, Clark and Sarah also just "clicked." They enjoyed the same activities, kept the same schedule, and valued the same financial priorities.

---

[1] I have worked with several couples who had struggles similar to the story told here. This case study combines details of these different situations. None of the identifying information in this chapter matches that of the real persons involved.

Their relationship was so strong and exemplary that I regularly pointed to them as a model marriage in our church.

I was only aware of one problem. Clark and Sarah both desperately wanted children, and they had some difficulty conceiving. They had never used any kind of birth control but "trusted God to give them children in his own time." They were not trying to conceive children, but neither one would have been disappointed if Sarah had become pregnant even within their first year of marriage. After five years, however, "not trying" turned into really trying. Their efforts at having kids grew into a shared concern that conceiving children would not be possible.

After taking Clomid,[2] however, Sarah became pregnant. In fact, just two weeks before the afternoon phone call I received from Clark, Sarah had given birth to a beautiful daughter named Zoe. Clark and Sarah were ecstatic. They were overcome with joy in God's grace to them. They were overwhelmed with thankfulness for a healthy pregnancy and a beautiful daughter. I visited them in the hospital and also stopped by their home soon after they were discharged. Everything seemed fine. Now, as I sat in my office waiting for them to arrive, I could not imagine what might be wrong.

As soon as Clark and Sarah walked in, it was clear that something was very wrong. Sarah looked like a different person. Her face was puffy, her eyes bloodshot, and she looked absolutely exhausted. Clark was holding her hand and looked scared. I noticed they did not have Zoe with them. They explained that they had left her with a friend because they had something serious to discuss. Based on their appearance, my first instinct was a sinking fear that Clark may have committed adultery. After praying together, I asked them what was wrong.

Little Bundle of . . . What?

Sarah said that these first few weeks with Zoe had been hard, but she could not finish talking. She began to sob. Clark picked

[2] Clomid is an ovulatory stimulant used to induce egg production in women.

up where she left off, describing a trying ordeal with Zoe. Like all newborns Zoe cried often, needed constant attention, and kept a remarkably inconvenient sleep schedule. For the most part Sarah was completely uncertain about what to do with Zoe when she cried. She tried to feed her or rock her, but the crying seldom stopped. Putting Zoe to bed resulted in more crying. They had visited the pediatrician who assured them that Zoe was just a normal infant and things would improve over time. It didn't. Sarah had not slept more than a couple of hours a night for three weeks. She was exhausted, stressed, sad—and angry.

She explained through tears that she actually had started to resent her baby. She felt no connection with Zoe and had been longing for her life to return to the way it was before Zoe was born. She missed the normal rhythm of work and her quiet evenings with Clark. She had assumed being a mother would be fun and would come naturally to her. It was not. She was now concerned that she was going to be a bad mother. Again Sarah began to sob.

Clark said that Sarah was bouncing between extremes of anger and sadness. He had never seen her this way. Clark and Sarah then began describing a serious situation: Sarah had been thinking about killing Zoe.

On one occasion Zoe had been crying and would not stop. After a long time Sarah grew past the point of frustration. Not knowing what to do, she started thinking about throwing Zoe up against the wall as hard as possible, "just so it would be quiet for a few minutes." Late one night Zoe was crying in her crib. Sarah "tried everything" to quiet her down, but Zoe would not go to sleep. After quite some time of just staring into the crib, Sarah began to fantasize again about throwing Zoe up against the wall.

Finally, on the afternoon that Clark had called me, Zoe had been crying as Sarah was beginning to prepare dinner. As Sarah held a knife, she began to plan a scenario of picking up Zoe, slamming her on the floor, and slitting her own wrists. At that point Sarah realized that she needed help. She picked up the phone and called Clark. He came home from work immediately, and Sarah told him everything. That is when Clark called me.

Sarah described a "dark side" of her personality, which she had not seen in quite some time. As a child she had a difficult relationship with her mother. They were never close. Her mom abused alcohol and had a terrible temper. Sarah observed her mother's fits of rage as she would yell and throw whatever was nearby. As Sarah grew up, she began to imitate her mother. Her life was marked by severe fights that would often result in yelling and throwing anything in sight. These incidents had subsided when Sarah became a believer. They vanished completely when she married Clark. "It is so easy being his wife that there has not been a reason to act that way," she explained. "But now I'm just so confused. I thought I had put this dark side of my personality behind me."

Clark displayed an obvious tenderness for Sarah which I had witnessed on numerous occasions. Even in our meeting he confessed his love for her several times and had one hand around her shoulders and another on her lap the entire time she talked. Clark obviously loved his wife. Nevertheless, he was a little upset over the angry outbursts Sarah had been directing at him in the last few days. She had never treated him this way, and he didn't like it. Clark was scared. He had seen the devastating news reports of women who killed their young children, and he was desperate to keep this from happening in his own family.

Sarah was terrified. Though she did not feel a strong bond with her daughter, she did not want to hurt her. She was now rightfully concerned that she might. She loved her husband, but she knew that her anger was damaging their marriage. Sarah looked at me and asked, "Why is this happening? What is wrong with me? What can we do?"

What Is Going on with Clark and Sarah?

This is precisely the kind of problem many pastors and counselors would observe, describe as an extreme case that stands outside the bounds of Scripture, and promptly refer to a secular psychological professional. But in our time together that summer afternoon, I carefully listened to them, and Clark and Sarah gave me all the information essential to understanding what was wrong with them and how to help. The Bible, rightly understood and lovingly lived out, is overflowing with principles to help this couple. Before I expand on the scriptural understanding of the problem and unpack the solution the Bible offers, we need to bear in mind that the biblical understanding has a fierce secular competitor.

The Secular Diagnosis

The American Psychiatric Association identifies Sarah's problem as a depressive mood disorder with a postpartum onset, or "postpartum depression" (PPD).[3] PPD is reported in 10–13 percent of women and stands as the intermediate diagnosis in a spectrum of postpartum struggles.[4] This disorder (often known as the baby blues) is thought to affect 50–75 percent of women after childbirth.[5] Postpartum psychosis (PP), however, is reported to afflict just a fraction of women. The problems described in a PPD or PP diagnosis are very serious, including high levels of anxiety, marked sadness, insomnia, not feeling connected to the child, thoughts of suicide, and thoughts of harming the baby—all occurring within the first four weeks following delivery. The main difference between PPD and the more extreme PP seems to be the presence of hallucinations.[6]

The psychiatric community believes that problems described in a PPD or PP diagnosis stem from (1) hormonal imbalances occurring in the aftermath of delivery, (2) the harsh life changes required by the entrance of another human being into one's life, or

---

[3] *Diagnostic and Statistical Manual of Mental Disorders: DSM-IV-TR* (Washington, DC: American Psychiatric Association, 2000), 386. "Postpartum" refers to the period following childbirth, so postpartum depression refers to the intense sadness women sometimes experience at this time.

[4] Michael W. O'Hara and Annette M. Swain, "Rates and risks of postpartum depression—A meta-analysis," *International Review of Psychiatry* 8, no. 1 (1996): 37–54.

[5] Michael W. O'Hara, Janet Schlechte, David A. Lewis, et al., "Controlled Prospective Study of Postpartum Mood Disorders: Psychological, Environmental, and Hormonal Variables," *Journal of Abnormal Psychology* 100, no. 1 (1991): 63–73.

[6] *DSM-IV-TR*, 386.

(3) a previously undiagnosed mental illness. In order to treat the problem, psychologists first seek to rule out organic or biological causes. A number of physical issues, such as hormonal, endocrine, and vitamin deficiencies, may contribute to problems like the one Sarah was experiencing.[7] Finding or ruling out any such problems is a critical first step. Next psychiatrists desire that women diagnosed with PPD or PP begin drug therapy using the same kinds of psychoactive drugs prescribed for other depressive, manic, and obsessive-compulsive problems. Finally, some would recommend a course of electroshock therapy.[8] Thus, after any medical problem is ruled out, some combination of drugs, counseling, and—in rare cases—electric shock would be recommended. Interestingly, although most psychologists believe that hormonal shifts have something to do with PPD/PP experiences, such a view has never been documented. The only hormonal treatments offered are uncommon and experimental.[9]

This thumbnail sketch represents secular psychology's basic portrait of Sarah and Clark's problem. The portrait is helpful in at least two major ways. First, it reminds us that Sarah is not unique or alone, and her situation should not come as a shock. Many Christians might be unaware of these more extreme types of problems and may be bewildered when they encounter someone like Sarah, but many secular thinkers have spent hundreds and thousands of hours listening, observing, and working with women just like Sarah. It is not essential to know this material to help

---

[7] Dorothy Sit, Anthony Rothschild, Katherine Wisner, et al., "A Review of Postpartum Psychosis," *Journal of Women's Health* 15, no. 4 (May 2006): 352–68.

[8] Paul Reed, Nicola Sermin, Louis Appleby, et. al., "A Comparison of Clinical Response to Electroconvulsive Therapy in Puerperal and Non-Puerperal Psychoses," *Journal of Affective Disorders* 54, no. 3 (Aug 1999): 255–60.

[9] Deborah A. Sichel, Lee S. Cohen, Laura M. Robertson, et al., "Prophylactic Estrogen in Recurrent Postpartum Affective Disorder," *Biological Psychiatry* 38, no. 12 (1995): 814–18; Channi Kumar, Ronan McIvor, Tony Davie, et al., "Estrogen Administration Does not Reduce the Rate of Recurrence of Affective Psychosis after Childbirth," *The Journal of Clinical Psychiatry* 64, no. 2 (2003): 112–18; Thomas Insel, "Spotlight on Postpartum Depression," NIMH [online] October 28, 2010 [cited December 2010]. Available from the Internet: www.nimh.nih.gov.

Sarah, but the experiences of such persons may supply some missing perspectives.

Second, this research reveals that there is nothing altogether unique about secular psychology's approach to the problem. Referral to a secular psychiatrist is not a referral to a medical guru with mystical and infinite knowledge about how to fix complex problems. Rather, it is a referral to someone who may have met with and diagnosed other women describing similar problems and will try to find a medical cause. When no medical cause presents itself, this professional will discuss Sarah's problem with her, experiment with medication that may or may not work, and/or engage in other therapies until the problem has improved.

The question before us is this: Can Christians do a better job of understanding and helping women like Sarah in their difficulties? I firmly believe that we can and that God's Word tells us exactly how to do so.

Word-Informed, Love-Motivated Ministry to Clark and Sarah

Many Christians would respond to Clark and Sarah's story with confusion, apprehension, and even horror. Obviously, thoughts of suicide and killing your own baby are serious issues that seem to go against the very nature of a mother's love. Many people are completely unaware that such a response to a new baby is possible (much less common). Further, many Christians are perplexed by the psychological lingo created by the secular mental health establishment. It is not surprising, therefore, that many would view Sarah's problem as a difficulty high above the pay grade of Christian ministers. What happens when this becomes the prevailing perspective? This couple is sent to an "expert" who supposedly possesses exclusive resources to help.

As Clark and Sarah shared their difficulties with me, however, they revealed most of the information that a wise and loving Christian—armed with God's Word—would need to help them. Christians don't need to be intimidated by technical-sounding labels and drug therapies. God understands this couple's problem, and he describes both the problem and the solution in his own terms. So the question becomes: How do we take God's perspective on helping this couple and wisely proceed in the most helpful ways? The rest of the story answers that question.

Candle in the Dark: Starting with Encouragement

Where would you start with Clark and Sarah? After a traumatic story ending with a distraught mother, a kitchen knife, and the momentary temptation to commit infanticide and suicide, Sarah needed me to start with encouragement.

Encouragement might sound like an odd first tactic given the desperate nature of this situation. Two passages of Scripture came to mind, however, as I began to respond to this couple. The first was Matt 7:1–2 where Jesus warns his hearers, "Do not judge, so that you won't be judged. For with the judgment you use, you will be judged, and with the measure you use, it will be measured to you." This passage is often misunderstood to mean that Jesus forbad making any judgments at all. Just a few verses later, however, Jesus assumed that Christians will make judgments of some kind as they discern who are "dogs" and "pigs" (v. 6) and who are false and true prophets (vv. 15–20). So what Jesus clearly meant here is that we should avoid judgmental and condemnatory attitudes that are harsh and critical, judgment where we are thinking the worst of someone instead of the best (Luke 6:37–38; 1 Cor 13:7).

Extending a measure of charitable judgment to Clark and Sarah meant that I needed to listen carefully to their story and try to understand how it made sense. People usually feel what they feel and do what they do for reasons that make perfect sense to them. Extending love and grace means listening carefully and trying to understand why people are doing what they are doing (especially those who have an "extreme problem"). Conversely, one displays arrogance in assuming the worst of people, silently accusing them of being kooks and giving up on them as hopeless cases simply because one is not in their situation or presumes that one's response in the same situation would be different.

The second passage that came to mind was 1 Cor 10:13 where Paul gave a powerful encouragement: "No temptation has overtaken you except what is common to humanity. God is faithful, and He will not allow you to be tempted beyond what you are able, but with the temptation He will also provide a way of escape so that you are able to bear it." Paul sought to give hope to those struggling with sin and temptation. The hopefulness of Paul's words rings loud and clear: there is no such thing as a unique struggler. Though people often feel alone in their difficulties, God gives hope to his people by declaring that no one is alone—no matter what we are going through. There is nothing new under the sun (Eccl 1:9–10). These two passages (Matt 7:1–2 and 1 Cor 10:13) collided together with explosive relevance for this couple.

The Bible teaches that Sarah was not alone in her difficulty no matter how extreme her problem. If I did not yet know this truth by experience, I could know it by faith from 1 Cor 10:13. Realizing this fact gave me a new, hope-filled perspective to offer Sarah—the same kind of hope Paul offered the Corinthian church. Sarah was not a solitary struggler, and God would give her the grace to change even in her desperate situation.

As Clark and Sarah finished telling me what they were going through, they each looked at me anxiously. Holding their breath and biting their lips, with furrowed brows and tense eyes, they were searching my face for a look of shock, disbelief, or disdain. They were expecting to hear me say (or see me thinking), "What a mess! You are totally insane and an unfit mother! What kind of crazy are you?" That was the last possible response on my mind. Instead they heard: "Oh Sarah, I am so sorry. It sounds like the last few weeks have been terribly difficult. I want you to know how sorry I am but also how encouraged I am that you came for help. I think we *can* help." At this point I opened my Bible to 1 Cor 10:13, read it aloud, and told them that they were not alone in this struggle. Their situation made sense to me, and I knew that God would certainly give them grace to navigate and overcome their problems. I encouraged them that together we would figure out how to lay hold of God's grace in this situation.

I wish you could have seen their faces. Clark and Sarah were expecting to be viewed as "freaks," and their demeanor displayed this fear. When I responded with encouragement and comfort, two things happened. First, the pressure in the room deflated. The embarrassment, awkwardness, and discomfort fled. Second, both Clark and Sarah began to cry. Although Sarah had cried earlier, the tears were different now. Previously, her tears had arisen from deep wells of despair and confusion, but now her tears were flowing from relief. Sarah wanted to be a good wife and mother, and now she saw a glimmer of hope that God could alter her previously hopeless situation.

First Things First: Triage in Counseling

With seeds of hope now sown in their hearts, Clark and Sarah needed a path forward. They needed care that rightly prioritized all of the various issues that were on the table.

Sarah was in a desperate physical situation. Two weeks earlier she had been through labor, one of the most physically challenging activities any human can endure. She had not slept more than one or two hours during the last ten days. On top of that, she was trying to figure out—without experience or help—the sophisticated and demanding task of caring for a brand-new baby. Her difficulty was entirely understandable.

The Bible speaks frankly about the importance of our bodies and the role they play in both our physical and spiritual well-being. The Bible teaches that humans exist in a unity of body and soul. For instance, the apostle Paul writes, "Even though our outer person is being destroyed, our inner person is being renewed day by day" (2 Cor 4:16). Again, "An unmarried woman or a virgin is concerned about the things of the Lord, so that she may be holy both in body and in spirit" (1 Cor 7:34). The Scriptures teach in the passages above that persons have two constituent parts that exist in one unique whole; these constituent parts are called the "body" and "spirit" or the "inner person" and the "outer person." The two elements may be distinguished but cannot ultimately be separated.[10] Both are an essential aspect of a human being. Christians, therefore, should never discount either the spirit or the body. We do not counsel people to overcome their physical distress with some sort of "mind over matter" willpower. Instead, in harmony with Scripture, we take the body seriously. Scripture affirms that people need food (Jas 2:15–16), water (Rom 12:20), and sleep (Eccl 5:12). Paul affirmed the use of medicinal substances for the body (1 Tim 5:23).

The life and ministry of Elijah clearly exemplifies this necessity to care for one's body. After God defeated the prophets of Baal on Mount Carmel, Elijah's life was in danger because of his faithfulness to God. He found himself running for his life:

> Then Elijah became afraid and immediately ran for his life. When he came to Beer-sheba that belonged to Judah, he left his servant there, but he went on a day's journey into the wilderness. He sat down under a broom tree and prayed that he might die. He said, "I have had enough! Lord, take my life, for I'm no better than my fathers." Then he lay down and slept under the broom tree. Suddenly, an angel touched him. The angel told him, "Get up and eat." Then he looked, and there at his head was a loaf of bread baked over hot stones and a jug of water. So he ate and drank and lay down again. Then the angel of the Lord returned a second time and touched him. He said, "Get up and eat, or the journey will be too much for you." (1 Kgs 19:3–7)

It is remarkable how much Sarah has in common with Elijah. Elijah had been through a physically and spiritually challenging ordeal—literally running for his life. In fact, his situation was so bad that he wanted to die, and he even asked God to take his life. God would soon teach Elijah some specific lessons too (vv. 9–18), but this was not the time. In this moment God provided for Elijah's

---

[10] Even though body and soul are separated at death, the scriptural expectation is that they will be reunited forever at the return of Jesus Christ (see 1 Cor 15:12–58).

physical needs—sleep, food, and drink. This demonstrates that care for one's body is a principle endemic to the Scriptures.

What did all of this mean for Sarah? This was not the time for much of anything on her part except for sleep and nourishment. Many issues would need to be addressed with Clark and Sarah as time went on. The only thing I did that afternoon, however, was to explain that other issues could be postponed while we made rest and food Sarah's priority. I also insisted that Clark make an appointment for Sarah to see her physician as soon as possible. The Bible's clear teaching on the importance of the body encourages seeking the assistance of trained medical professionals in situations such as this.[11]

After describing all of this to Clark and Sarah, I explained that beginning at that moment, Sarah was off-duty until the next day. This meant that Clark was responsible for dinner that night, caring for Zoe until the next morning, and getting a babysitter for Zoe so we could meet the following day.[12] Being off-duty also meant that Sarah was not allowed to get up with Zoe during the night. That would be Clark's job. I also asked Clark to take the day off work tomorrow. He needed to be available to help out around the

---

[11] Sarah did go to see her OB/GYN the next day; but unfortunately, the visit did not go well. There are medical tests that might have been performed, but her physician performed none of them. After asking her a few questions, her doctor insisted that Sarah seek psychiatric help. He informed her that he would check up on her in coming days, and if she had not contacted a counselor in the next day or so, he would be forced to report her to Child Protective Services. Thankfully, he was satisfied when they informed him that they were already meeting with a counselor, and they never heard from him again. I have heard similar stories from numerous families I have counseled. In one particularly unfortunate situation, a physician had a young woman placed in a psychiatric hospital after merely reading her answers on a questionnaire. I was deeply disappointed that this highly trained professional failed to provide us with the benefit of his medical expertise—which is what we needed from him. I say this not to insinuate that such responses from professional medical personnel are normal; I hope they are not. However, I say it to encourage women who are experiencing similar difficulties to avoid merely reporting their situation to their physician. In such instances a couple should demand that their medical providers administer physical exams and appropriate laboratory testing to rule out any organic causes for their problems.

[12] Clark and Sarah had made the decision to bottle-feed Zoe, but in some instances a mother might have to remain available to feed or pump.

house and to return for another meeting with me. Clark seemed a bit concerned about this request, but I explained that this was an emergency. He needed to take serious and deliberate action to bring relief to this desperate situation.

I framed my instructions to Clark and Sarah in this way because I wanted to guarantee that Sarah would get some much-needed rest. Sarah's physical recuperation was not my only goal. I did not go into detail about this at that moment, but I wanted Clark to begin serving his wife and daughter. This was not the time to address the issue in a direct way, but I was concerned that for two weeks, in the face of his wife's mounting exhaustion and increasing irritation, it had not occurred to Clark to help Sarah so she could get some sleep. Giving them basic instructions the way I did helped me begin addressing the issue even before we unpacked it together. Giving Clark responsibility for Zoe also ensured that Sarah would not have the opportunity to harm Zoe if she was tempted again.

After these instructions, we prayed together and set up a time to meet the next morning. I told Clark and Sarah that I would handle everything else.

Surrounded by Love: The Hands and Feet of the Local Church

Clark and Sarah desperately needed help, and God in his providential care had raised me up to walk with them during their time of need. I was not going to be able to minister to them alone, however. I also would need help. Anticipating events like this one, the Holy Spirit inspired 1 Pet 4:9–11:

> Be hospitable to one another without complaining. Based on the gift each one has received, use it to serve others, as good managers of the varied grace of God. If anyone speaks, it should be as one who speaks God's words; if anyone serves, it should be from the strength God provides, so that God may be glorified through Jesus Christ in everything. To Him belong the glory and the power forever and ever. Amen.

This passage is about the glory of God. God desires to receive glory through Jesus Christ, and the way he gains glory in this passage is through his people's mutual service to one another. For the apostle Peter, the glory of God is at stake in whether a Christian shows joyful hospitality and performs God-empowered service. For Clark and Sarah the service of the body of Christ was potentially a matter of life and death.

Clark and Sarah needed more than mere talk. They did not need counsel alone but ministry that springs to life in tangible ways. They needed *help*. In desperate situations like theirs, there is no place for the lifeless faith that wishes someone well while doing nothing practical to assist them (Jas 2:14–17). This was a time for the body of believers to come to the aid of Clark and Sarah.

The first thing I did after Clark and Sarah left my office was to call Sherry, the leader of our church's care ministry. The care ministry traditionally organized one week of meals for families who had just given birth. Clark and Sarah had already received these meals, but I requested from Sherry that they needed meals for at least another two weeks starting tomorrow. I did not go into details. I simply explained that they were going through a difficult transition and could use some more help. Sherry did not ask a single question but affirmed that she would get right on it and have a meal there the next day. I also asked her to be thinking about some people who would help clean and assist in other ways around the house. Sherry said she knew of some ladies who could help, and she would wait to hear more from me.

The next person I called was my wife, Lauren. I am married to an amazing woman. We have three children, and the Lord has gifted my wife with an amazing and uncanny ability to care for little ones. On countless occasions I have been thankful that my wife always seems to know just what to do with our children. I shared Clark and Sarah's story with Lauren and asked her to be available over the next couple of days to help out and give Sarah some wisdom as she figured out how to be a new mom. As I anticipated, Lauren was happy to help in any way she could.

After these two important phone calls which mobilized the help of the church, I spent some time in my office praying, going over the notes I had taken during our conversation, and developing a plan for how to help this couple. A number of themes had surfaced that needed attention. In addition to the emergency help that was needed to get Sarah on an even keel mentally, it was necessary to address some doubts that she had expressed about God's goodness toward her. I knew that I also needed to speak to her fits of anger, among other things.

The next day when Clark and Sarah arrived at my office, Sarah's improvement was noticeable. After our first meeting they had returned home, and Clark had ordered a pizza. Sarah ate and collapsed into bed. She said she felt relieved to have "permission" to take a break, knowing that Clark was caring for Zoe. She slept for 12 hours. Though she felt somewhat "guilty" for resting so long, she admitted that she felt much better.

I was glad to hear that she had rested well. I explained that it would be wise for them to spend the rest of the week getting stabilized. Some women in the church would provide meals as well as help out around the house when Clark went back to work the next day. I also told them that Lauren was available to help Sarah adjust to motherhood.

Sarah seemed concerned. I could tell she was not comfortable with what I was saying, so I asked her what she was thinking. She said that this was one of the things of which she was afraid. She seemed to see these women's help as "proof" that she was a parenting failure. "I'm Zoe's mommy," she said. "I'm supposed to know how to take care of her, and I don't. I'm just a bad mother."

"Sarah, let me read you something," I responded. I turned to Titus 2:3–5 and read it aloud:

> Older women are to be reverent in behavior, not slanderers, not addicted to much wine. They are to teach what is good, so that they may encourage the young women to love their husbands and to love their children, to be self-controlled, pure, homemakers, kind and submissive

to their husbands, so that God's message will not be slandered.

Titus 2:3–5 was powerfully relevant for Sarah. When she protested against offers of help, she was overlooking two fundamental realities. First, she was missing the fact that Paul unashamedly identified two kinds of women: older and more experienced women, and younger and less experienced women. The mature women were to mentor the younger women, and the younger women were to open their minds, hearts, and hands to the practical wisdom of their seasoned older sisters. Sarah's willingness to receive help from her older sisters in the Lord was not a mark of shame. Rather, her humble acceptance would affirm God's design and allow for the proper functioning of his redeemed community.

Second, Sarah was overlooking the reality that good mothering is *learned*. Paul clearly stated that young women need to *learn* how to love their husbands and their children. Young women need to *learn* how to be good homemakers. Sarah's misplaced feelings of guilt grew from frustration that her maternal love had not morphed instantly into maternal skill.

Many women who share Sarah's struggles possess an overly romanticized view of motherhood. They imagine the gentle cooing and tender caresses of their soft, content baby. They envision the bubbly giggles and waddling first steps of a model toddler. They dream of the Christmas photo with three beaming faces broadcasting to the world a picture of familial perfection. They fail to consider the latching problems, the sleepless nights, the relentless fatigue, and the annoying smell of spit-up caked on two dozen shirts of yet-to-be-done laundry. Not in a million years did they imagine that they might not feel like making dinner on many nights or that they could go five days without a shower due to the tyranny of the urgent. They do not consider that many aspects of motherhood do not come naturally. They do not realize that the deepest joys of mothering and the lasting bond between mother and child are hard-won through days, weeks, and months of steadfast travail with their little one.

As we discussed motherhood from these angles, Sarah was not fully convinced, but she was willing to trust me. Together we developed a plan for Sarah to spend the rest of the week getting adjusted, receiving help from the ladies in the church, talking to Lauren, relying on Clark to help out on some nights, and hearing the results from her doctor's visit. I would check in with them every day either personally or through Lauren, and the three of us would sit down together in a week unless we needed to do so earlier.

The rest of the week progressed well. Families in our church provided abundant food each day. Sherry, the director of the care ministry, volunteered as an extra set of hands the first day Clark returned to work. She cleaned dishes, washed clothes, and bottle-fed Zoe while Sarah napped in the afternoon. Most importantly, she and Sarah sat and talked while Zoe slept, and Sarah began confiding in Sherry about all that had been happening. Sherry listened and responded graciously. It was the beginning of a close relationship.

Lauren also began to help Sarah get Zoe on a basic schedule. The purpose of the schedule was not to enslave Sarah but to serve her. Sarah began to see how helpful her new schedule could be because it helped her rule out options when Zoe was crying. For instance, if Zoe had just eaten well but had not slept at all, Sarah could know that it was her naptime. The schedule added some predictability to a normally chaotic time.

Lauren also told Sarah to call anytime she had questions or was upset. One afternoon Sarah called in tears. Zoe had slept well that morning and had eaten a full bottle, but she still would not stop crying. Sarah was not "freaking out" like before, but she was at her wit's end and didn't know what to do. After some investigative conversation, Lauren suggested that Sarah lay Zoe on the floor and alternately push her legs up to her chest and then stretch them back down. Shortly after starting these exercises, Zoe began passing gas and stopped crying. Sarah joked that flatulence never brought such relief to a mother!

By the time the next week rolled around, I found myself sitting in my office talking with a different couple. Sarah had not thought about harming herself or her baby since the afternoon of our first meeting. Naturally, she was still fairly stressed out, but her confidence that she could grow into a good mom was increasing. She was thankful for the friendships she was developing with Lauren and Sherry. Both she and Clark were each overwhelmed with gratitude for the cooking, cleaning, and counseling they had received from so many in the church. They were each tired, but neither was exhausted. Both felt encouraged that they were making progress.

In only a week God had showered his grace on Clark and Sarah, and they had come a long way. Their journey was not finished, however. There was more work to be done. There were still areas we needed to discuss to build on the good gains of their grace-filled first week.

Struck Down but Not Destroyed: Rejoicing in Suffering

Zoe's birth had brought a unique blend of joy and turmoil into their lives. Much of this turmoil was simply due to their natural lack of knowledge about caring for a new child and the stress that attends this great responsibility. Much of the turmoil was related to Sarah's physical condition. She needed food and sleep, and she had a deficit of both during the early days after Zoe's birth.

Sarah's challenges were not only relegated to circumstantial and physical issues. She was not merely an organism that required food and sleep for proper functioning. As her pastor, I was not merely a life-coach providing tips on how to care for infants. Sarah was a human in desperate need of an encounter with Jesus Christ, her King and Savior. I was a minister of the gospel of Jesus with a divine mandate to preach the gospel of grace to her in the context of our personal relationship. This means that if all I did was make sure she napped at the right times and received some guidance regarding infant care, I would have failed. Even if she stopped contemplating harming herself and her baby, such "counsel" would be incomplete.

Helping Sarah encounter her Savior meant at least two things in this situation. First, she needed help in understanding how Jesus wanted her to process her suffering. Second, she needed help in understanding how Jesus wanted to deal with her sin. We started with suffering.

Sarah was legitimately suffering in the aftermath of her daughter's birth. The significant challenges she was facing were causing her to ask significant questions about God. Sarah was wondering why God would do this to her—how he could possibly care in light of all he was allowing her to go through. Sarah's questions were not the fiery questions of a rebellious teenager shaking an angry fist in the air. Hers were the questions of an injured toddler who was feeling pain. She simply did not know where it was coming from or why it hurt so much. Sarah needed the reminder that, by the grace of Jesus, God was up to something good in this difficult time she faced.

To see this reminder, one of the many passages we looked at together was Rom 5:1–5:

> Therefore, since we have been declared righteous by faith, we have peace with God through our Lord Jesus Christ. We have also obtained access through Him by faith into this grace in which we stand, and we rejoice in the hope of the glory of God. And not only that, but we also rejoice in our afflictions, because we know that affliction produces endurance, endurance produces proven character, and proven character produces hope. This hope does not disappoint us, because God's love has been poured out in our hearts through the Holy Spirit who was given to us.

Paul declared that because we have been justified by faith in Christ, we can rejoice in the hope of the glory of God as well as in our sufferings. Paul's perspective is astounding. We can all agree that Sarah should rejoice in the positive hope of the glory of God, but urging her to rejoice in her negative sufferings is so shocking it's almost offensive. How could I help Sarah make sense of this divine exhortation?

I began by clarifying that Sarah was not called to rejoice *at* the suffering but to rejoice *in* the suffering. This distinction is essential. In other words, we are not called to rejoice *at* suffering in and of itself. Suffering is bad, suffering is hard, and suffering often comes at the hands of wicked people (though not in Sarah's case). Therefore, we do not rejoice in suffering because we love the suffering in and of itself. We rejoice in suffering because we look forward to what God is able to do through our suffering. Paul celebrated the fact that through our sufferings and afflictions God is bringing about endurance, proven character, and hope.

This progression may sound strange. It makes sense that suffering would produce endurance. When a person bears up under burdens and challenges, endurance is a natural result. It also makes sense that endurance would produce proven character. When people learn to endure through trials and hardships, it bolsters their strength of spirit. It may seem less reasonable, however, that proven character would lead to hope. How can proven character lead to a kind of hope that does not disappoint (v. 5)? This question is answered in verse 2 when we see what kind of hope Paul is talking about. It is the hope of the glory of God.

The hope in Romans 5 is not the hope that we will someday escape our sufferings (though Romans 8 teaches this truth). The hope in Romans 5 is that our sufferings will lead to God's being glorified. When God gives Sarah the strength to endure and graciously forges proven character in her through her afflictions, he gains glory for himself. This promise had the power to produce great hope in Sarah.

For this to work, Sarah must realize that her life and her situation were not ultimately about her but about her Lord. God was writing a redemptive story with her life in order to gain glory for himself. Because Jesus understood this, he taught his followers, "Let your light shine before men, so that they may see your good works *and give glory to your Father in heaven*" (Matt 5:16, emphasis added). Our lives and our works are not ultimately about gaining glory for ourselves but for our Father in heaven.

Clark, Sarah, and I sat together for weeks discussing these themes. We spent hours contemplating the comforting presence of Christ in our difficulties. We dwelt for a long time on the goodness of God in trials. We talked often about how Sarah could learn to view her times of difficulty as opportunities to trust the gentle grace of Jesus who was working to make her like himself (even in her hardest days), all for the purpose of blessing her and honoring his name. Sarah learned that she could call out to God in her darkest moments and receive timely help (Ps 46:1). She learned that she needed to start judging the degree of her blessedness not by the ease and comfort she might be experiencing at any given moment but by the degree to which she was being conformed to the likeness of Christ. Sarah began to gain confidence in the Lord's care for her, and she was emboldened as she realized that this intense season of difficulty was not a horrible interruption in her life. Rather, it was a prime example of God's gracious commitment to make her more like Christ and bring himself glory.

The Enemy Within: Fighting Against Sin

After a couple of weeks, as Sarah was more rested and had more confidence as a mother, she was increasingly encouraged about God's love and care for her in the midst of her trial. It was now time to address another area where Clark and Sarah needed to encounter Christ. Until now we had been addressing Sarah's physical needs and equipping her for motherhood along with providing spiritual comfort. I now needed to shift to another area—the ways in which Clark and Sarah had each sinned against God and against each other in their situation.

Sarah was not guilty of sin because she did not have mothering down pat or because she was sleep deprived and physically weakened, but there were aspects of Sarah's response to her suffering that needed to change. When the biblical authors talk about change in the area of sin, they speak of *confession* and *repentance*. First John 1:7–9 reads,

> If we walk in the light as He Himself is in the light, we have fellowship with one another, and the blood of

> Jesus His Son cleanses us from all sin. If we say, "We have no sin," we are deceiving ourselves, and the truth is not in us. If we confess our sins, He is faithful and righteous to forgive us our sins and to cleanse us from all unrighteousness.

The apostle John taught that walking in the light does not mean enjoying a sin-free existence. Rather, walking in the light means that we confess the sins we are sure to commit. John also said that when we confess those sins we will be forgiven because God is a faithful and righteous God who will never fail to accept Jesus' payment for sin.

Someone like Sarah can find great encouragement here as she deals with her sin. Forgiveness is guaranteed for those who are trusting in Christ. They only need to walk in the light and confess their sins. The same logic is seen in the promise of Jas 4:6, "God resists the proud, but gives grace to the humble." If Clark and Sarah were to know the forgiving grace of Jesus, humble confession and repentance were the steps to freedom.

There were definitely specific areas where Sarah needed to pursue confession and repentance of sin. One area was her responses of sinful anger toward Clark and Zoe. Yes, Sarah had been stressed and fatigued, but the Bible teaches that sinful anger is a spiritual problem before it is an emotional or physical issue (Mark 7:20–23; Gal 5:19–21; Jas 4:1–2). Even in a physically weakened condition, it is possible for Christians empowered by the Holy Spirit to respond to their physical trials with faith, hope, and love (Rom 8:9–11; 1 Cor 13:4–7; Gal 5:22–26). This reality was as true for Sarah as for anyone else. Sarah began to realize that she had never dealt with the patterns of anger she learned in childhood. Instead, they had just gone dormant. When she was living with her mother, Sarah's anger would constantly flare up. While living with Clark, her external circumstances had changed, and the temptation had abated. Now that her temptation had returned, the sinful disposition of her heart reared its ugly head and revealed her need to repent.

As Sarah began the process of confessing her sin to God, to Clark, and even to Zoe (why not?), Jesus began to expose in her heart other patterns of pride and selfishness. Sarah came to realize that she had waited far too long to seek help because of her pride. Sarah had not wanted to admit that she needed assistance, advice, mentoring, or even a listening ear. She was reluctant for anyone to know that there were significant areas of ignorance in her life when it came to motherhood.

Sarah, like many mothers, wanted everyone to think that she was the perfect mom with the perfect family. She began to recognize that much of her physical suffering was the result of her own pride that refused to admit weakness or ask for help. Sarah began to repent of this pride, and the fruit of her repentance grew ripe as she began to request and accept help from our church.

Yet Sarah was not the only one who needed to draw near to Christ in a humble process of confession and turning from sin. Clark also had his problems. Clark and Sarah had a solid marriage, but Zoe's birth had exposed patterns of selfishness for both of them.

It was strange to me that Sarah's distress had to reach emergency status before Clark got involved. During one of our times together, I shared my concern. "You know, Clark, I wonder how you missed all of Sarah's struggling going on right under your nose?" This question cut Clark to the core. He was deeply broken and began to see and confess his own selfishness. Without much thought, he had assumed that Zoe was exclusively Sarah's responsibility. Whenever he heard Zoe crying, he expected Sarah to handle the situation. At night he thought only about getting to bed himself so he would feel ready for work the next day. After all, he reflected, "I assumed that since Sarah was staying home, she could take a nap whenever she wanted." When Clark noticed that Sarah seemed sad and distressed, he simply assumed that this phase would pass and made no real effort to understand or resolve the problem. Clark was now realizing that his presumptuous behavior was recklessly selfish and unloving (1 Cor 13:5). Clark humbly sought forgiveness from God and Sarah for his culpable thoughtlessness.[13]

As the weeks and months progressed, I met with Clark and Sarah less and less until finally we were not meeting regularly for "counseling" at all. During this time each of them was growing first and foremost in their trust in God and their walk with Jesus. They were also growing in their facility as parents, in their love for each other, and in their connection to their church body who continued to serve them well. The willingness to accept ministry from others was a huge change for this couple who had been in the habit of serving but not being served. This role reversal was necessary and humbling, and later it would help them return to their serving roles with a new love for those who had walked with them so faithfully. My time with this couple turned out to be a remarkable demonstration of the power of Jesus as he showered them with grace and life, perspective and perseverance in suffering, escape from sinful ruts, practical maturity in parenting, and vibrant connections among their brothers and sisters in our local church.

Conclusion

Are you equipped to help a young woman wrestling with thoughts of killing her baby and herself? As I have tried to demonstrate, I believe Christians are equipped to help in this way, but the great concern of my ministry is that many Christians never even would have tried to help Sarah and Clark. Most Christians would have dropped their jaws at one of Sarah's siren phrases like "kill my baby" or "cut my wrists" and would have immediately passed this couple off to a secular professional. I understand that. Such phrases are alarming.

---

[13] Clark and Sarah worked on a number of issues between sessions as well. They each practiced confessing and forgiving their sins to each other. They also worked together to develop a list of clear responsibilities for each of them so that neither would assume that a particular task was the other person's responsibility. They also read Robert D. Jones's book *Uprooting Anger: Biblical Help for a Common Problem* (Phillipsburg, NJ: P&R, 2005). We discussed this book in order to help Sarah respond in the power of the gospel whenever she was tempted toward anger.

Having noted that, I really believe the key to Clark and Sarah is found in Jas 1:19, "My dearly loved brothers, understand this: everyone must be quick to hear, slow to speak." The principle of this verse is that we should listen first and speak last. Many Christians would encounter Clark and Sarah and be too quick to say, "I can't help." Look back at the story of Clark and Sarah. When you take time and listen well, Sarah's extreme problem becomes understandable. When you push past the scary headlines and read the details of the story, the frightening buzzwords give way to understandable themes: rest, nutrition, practice in acquiring skills, and—most importantly—Jesus' power to slay sin and bring solace in suffering.

One of my aims in describing my relationship with Clark and Sarah is to demonstrate how a big and frightening problem can actually become manageable when you take the time to listen carefully and commit to help. "Manageable" does not mean easy. Problems that require in-depth counseling are never easy. Rather, "manageable" means that with Scripture, wisdom, and thoughtful input from other Christians, you can handle each situation by God's grace. I pray that meeting Clark and Sarah encourages you to accept that with your eyes open to Scripture and your ears attentive to the situational struggles of people, you can minister real help even in a hard case like this one.

Chapter 5

"Mary" and Paralyzing Fear

Dan Wickert[1]

I HAD NO PLANS TO WORK as a counselor when I was completing my last year of medical school at the University of Illinois in Champaign. My medical pursuits were still clearly in place as I finished up my residency in obstetrics and gynecology (OB/GYN) in Grand Rapids, Michigan. Soon I moved to Lafayette, Indiana, where I have worked as a general practice OB/GYN since 1985. During my first few years of medical practice in Lafayette, I did not see the parallel between my career as an OB/GYN and my future career (unknown to me) as a biblical counselor. But Bill Goode did.

Bill was the senior pastor of Faith Baptist Church in Lafayette. He talked to me frequently about biblical counseling and consistently expressed his desire to train me as a biblical counselor. He called me when he encountered counseling cases with medical histories and jargon. He invited me to observe counseling sessions. He perceived my education and experience as a physician to be useful tools in the counseling room. He encouraged me to consider expanding my ministry.

---

[1] This chapter was written with significant help from Rebecca Thomas.

"Why are you here?" Pastor Goode challenged me. "What will you do with your life?" He encouraged me to contemplate how I might make the greatest investment in God's kingdom. He urged me to use my talents and skills not only in the honorable practice of medicine but also in the ministry of the Word. Fueled by a growing desire to advance the glory of God and encouraged by the Holy Spirit, I began gradually to serve in the counseling ministry under Pastor Goode's oversight. I have been counseling and rejoicing in God's grace since 2001.

Though I never had any personal plans to serve God through biblical counseling, I now see how he was preparing me through my seemingly unrelated medical practice. I say *seemingly* because the parallels between a medical doctor (who cares for the body) and a biblical counselor (who cares for the heart and mind) are strong and instructive. Three specific parallels are worth highlighting to set the stage for one of my earliest counseling cases.

From Medical Doctor to Biblical Counselor: Practices and Parallels

Listening First

As a physician I always spend my first appointment with a patient "taking history," a priority that finds echoes in the counseling term "gathering data." Taking history involves a detailed foray into each patient's medical past—her medical diagnoses, prescriptions, concerns, and complaints—in order to better understand her personally, to better understand her unique situation and circumstances, and to better determine how I can help her. Solomon wisely said, "The one who gives an answer before he listens—this is foolishness and disgrace for him" (Prov 18:13). It would be foolish for me to write out a prescription for a patient before I have taken the time to read or investigate her medical history. Without enough background information I could give her the wrong medicine. I could give her medicine that does nothing to solve her problem, or worse, medicine that intensifies her problem.

Gathering data in the counseling office is just as important (if not more so) as taking history in the physician's office. The heart and mind are complex and difficult to understand, and the symptoms of an unwell heart are wildly diverse. Counselors have a daunting task: They seek to understand aching and fractured, angry and despairing people, and try to offer help. This is impossible, of course, without prayerful, Spirit-endowed compassion along with a careful, attentive, empathetic investigation into each counselee's history.

Hope Is Help

A second similarity between my OB/GYN practice and my counseling ministry is the emphasis on hope. A good doctor does not examine a complaining patient and conclude her first appointment by saying, "There's no hope for you; you're going to be miserable forever. Don't bother scheduling another appointment." Sadly, in the medical world, some conditions are chronic or even terminal; still I would be a terrible (and short-lived) doctor if I preempted all treatments and discussions about medical options by saying, "There's no hope for you."

Of course, a physician must be honest and not misleadingly optimistic. Saying to a sick patient, "You're doing great! Go home and relax!" would be just as detrimental as pronouncing her hopeless. Real hope is not about faking optimism, turning a blind eye to the problem, or lying to the patient. Rather, hope is rooted in truth. In the medical field the truth is that God is sovereign, and I can offer information, options, medication, surgery, perspective, and other solutions to my patients. In matters of the heart, the truth again is that God is sovereign, and the Bible offers information, redemption, encouragement, rebuke, perspective, and other solutions to my counselees. Even more holistically, the Bible offers insight into the nature of God, the nature of man, the nature of living, and the nature of the joy and complete satisfaction we find only in God—only through our redemption by Jesus Christ. Medical treatments may fail. Disease can surpass the level of medical technology accessible to professionals. But God does not fail. His revealed Word is flawless and timeless, and his purposes for his people are good.

A medical doctor does not offer hope by denying or ignoring pain. Chemo aches, surgery hurts, and hospitals are lonely. Neither should a counselor ignore or discount the present, prolonged suffering of the person he is counseling. Hope is not defined by the absence of hardship. Rather, hope is found in God's grace in the midst of hardship. Hope is found in his promise to give us a future. God offers hope to Christians when he promises, "I am persuaded that not even death or life, angels or rulers, things present or things to come, hostile powers, height or depth, or any other created thing will have the power to separate us from the love of God that is in Christ Jesus our Lord!" (Rom 8:38–39).

Assigning Homework

The third similarity between my practice as an M.D. and my practice as a biblical counselor might be considered a small thing: As a physician I cannot change people. If they are to change, they must put forth effort, so I give homework. At a basic level I instruct my patients to eat well, exercise regularly, sleep sufficiently, and drink lots of water since these practices reflect fundamental stewardship of the body. I also assign and record a specific course of treatment with medication that is relevant to each patient's specific medical problem. If someone cannot be healthy at home, she will not be healthy at the doctor's office.

Spiritual health is similar. Most of the counselee's progress will be made at home, decision by decision—*not* in my office. Assigning homework helps the counselee make right decisions and develop good habits of thinking and acting at the most important times—when she is not sitting across from me but is alone at work or home. I often assign my counselees specific ways to measure and record their progress as well because specific results are more informative for me and are often more encouraging to the counselee.

The Greater Need

While there are many strong parallels between my medical practice and my service as a biblical counselor, I have also identified important distinctions between them. The most significant is that medicine often treats symptoms but cannot meet the patient's greater need. Medicinal treatments cannot transform the soul.

I have great respect for science and medicine. I have devoted decades to my medical practice precisely because I see the field as important and useful. I can testify, however—in spite of all the literature published in medical journals by top-flight scientists—that the right pills, the right operations, the right diet cannot turn dissatisfied people into content people. A woman who is anxious and depressed when she struggles to conceive will be an anxious mother who struggles with depression. Her greatest need is not medical in nature; she needs the power of God's *transforming* gospel.

Although my medical background has given me helpful insights into medical counseling cases, I do not believe that one needs an M.D. or a Ph.D. to identify the greater needs of people. *Non*-doctors are not disadvantaged in any substantial way. All Christians—regardless of their formal academic training—have access to God's power: "For I am not ashamed of the gospel, because it is God's power" (Rom 1:16). Transformative power is not in one's title or background; it is not in a degree or a list of experiences. Rather, the power that meets the greater needs of all people is found in Jesus Christ and his gospel.

In my years of counseling, I have seen this gospel power unleashed many times to save, heal, change, and help even the severely broken. Such changes are rarely instantaneous, but God is faithful. He loves to use believers like me and you to bring his life to hurting people through conversation, prayer, relationships with others in the body of believers, the preaching of the Word, the commemoration of the Lord's Supper, and a thousand other graces in the community of faith. Our great God who is sovereign and holy gains glory for himself as he works to make his people free, forgiven, flourishing, and happy using all the graces available to us in Christ. These graces—purchased with Christ's precious blood—ultimately transformed the desperate woman who came to my office as one of my first counseling cases.

Mary

Mary was nervous. Danger and disease were everywhere: stained carpets, spotted ceiling tiles, my black ink pen lying conspicuously on the worn desk between us. As far as she could see, every object in my office was crawling with germs and contamination. Although she was frightened as she settled into my office for that first evening session, she still managed to be friendly and talkative.

"I'm depressed," Mary began. "I'm anxious." This confession was the understated introduction to the last four years of Mary's life. During this time Mary's life had been characterized by an irrational, debilitating, and intensifying fear of AIDS.

Four years earlier Mary had married her husband, Ben. When they met, Mary and Ben were each deeply committed to Christ and Ben was pursuing a ministry degree at a Christian university. Before they met, Ben had been sexually immoral; but Mary was in love with the man he had become. They each wanted to spend their lives together pursuing Christ, so when Ben asked to marry her, she was delighted. The possibility of HIV/AIDS was particularly concerning for Mary, so in preparation for marriage, Ben was screened for sexually transmitted diseases. Ben's tests would eventually prove that he was free from any such diseases; but while they waited for the results, Mary learned some upsetting medical news of her own: she would have difficulty conceiving.

The news devastated Mary. She had always imagined herself with children, and suddenly she felt fearful. She was fearful that she would not get the family she had always dreamed of having. She was fearful that she could not be happy without the family she had always wanted. She was fearful that she might have to *settle* for a life that did not give her all she desired and deserved. She also feared disappointing Ben, as well as her parents. Mary pictured herself in five years, watching her friends cooing at their chubby infants and scooping happy toddlers into their minivans. She could already feel the claws of jealousy and bitterness closing around her heart, which was throbbing with the ache of despair. Mary was crushed and was becoming increasingly listless. She couldn't pick out clothes to wear in the mornings and didn't want to go to work. Mary was shutting down.

This development is common in cases involving depression over medical complications. The mind affects the body, the body affects the mind, and a downward spiral begins. In Mary's case the anxiety invoked by her potential infertility and Ben's potential STD began to manifest itself in her body: She felt a disabling lack of energy and an overwhelming desire to stay in bed. These affectations of the body—the lack of physical activity, the listlessness—then affected Mary's mind, making her more depressed.

By the time Ben's tests came back negative, Mary was severely depressed. She was spending days curled up on her bed, in the fetal position. The depression, however, was only the beginning of Mary's emotional turmoil. She was constantly anxious. In spite of Ben's safe test results, Mary's fear lingered and began to grow. Over a period of two months, she began isolating herself from her friends and shedding her church and ministry commitments. By the end of these two months, she couldn't even bring herself to get dressed, leave the house, go grocery shopping, or run errands of any kind.

Mary's isolation and lethargy were naturally straining her relationship with Ben. In spite of the difficulties, they managed to get married, but now he was striving to be a patient and understanding husband who was discouraged by his wife's emotional collapse. After long days at work, he would return home to a dark, dirty house. Mary's fears were debilitating. Fear dominated her mind and dictated her schedule.

When Help Hurts: The Failure of Superficial Solutions

Biblical Counsel?

Over time Mary sought various kinds of counsel. When she first began to struggle with anxiety, she spoke to a pastor affiliated with the Bible school her husband attended. Mary felt that this pastor didn't try to understand her situation and her feelings. She did not sense that he appreciated the severe weight of anxiety she was carrying. His advice seemed superficial. His words rang hollow. This pastor certainly meant well, and he may have done a better job than Mary indicated with what was—at the time—fairly rocky soil. Still, Mary's recollections of her experience present a sad but common stereotype of biblical counselors.

It can be easy for some counselors to treat the Bible like Tylenol, but Scripture was never intended to be prescribed for mechanical ingestion every six hours to make people feel better. This is where my earlier comparison between physicians of the body and physicians of the heart begins to break down. Counselors who *prescribe* Scripture are in danger of approaching their counselees in a routine, uninterested, and dispassionate way. They instruct counselees to memorize this verse and to write out that verse, but they don't use the powerful Word as a dynamic means to encounter the living Christ. They rarely delve into the depth of biblical passages, the character of God, the beautiful implications of the gospel, or the nature of the sinful heart that fuels idolatry and deception. It is spiritual malpractice. At the end of the day, this pastor was well meaning, but he simply did not offer Mary the deep wisdom required of a complex problem like hers.

Just Have a Baby?

After the pastor, Mary sought the advice of a doctor who advised her to pursue pregnancy. He reasoned that Mary's negative emotions were most likely the consequence of some hormonal inconsistency that would correct itself during a pregnancy. He believed that because Mary *wanted* a baby, a baby would make her happy. Naturally, Mary agreed, and she soon found out that she was pregnant! The immediate excitement of pregnancy along with the attention Mary received from her family and friends were enough to quell her depression and anxiety—temporarily. After the enthusiasm wore off, however, Mary's old habits of sinful thinking began to creep back to the forefront of her mind.

In her second trimester Mary accidentally cut her finger at a nail salon. The tiny cut reminded her of AIDS. She remembered, specifically, that AIDS is transferred and contracted by blood. Her fear came rushing back.

Over the next few months, Mary's fear of both blood and AIDS escalated far beyond reason. Trying on clothes at the mall became a terrifying risk. Mary felt contaminated because she didn't know where the clothes had been or who had tried them on before. She began to see her own hands as potential carriers of AIDS. Because of this she pursued the comfort and control of cleanliness and began to wash her hands obsessively. She believed that with a little soap she could wash away the threat of disease. Objects in her home that she frequently touched began to lurk in her consciousness like closet monsters, crawling with the possibility of AIDS. Mary began to regard an ink pen in her home with suspicion, washing it as frequently as she washed her hands.

The fear was suffocating. Mary couldn't use her toilet seat one morning because she believed an intruder had broken into her home while she was gone and contaminated the toilet seat with HIV. By the time her son, Daniel, was born, Mary was miserable. She was tormented in her own house and confined to her bed, which was the only "safe place." She was imprisoned in a home speckled with mysterious stains and everyday spots, all of which Mary now associated with AIDS. She even collected her family's laundry under the bed because her fear of the dirty clothes prohibited her from washing them.

Like the pastor Mary met with, this physician also meant well, but his solution of having a baby does not decrease anxiety or remove depression. Babies are entirely vulnerable to harm, are prone to illness, need constant attention; and since they are unable to communicate verbally, they raise millions of questions about what they want. Babies create a steep learning curve. A newborn baby *increases* a woman's concerns. New babies also do not solve depression. If Mary could not care for herself or make dinner for her husband under the regular stress of life, how could she care for an infant under the sleep-deprived stress of a first-year parent?

Mary's pregnancy was a tremendous gift from God, but it did not rid her of all her problems as she had thought it would. It made her problems worse. God had not intended the blessing of pregnancy to redeem Mary from her crippling fears. He cared too deeply about her soul to mask her problems even with good things.

Medicate the Problem?

Once again Mary was left searching for a solution. As a last resort she began taking Prozac and Valium for her depression and anxiety. Such a decision is not uncommon. In fact, most of the men and women whom I counsel are taking or have taken multiple antidepressants, along with other medications intended to help them feel better or to treat a specific psychiatric diagnosis. As a physician I am always familiar with the details of my counselee's medications. I recognize most antidepressants; I know how they work, the common side effects, and the mental and physical dependency that many of these drugs cultivate. Because of my knowledge in this area, many counselees want my medical advice concerning whether they should continue with their medication.

As a rule, I never advise or require counselees to stop medicating because I am not *their* physician. I don't know their complete medical history, and it would be irresponsible for me to advise them out of ignorance. In many cases patients who stop taking their medication cold turkey will suffer severe withdrawal symptoms that make it even more challenging to think and act rightly. Sometimes, however, a counselee will inform me that he is ready to stop taking medication. In these cases I am always curious to hear his reasons before I advise him to talk to his doctor about stopping.

One question I typically ask is, "Why do you want to stop?" Often a counselee wants to get off medications because they do not want to be judged by their friends or family. This is not a good reason because the person is often more concerned about his own glory than the glory of God. A second question I consider is, "How are you handling life *on* the medication?" Are they handling the normal problems of life in a biblical, God-honoring way while they are *on* the medication? If not, then taking them off the medication usually will not help the counselee to please God.

Does medicine ultimately solve heart problems? No. But is God's will ultimately going to be hindered by medicine or a lack of medicine? No. God will work his will in a counselee's heart regardless of whether they are medicated. My goal and responsibility are to cultivate hope, to help people grow in Christlikeness, and to help them prosper in the freedom of the gospel and in God's rich purpose for their lives.

After a desperate struggle with fear and despair, Mary got the best advice she could find, and it was all an inch deep. From a pastor she got shallow spirituality; from one physician she got bad advice ("have a baby"); and from another physician she got medication. Such wisdom, as it turned out, had no power to help Mary. I do not say this to mock Mary and the men who honestly wanted to help her. I only want to illustrate the superficiality of much advice—even when that advice parades as medical expertise and biblical counsel. *Any* counsel unhinged from the riches of the gospel and unplugged from the divine power of the Holy Spirit can only deal with surface issues.

Understanding Mary: Mind and Body

Before addressing how to help Mary, it is important to understand how her mind and body work together. From an anthropological perspective, a human being includes these two distinct components. What we call the "heart," "soul," or "mind" is the *inner man*; what we call the "body"—including its chemical processes—is the *outer man*. These two components function closely together, and Scripture often addresses them together. Deuteronomy 6:5 says, "Love the LORD your God with all your heart, with all your soul, and with all your strength." Moses urged

Israel to pursue God with all the facets of their inner man (heart and soul) and with all the functions of their outer man (strength).

There are many pathophysiological cases—cases in which the mind affects the body and the body, in turn, affects the mind. For example, an abnormally low-functioning thyroid will produce physical consequences such as decreased energy, cold intolerance, and weight gain. But it can also have emotional ramifications (depression) and mental ramifications (difficulty concentrating). A low hemoglobin level (the result of blood loss) yields similar consequences: energy loss, lightheadedness, and headaches, which combine to make it difficult for the patient to think rightly.

A much more common example of the mind-body relationship is stress. Everyday stress begins as a mental experience that is manifested in the body. When a person is stressed, his heart rate speeds up, muscle tension increases, and the digestive system is affected, all in response to stress hormones released by the body as it responds to the mind. Some people begin to perform ritualistic behaviors, like scratching one area of their body over and over again until they develop a persistent rash. Notably, the *body* rarely initiates stress; the *mind* perceives the danger, discomfort, deadlines, pressure, or confrontation in accordance with God's design. The body merely reacts to the mind's perception.

A final example of the mind-body relationship is grief. Anyone who has experienced severe grief understands the mental and physical effects: feelings of emptiness and sorrow, fatigue and weight fluctuations. The mind and body are connected in a wonderful, intricate, cyclical way.

This relationship illustrates the serious ways a counselee's thinking can affect his physical well-being, which then makes it more difficult to think rightly, which in turn causes more physical consequences—and so on. The mind-body relationship is beautiful, but sin can turn it into torture. Persons who are stuck in patterns of sin and who are suffering mental and physical consequences should evoke a counselor's deepest compassion. Their suffering, even when self-inflicted, is real. David mourned over such suffering in Ps 31:9–10 after his adultery with Bathsheba. He cried out, "I am in distress; my eyes are worn out from angry sorrow—my whole being as well. Indeed my life is consumed with grief . . . my strength has failed because of my sinfulness, and my bones waste away."

Mary was experiencing the mental and physical consequences of her sinful failure to trust God. But God, who is full of grace and mercy, often uses trials to transform us into the image of his Son and to bring us into a closer, joy-producing relationship with him. She needed to experience the hope of this truth and the truths of Rom 15:13 to set her free from her enslaving fears: "Now may the God of hope fill you with all joy and peace as you believe in Him so that you may overflow with hope by the power of the Holy Spirit."

Starting with Good News

My counseling relationship with Mary began at the request of Ben's employer. Mary, Ben, and Daniel had just moved to Lafayette, where Ben had secured a job teaching at a Christian high school. Mary and Ben were both Christians, and Ben was enthusiastic about his new ministry job. During the job interview Ben had been honest and straightforward about his family's struggles. He had shared openly with the school administrator, but he had also expressed confidence that God would give them victory together. The administrator was impressed with Ben's honesty and faith. When he offered Ben the job, he also referred Mary to the counseling ministry of Faith Baptist Church. Because Mary's case had a medical angle, she was directed to me, one of several physicians on staff at FBC.

As Mary was telling me her intricate story in our first counseling session, I focused on her understanding of the gospel. Her level of understanding in this area would determine the trajectory of our time together. Milton Vincent joined the rich chorus of contemporary authors calling on believers to preach the gospel to ourselves every day:

> Over the course of time, preaching the gospel to myself every day has made more of a difference in my life than

> any other discipline I have ever practiced. I find myself sinning less, but just as importantly, I find myself recovering my footing more quickly after sinning, due to the immediate comfort found in the gospel. I have also found that when I am absorbed in the gospel, everything else I am supposed to be toward God and others seems to flow out of me more naturally and passionately. Doing right is not always easy, but it is never more easy than when one is breathing deeply the atmosphere of the gospel.[2]

Mary professed that she had trusted in Jesus as her Savior and had bowed to him as her Lord. She understood the desperate condition of her heart and life without Christ. She acknowledged the pervasive necessity of the gospel in her sanctification and knew that a growing believer should overflow with the fruits of the Spirit. Mary was a believer. She trusted in Christ. As true as that was, she had been shackled to her fears for over four years. There was no satisfaction or joy in her life. What was wrong?

Mary wasn't satisfied with her life because she was trying to locate satisfaction in temporary things that only dazzle the heart in a temporary way. She was not finding joy, hope, and satisfaction in a living Savior who could justify, adopt, and sanctify her. As a result she was unhappy and anxious. What temporary object was Mary looking to in order to be satisfied? In that early meeting one thing was clear: Mary was desperately discontent because she was seeking satisfaction in an elusive assurance that she would not get AIDS. Though Mary was a believer, she was actively pursuing an AIDS-free life more than she was pursuing Christ. This was a serious problem, but even in her deep distress, the God of steadfast love was drawing Mary back to himself.

As Mary and I began our counseling relationship, I knew God had brought us together so she could learn that her greatest need was to find her satisfaction in Christ alone. Mary needed to desire him, trust him, and seek him more than she valued protection from AIDS. She was learning the hard way that medication

---

[2] Milton Vincent, *A Gospel Primer for Christians: Learning to See the Glories of God's Love* (Bemidji, MN: Focus, 2008), 6.

and a newborn would never fulfill her. Shallow spiritual balms did not take her deep enough into the riches of grace. Constant efforts at cleaning and avoiding "contaminated" objects were false refuges that would never provide the security for which she longed. I began to pray that through our times together Mary would encounter Christ and the peace which only he can provide.

Making Sense of Mary's Fear

During our first session I asked Mary to explain exactly *why* AIDS was so terrifying. I learned that most of Mary's dread stemmed from three places: a calculated fear of death, a fear of contaminating her family, and fear of her friends' judgment. Mary did not share in depth about her fear of death, but she spoke at length about how AIDS might affect her family and her friends. The worst part about contaminating her family, she expressed, was that she would feel guilty and she would lose them. Her fear of her friends' judgment sprang from a similar thought. They would make her feel guilty and dirty for having AIDS, and then she would lose them.

Although this fear of losing family and friends can sound natural and right, it is typically founded on a premise of entitlement. The unstated assumption is that "I deserve to have a healthy family and nice friends" or "I *don't* deserve a sick family and judgmental friends." For Mary this assumption turned into a stronger conclusion: "I *must* have what I deserve or I cannot be happy. I *must* have what I deserve or God is not good." This demand led to crippling anxiety. Mary could not absolutely guarantee that her family would avoid contracting AIDS so she became increasingly fearful. As Mary finished describing her situation, she sighed, "I don't know how to let it go."

Mary's obsessive thinking was negatively affecting both her mind and her body. As she looked at me from across my desk, hands folded neatly in her lap, I felt the crushing weight of her fear. I recognized its folly, but I was also moved by her vulnerability, her admission of weakness, and the misery of her self-induced captivity.

Who Is God? Faith Versus Feelings

In our second counseling session, I wanted to establish further the disconnect between a robust belief in the gospel of Jesus and Mary's patterns of behavior. Often counselees are so fixated on their *feelings* regarding their situation that they ignore the truths God has clearly revealed in his Word. These counselees are operating under the unstated assumption, "I feel it to be true; therefore, it *is* true." Such patterns of belief are a poison to trust in Christ and his promises. It is deceptive and precarious logic; it elevates a sin-cursed person's perception of circumstances above the absolute truth that God has established. To ignorc this absolute truth is to say, essentially, "My perception, my logic, and my thinking are just as good, accurate, and credible as God's." In contrast the imprisoned apostle Paul urged believers to set their minds not on their feelings but on what is *true* (Phil 4:8).

In response to my questions, Mary claimed to know that God was holy, good, kind, sovereign, gave believers joy, and worked all things for the good for those who love him. I asked if Mary *really* believed these things. She nodded. I asked if she believed them last week when she felt fearful. She shook her head. The truth was that Mary knew those truths intellectually and generally but was not pondering and embracing them daily; instead, she was focusing on her weaknesses, her fear, and her discouragement.

Thinking only on what is true is impossible because we are fallen creatures. We were born in sin, and although believers are now counted righteous before God and possess Christ's power to obey, we will wrestle with our sin until we are perfected in heaven and our transformation into the image of Christ is complete. As we await that transformation, we still struggle against deception deep in our hearts. Mary's heart was telling lies, and she was falling for those lies. She was basing her decisions on her *feelings* about what was true, rather than on the established truth of God's Word. I pointed out to Mary that her wavering emotions were founded on shifting lies.

In fact, every sin is founded on a lie—the lie of unbelief directed toward God's Son and his declared truth. For example, we often fail to believe that God is who he says he is. We do not believe that God will really do what he has promised to do; we suspect that God might not know or will not do what is best for us; and we doubt the way that God has ordered the world. When we believe lies and choose to sin, we experience emotional consequences such as depression, anger, anxiety, hopelessness, and many others.

Mary had not been abiding with Christ by dwelling on the truths of God's Word. She was not trusting in God's sovereignty or his goodness. Instead she believed the lies that she could protect herself better than God could and that she could manipulate a healthy future for herself. She did not believe God would satisfy her with his presence, love, and care. Rather, she was deceiving herself into thinking that control and good health would satisfy her. As a result, Mary's fears escalated as she realized that she could not guarantee herself the control and protection she was craving.

Mary needed to see the infinite riches of Christ, she needed to rest in those riches, and then she needed to learn to remind herself of those riches when anxiety threatened her trust. Just like the rest of us should do, she needed to preach the truth to herself daily (starting with the gospel) instead of listening to the constant refrain of lies streaming to her from without and from within.

Laying a Biblical Foundation

If lies come from our selfish hearts, our sinful world, and our deceptive adversary Satan, then where does the exclusive and inerrant truth come from? I shared with Mary the declaration of Hebrews: "For the word of God is living and effective and sharper than any double-edged sword, penetrating as far as the separation of soul and spirit, joints and marrow. It is able to judge the thoughts and ideas of the heart" (4:12). The author of Hebrews connects this living, effective, sharp, penetrating, judging word to Christ (Heb 4:14). That means that if Mary is going to encounter her Savior she is going to need to turn from her feelings to the Word, which leads her to the Savior of her soul.

With this in mind, I challenged Mary to put her hope in Christ by looking to the truth and authority of Scripture, even when she *felt* the world was dangerous, even when she *felt* lonely or purposeless, even when she *felt* victory was a lost cause. The Bible would be *critical* in helping her determine the truth about herself and her situation. Without a standard of truth, how was Mary to know what was true about her circumstances?

Thankfully, Mary claimed the Bible as her source of truth and admitted that her feelings were not a trustworthy source of confidence. Because Mary was already a believer with confidence in Scripture, she was quickly encouraged as she saw where the Bible directed her hope in our discussion of the truth of the gospel and the reality of her redemption. We read Rom 8:28–29 together: "We know that all things work together for the good of those who love God: those who are called according to his purpose. For those He foreknew He also predestined to be conformed to the image of his Son, so that He would be the firstborn among many brothers." As we unpacked these verses together, Mary began to have hope that God's plan for her future in Christ was good, holy, and wonderful—even when she could not see it at the time.

"You already know what's true," I told Mary. "We've talked about all of these true things. Now you have to decide, and you'll have to decide every day and maybe even every half hour, whether you're going to repent of your unbelief and trust Christ and believe what is *true* or whether you're going to believe lies. Truth leads to repentance, restoration, satisfaction, and joy. Lies only lead to destruction."

Mary understood. She knew that continuing in her wrong thinking would mean forfeiting victory and reembarking on a gloom-filled, fear-laden, unproductive life spent in the fetal position. She admitted that without the hope of God's truth, her future was one of loneliness and perhaps eventual institutionalization.

"But the lies are just so overwhelming," Mary confessed. "When I start to feel afraid, I feel like I can't stop. It just gets worse and worse." I sympathized with Mary's feelings of helplessness; but for her own good and growth, such lies had to be challenged: "You *feel* like you can't stop, but what is *true*?" I pressed. Mary shrugged.

So together we looked at 1 Cor 10:13 where Paul wrote, "No temptation has overtaken you except what is common to humanity. God is faithful, and He will not allow you to be tempted beyond what you are able, but with the temptation He will also provide a way of escape so that you are able to bear it." I explained that even when the temptation to fear seemed overwhelming, God had promised her a way of escape. God is faithful. He cares for his precious daughter. He would never allow her to face more than she could handle with his help. I asked Mary to memorize this verse so that she would be prepared the next time she faced fear and the corresponding temptation that she could not escape it.

Scripture memory is a sharp, shining weapon against temptation. Memorizing Scripture invokes the aid of the Holy Spirit—God-on-the-scene in our struggles. The Spirit who dwells within us has the power to strengthen and comfort and gladden our hearts with his Word. The psalmist says in Ps 119:11, "I have treasured Your word in my heart so that I may not sin against You." By the power of the Holy Spirit working through the Word, we are set free from the slavery of our sinful nature (Rom 8:2, 10–11; 2 Cor 3:17), we are convicted of any hidden sin (Ps 19:12), we abound in the fruit of the Spirit (Gal 5:22–23), and we abound with hope (Rom 15:13)!

Loosening the Grip

Over subsequent sessions Mary's progress was slow but significant. In our fourth meeting we discussed her craving for control. All of Mary's fears—her fear of death by AIDS, her fear of infecting her family with AIDS, her fear of her friends' judgment if she were to contract AIDS—stemmed from a desire for *control*. Mary wanted to control her future. She wanted to control her family's health and well-being. She wanted to control her friends' opinions of her. Of course, our natural desires for safety, comfort, and health are not inherently wrong. But Mary was willing to sin to get what she wanted. She was willing to stop serving her family, her friends, and her church in order to maintain her safety, comfort, and health. She was motivated, driven, and striving for control over her circumstances.

As we talked, I pointed out to Mary that she had erected an idol in her heart. Where the living God should have been—in the center of Mary's consciousness and at the center of each of her endeavors—an idol of control received her worship.

John Calvin once said that the human heart is a "factory of idols."[3] This is a frighteningly accurate metaphor. Just as every sin is the fruit of unbelief, at the heart of every sin is an idol. If I believe a lie about God, then I am not worshipping him; rather, I am belittling him, casting him from the throne of my heart. Man was designed for worship, so if I am not worshipping God, I am worshipping something or someone else. Mary was worshipping control. She believed the lie that having control would make her happy. She believed that having control would keep her safe, that having control would keep her family safe, and that having control over the opinions of her friends would keep her from being lonely.

Idols are powerful, but two realities cause our hearts to become dissatisfied with idols. The first is that we are created in the image of God and created for God; nothing else will give us eternal purpose or everlasting joy. When we choose to set up a dead, powerless idol and worship at its feet, then we are attended to by a dead, powerless idol that pleases temporarily and superficially. Money disappears. Fame fades away. Children grow up and leave. Our friends fail us. Control is elusive. God alone—in all of his beauty and grace—can promise us joy forever.

The second reality that causes our hearts to grow dissatisfied with idols is the grace of God. God is too good to allow his children to worship something or someone that will not satisfy. He is so good that he either wrenches our idols from our hands or makes us miserable as long as we clench and grasp. Mary was seeking her happiness, her safety, and her fulfillment in her own ability to

---

[3] John Calvin, *Institutes of the Christian Religion*, ed. John T. McNeill, trans. Ford Lewis Battles, Library of Christian Classics, vol. 20 (London: SCM Press, 1960), I.XI.8 (108).

control her circumstances. Ultimately, her warped belief that she *could* control her circumstances revealed Mary's prideful worship of *self* in addition to her worship of control.

When the threat of AIDS exposed her illusion of power, Mary crumbled. The fear of AIDS threatened Mary's gods, the idols of her heart: her own self and her lust for control. As a result she isolated herself and stayed in bed—her best attempt to achieve safety and relief from her fears. Living for a false god will bring each of us to this point, one way or another: a lonely, fearful life lived in the fetal position.

Is God Good?

Not only was Mary willing to neglect her family in her desperate chase for safety, but her lust for control also presented yet more evidence of her self-deception. Mary was not believing that God was good. When I challenged her with this reality, she admitted that she had difficulty surveying her circumstances and concluding, "God is good."

"I wouldn't say, 'God is *not good*,' said Mary, "but it's just hard to believe that *what he's putting me through* is very good." I appreciated Mary's honesty. She was only expressing what many believers feel in the course of suffering: How can a good God allow people to suffer? We made this a matter of discussion in our times together. I also had her memorize Ps 119:68, "You are good, and You do what is good; teach me Your statutes." Additionally, I encouraged Mary to read *Trusting God* by Jerry Bridges to bolster her understanding of God's love, his providence, and his sovereign control. This book addresses at length her major questions about God's goodness and sovereignty. Mary was to read one chapter each week, underline anything that seemed pertinent to her situation, and we would then discuss it in our weekly meetings. This detailed process of reflection made our discussions more thoughtful, substantial, and relevant.

"We both know that the Bible portrays a good God," I reminded her. "Do your feelings or your circumstances change that truth?" I explained that according to Ps 119:68 (and many other passages),

God not only exercises sovereign control over every event in our lives, and he is not only good in the essence of his being, but he is also *doing good* in our everyday lives. It might not seem good, and it might not feel good. But the *seeming* and the *feeling* are not definitive.

"Think of the crucifixion of Christ—was that good?" I asked Mary. "No," she immediately replied. Then she caught herself and continued, "Well . . . yes." I watched the light go on in her mind. Mary knew that God had sent Christ to suffer and atone for our sins. He was tortured. He was mocked. He bled. Had Mary and I been present at his crucifixion, we would have stood beneath the cross and asked, "Why? Why is God making him suffer like this?" But the beautiful truth is that God's ways are higher than ours (Isa 55:8–9). Our sovereign God transformed the brutal, horrifying death of his innocent Son into the best good his people could ever experience.

"What if you *did* get AIDS," I asked Mary. "Is God still good? Romans 8:28 says that he works *all things* for your good. Would that include AIDS?" I pressed Mary to recognize that God is always good—even in the shadow of her darkest circumstances. If she were not sick for a single day of her life, God would be good. If she and her entire family contracted AIDS, God would be good. God was always working for her good.

"Isn't he working to give me a better life?" objected Mary. "I don't understand how that works if I get AIDS."

"He's working to make you more like Christ," I explained. "He's working to draw your heart closer to his. There are rich, popular, healthy people all over the world who are miserable; but if you are trusting in Christ, thanking him for his goodness, rejoicing in the truth of your salvation, and serving and encouraging others, then you will experience joy and satisfaction in Christ—even if you have AIDS. I can promise you that."

Mary was beginning to learn that until she cultivated a submissive heart to the truth of God's goodness and the rightness of his plan, she would not rid herself of fear in any long-term way. So long as an idol occupied her heart, she would remain fearful and discontent. As Mary grew in her understanding of the goodness of God, she began to taste the bitterness of her unbelief and to recognize her consuming fears as sin and rebellion. Where sin had multiplied, God's grace multiplied all the more (Rom 5:20).

From Fear to Love

Over our next few sessions, Mary and I discussed 1 John 4:18: "There is no fear in love; instead, perfect love drives out fear." I read this verse aloud to her and explained that the antidote to fear was not courage but faith in the bold and persevering love of God.[4] If Mary would entrust herself to God's love, her fears would be driven away. As she began making progress in her thinking, I challenged her to follow Christ's example of love by living her own life in love. This would help her begin thinking of others instead of only herself, a process which, by God's grace, would mean a complete turnaround over time. I explained that fear drives us to self-preservation but that love seeks to understand others and sacrifices to meet their needs. Fear had led Mary to avoid unpleasant situations and to expel discomfort at all costs. Now love would move her to dwell on God's grace and thank him for the intimidating situations which were designed to mold her into the image of Christ.

With this new purpose Mary continued to make progress. Over the next month she faithfully completed the counseling assignments I gave her, some of which were service projects. She planned out two serving opportunities along with keeping a journal in which she recorded events throughout the day that triggered her fear. Then she wrote out the truths that she could turn to as weapons in the battle against fear. I urged her to repent whenever she became sinfully fearful and to thank God for each "fear trigger" which God was using to shape her. Each assignment was

---

[4] The primary fear here in this passage is God's judgment that has been dispelled when a person places faith and trust in Jesus for salvation. The secondary application is that fear is basic unbelief and loving trust will help Christians deal with their fears.

designed to help Mary ponder truth, cast down idols, focus on others, and rest in Christ.

After five weeks of counseling, Mary finally washed the clothes under her bed. In our eighth week together, she took her son, Daniel, to a nursing home where her goal was to visit with the residents and bring joy to their day. Throughout the afternoon she struggled to remember that God was protecting both Daniel and herself, but she persevered in faith and even touched one of the residents on the shoulder in a comforting gesture of love. Her heartfelt love and her mission to serve enabled her to overcome her fear of this sort of contact. Rather than viewing the nursing home residents as threats to her and her son's safety, Mary was viewing her afternoon in the nursing home as a ministry, an opportunity to share her joy in the Lord. Jesus Christ defeated Mary's lust for control as she trusted him in obedient faith. She went home happy, reaping the blessing of joy for her grace-empowered obedience.

Journaling for Growth

As we continued to meet, guided journaling became a key element in Mary's process of change. In addition to recording her "fear triggers," I also asked Mary to write out what she was thinking and wanting each time she saw fear in her heart and to describe how she handled each encounter with fear. Did she succumb and spiral into depression? What truths from God's Word did she remember and preach to herself? This assignment not only helped Mary take "every thought captive to obey Christ" (2 Cor 10:5), but it also helped me follow her progress closely. She was encouraged as she flipped back through the pages each week, reading in her own writing how God had been faithful and victorious. Soon I asked Mary to add blessings and praises to her journal. "Stop and praise God for each trial you encounter," I suggested.

Through Mary's journaling, I could see that she was beginning to approach her life in an entirely new way. Every week we celebrated her victories, large or small, knowing that change was a gradual process and that even the small steps were worthy of celebration. In one of her entries, she wrote:

> When I woke up, I was fearful for the coming week. I repented to God for my rebellion and submitted myself to Him. I'm looking at just today knowing that there will be sufficient grace for me for today. Today I became fearful about something I cut myself with. I repented to God that I want to be in control of my own life and thanked Him for all the ways He reminds me that my protection is under His control.

After a month and a half Mary met with her physician and received his approval to begin reducing her anxiety and depression medications. This was yet another victory to celebrate in the journal:

> This was a victorious day, and I thanked God for his mighty power and grace that he has brought to my life. . . . I've had no medication this week. . . . The clothes previously under the bed are clean and worn. I can put my son in the grocery cart without wiping it down now.

Blood: The Final Proving Ground

As Mary progressed, I was fascinated by the way God designed unique trials specifically to refine her. For example, Mary feared the sight and even the concept of blood. During her nine months of counseling, she accidentally cut her hand twice at the nail salon and several more times at home. The cuts were small with no risk for infection, but these events were opportunities for her to entrust herself to God's goodness by trusting his Son and believing his truth. After all, how often does a nail salon worker cut a client's finger? I knew these "coincidences" were being orchestrated by Christ, the Wonderful Counselor (Isa 9:6).

Four months into counseling, Mary visited her local cable company to pay the family's cable bill. She was running errands that afternoon, helping her husband and serving her family, and probably celebrating her recent success as she walked confidently into the poorly maintained building and paid her bill. As she finished the transaction, she heard a sharp cry. Turning abruptly,

Mary saw a pale face in the doorway; the woman grimaced and held her elbow. This stranger had managed to slice her arm on a metal latch in the doorway, and a deep cut was bleeding down the length of her arm. Blood was already on the floor, on the doorframe, and on the woman; and she was standing in the middle of the only exit. Mary felt the familiar ache of fear knotting up in her stomach. The flickering exit sign over the door, however, reminded her of something.

First Corinthians 10:13, thought Mary. *God will provide a way of escape.* The truths she had been stockpiling in her mind flashed into action: *God is good. God would never give me more than I can handle with his help. God knows I can handle this. God has prepared me for this trial. It didn't come earlier because I wasn't ready. But now I can please him through this and become more like Christ.* God would give Mary the courage to walk through this trial as through an exit door, without being derailed by fear and self-protection.

It would not be simple or easy. Mary swallowed hard, her stomach sick and sinking. She glanced down at her feet and her strappy summer sandals, then back at the blood between herself and home. Maintaining a calm face, she walked straight past the woman and through the bloody doorway, her limbs cold and heavy. Outside the building now, she contemplated running to her car.

"Miss?"

The voice startled Mary. She turned around. The woman was calling from the doorway, white-faced and wide-eyed.

"Do you know first aid? It's bleeding a lot." The woman pointed to her cut. "Would you help me get to my car?"

Mary set her mouth in a shaky line, and shockingly started walking back toward the woman. Naturally she was extremely careful and made no direct contact with the woman's blood, but she still helped this stranger apply pressure to the wound with clean bandages, and then walked her to her car. As Mary walked back to her own car and drove home, her mind was blank.

When she pulled into her driveway, she was overwhelmed with anger. She knew God had put her in this situation. He had given her another difficult opportunity to trust him, and Mary was furious with God for making her do something so awfully hard. She ripped the floor mats out of her car and peeled off her shoes and stuffed them into the trash. She went inside and tried to sleep but couldn't—she felt overwhelmed. Eventually, with Ben's loving, gentle encouragement, she was able to accept God's love for her in arranging this monumental event. God had not abandoned her in her moment of need and weakness. God had used her to share his love and compassion with a stranger. God had brought her through blood.

As Mary related this story to me over the phone, I was astounded by God's grace lavished on her life, far more abundantly than she could ever have imagined. Over time, as she continued to learn how to rejoice in God's goodness toward her, she discovered a deep and thrilling paradox: All her hope—her sanctification, her joy, and her eternal satisfaction—was secured by Christ's *blood.*

Not only had God brought her through blood and taught her through blood in the cable company building, but he had also first *bought* her with blood at the cross. The thing she feared most—an encounter with blood—is what God had planned since before creation to redeem her—not only for a delightful eternity but for God-glorifying growth in daily living. In one of her final journal entries, Mary wrote: "I *know* that nothing happens to me by chance. God is actively involved in each and every experience I have to make me more like Christ, . . . and every time he calls me to sacrifice or deny myself, he plans to give me more than I had to start with."

Concluding Reflections

By the end of nine months, Jesus was transforming Mary as her mind was renewed (Rom 12:2). Of course, renewing the mind is a lifelong endeavor, and Mary would continue to wrestle with fear. But now she was equipped with God's Word and knew how to lay hold of God's power in the Spirit. She was much quicker to embrace God's gracious purposes in using her temptation to strengthen her faith and dependence on Christ.

Looking back, I see at least two major ways in which God enabled me to help Mary. First, Mary and I went directly and consistently to the cross and the core work of atonement that God had accomplished in her life. This gospel perspective freed Mary to understand her identity in Christ and her purpose in life. To this day I am still astounded by how the gospel intersected with Mary's sin. The one thing Mary feared the most, the one thing Mary ran from and hated—*blood*—was the exact thing God had used to save her forever. Blood had rescued her from a *truly* terrifying life and an eternity without him, and blood had given her hope for *today*.

Second, I chose not to focus on secular labels for Mary's unusual behavior. When referring to her problems, I purposefully avoided all terminology outside of biblical terminology. Others (especially secular specialists) might have labeled Mary's behavior obsessive-compulsive disorder (OCD), but I chose not to label her behavior as OCD in our counseling sessions because this label often weakens a person's sense of responsibility and indirectly undercuts hope. People who embrace these labels may conclude, "I was born with OCD, and there's no cure for that. I can't help the way I think and behave."

Although Mary's struggles should not be taken lightly, the Bible is *always* full of hope for believers, regardless of their mental and physical circumstances or setbacks. In Mary's case her OCD was the *symptom*, not the *source* of her struggles. Focusing on the deception of her sin nature, the sovereignty and goodness of God, and her tendency to become self-absorbed enabled Mary to see how the Bible was relevant for her problems. The Bible does not speak to OCD in contemporary medical terminology, but it does talk about the thoughts, motivations, and behaviors our culture uses to describe OCD. In other words, the Bible has a lot to say about fear, anxiety, trusting God, and loving others.

Finally, what would I have done differently? Thankfully, more than 10 years later, I am far more equipped today to help someone like Mary. Not only have I accumulated more experience, but I have also watched dozens of helpful contemporary resources stream into the hands of counselors and counselees. I did not have the following books on hand when I counseled Mary, but I would have been delighted to use them. *The Cross-Centered Life* and *Living the Cross-Centered Life* by C. J. Mahaney unpack the necessity and centrality of the cross in interpreting and living life to the glory of God. *A Gospel Primer* by Milton Vincent beautifully details the nonnegotiable task of preaching the gospel to oneself day by day and hour by hour. John MacArthur's *The Murder of Jesus* and *Hard to Believe* and James McDonald's *Gripped by the Greatness of God* serve as further reminders of the significance of our atonement in Christ as well as the practical implications of God's glorious attributes. Beyond material resources, connecting Mary with one or two female mentors also would have been beneficial. Walking closely alongside godly women would have been an effective way to encourage and inspire growth in her life.

This was a lengthy and memorable case that God used for good in both of our lives. After nearly a year of counseling, Ben found a job in the south that was a better fit for the family, so he, Mary, and Daniel moved on. Although Mary still struggled occasionally with fear, she was now equipped with the theological truth and practical tools to confront temptation through Christ's grace.

As one of my first cases, Mary's transformation solidified my desire to serve the Lord through biblical counseling. I was inspired by her growth, by her newfound passion for truth, and by her blossoming desire to know and worship God. God had drawn her near to himself, and her joy now warmed her home and lit up her family and transformed her relationships. Mary was shining like a light before us; and because of the Holy Spirit's work in her life, we were glorifying our Father in heaven (see Matt 5:16).

When Mary moved away at the end of nine months, a happy creature in Christ, she was neither fearless nor brave. She was, however, full of God's love and covered in his grace.

How is Mary doing now? Just last week I contacted her, and her response beautifully portrays the transforming power of God:

> My life is not my own. I daily choose to submit it to my Creator, and I have no limits or expectations for what He will do with it. . . . I only know that it will be good. It has

> been in that state of submission, I have been freed up with amazing energy to work with our local hospice. I have yet to get a terminal AIDS patient, but I can't wait! I've also been able to love and counsel many who are troubled with addictions and are potential intravenous drug users, and it is my greatest joy to hug them and love them and partner with them toward recovery. I have been able to work with the local Child Protective Services to care for a foster boy who was a drug baby, and I adore him as my own without one moment's regard for his health and how it could affect mine. The list goes on, and I hope it will continue to grow. The first major part of my life was consumed with thoughts of myself, my safety, and my happiness. I had built my own personal "kingdom" and was unwilling to accept anything less. Now I'm free. Free to serve, free to love the unlovely, free to offer hope to the hopeless, free to get dirty in people's lives. Free to say yes when my God calls me! My greatest passion in life is to lift Jesus high. If that is with AIDS or any other disease or loss—bring it on. My Most High God looked upon me and declared me righteous by Christ's blood, and there is nothing I will not suffer for Him and His glory.

God is faithful. His grace sustained Mary through every moment of weakness, raised the banner of hope in her heart, and exploded like fireworks in the dark skies of her fear. Now he will continue to work great and beautiful things through her compassion toward others.

Grace—how illuminating.
Freedom—how bright.
Blood—how cleansing!

Chapter 6

"Ashley" and Anorexia

Martha Peace

"911—What's your emergency?" answered the dispatcher. "One of our students has collapsed in the university library and isn't waking up," said the caller. "Her pulse feels fast and weak. Please hurry!" The library staff and fellow students had begun to gather under the curious silence that hovers over public medical emergencies. Hushed onlookers tried to put together the few puzzle pieces they saw scattered before them in the form of a thin 20-year-old sophomore English major. The full picture, however, would not emerge until the dust had settled.

How Image Became Everything

Up to this point Ashley's brief college career had been a success. She had enrolled at a major state university close to home and had earned a 4.0 GPA her freshman year. She had grown up in a Christian home and had thought often in her teenage years about how she could serve the Lord. Her parents were happily married and had taken good care of their three children. Dad was a businessman, and Mom had stayed at home with Ashley and her two younger brothers (ages 14 and 12).

During her senior year of high school, Ashley had begun to grow concerned with her weight and appearance. At a petite five feet three inches, she felt like she needed to trim down, especially as she carried around the mental image of a best friend whom Ashley considered more attractive than herself. She did some research, set some goals, changed her diet, and kept up an exercise routine. What began as a desire to eat healthily eventually led to this otherwise successful college sophomore lying unconscious on the floor. It had now become a "911 emergency!"

The paramedics arrived and quickly took control of the scene. They immediately saw that Ashley was extremely underweight. Her pulse was weak and barely palpable, her breathing was rapid and shallow, and she seemed dangerously dehydrated. She remained only semiconscious as the paramedics inserted an IV, fitted her with an oxygen mask, hooked up a cardiac monitor, and rushed her with lights glaring and sirens blaring to the nearest emergency room.

The ER doctor ordered immediate blood work and soon diagnosed that Ashley was severely dehydrated and her electrolytes were abnormal. This affected her heart rhythm and her ability to think clearly. She was so weak she could not sit up, and she weighed only 85 pounds.[1]

After her fluids and electrolytes were replenished by an IV, Ashley regained consciousness and was able to answer the doctor's questions. He finally diagnosed Ashley with "anorexia nervosa" with secondary electrolyte imbalance and dehydration, but the ultimate diagnosis would run much deeper.

Bound for Beauty: What Is Anorexia?

As soon as Ashley's parents received the diagnosis, they jumped online and began researching "anorexia nervosa." What they discovered about their oldest child was shocking:

> Anorexia is an eating disorder characterized by markedly reduced appetite or total aversion to food. It

[1] According to standard height/weight ratios, Ashley was at least 25 pounds underweight, regardless of her frame.

> is a condition that goes well beyond out-of-control dieting. . . . The individual continues the endless cycle of restrictive eating, often to a point close to starvation. This becomes an obsession and is similar to an addiction to a drug. Anorexia can be life-threatening.[2]

After discussions with university administration, Ashley's parents and school officials made the joint decision to withdraw Ashley from school temporarily so she could be cared for in the comfort and familiarity of her own home. Once at home, she admitted to her parents that she had no energy and was frightened. Like any faithful mother would do, her mom began regularly preparing Ashley's favorite foods; but most of what was placed before her she would only pick at or refuse to eat.

Her parents grew increasingly worried. As the days and weeks passed, they would cry, beg, or threaten Ashley with hospitalization or pretend not to notice her miniscule eating habits. Neither approach was working. Nagging only exacerbated the issue, and ignoring it was only going to lead back to the ER—or worse.

Thankfully, Ashley's mother knew about a biblical counselor in a neighboring town. The first responders had been lifesaving, the medical diagnosis was essential, the Internet research had been enlightening, and the commonsense steps Ashley's parents had taken at home were right and reasonable. Now that they were a few steps removed from the library floor, the ambulance, and the ER, more was needed for this "anorexia nervosa" than the medical world was able to offer.

Ashley's mother called the biblical counselor and made an appointment.

Asking, Listening, and Understanding

After listening to Ashley's mother explain what happened, I encouraged her that both she and her husband needed to come

---

[2] Ashley's parents found this definition of anorexia from *www.medicinenet.com*. For more information about the secular description of this problem see *Diagnostic and Statistical Manual of Mental Disorders: DSM-IV-TR* (Washington, DC: American Psychiatric Association, 2000), 583–89.

with Ashley for at least the first few sessions. Ashley tried desperately to get out of the appointment by promising that she would do better. Her parents wisely recognized the need for biblical counseling and gave her no choice.

The next day Ashley and her parents walked through my door looking discouraged and downcast. All three had been jolted by Ashley's medical emergency and serious diagnosis, and her return home had been punctuated by constant conflict about her dangerous habits. Their previously stable family had been rocked by this life-threatening sin that made everyone, including Ashley, dread the next meal.

I could tell from the beginning that Ashley would be a hard case and immediately recognized two simultaneous emergencies: Ashley's life and Ashley's soul. I had counseled many other women who struggled with anorexia, and I learned to begin the process by asking questions, listening carefully, and attempting to understand them. Only then could I offer her biblical hope and guide her toward practical steps of obedience and wisdom.

At our first meeting I began to ask questions and gather information about Ashley's life. She shared that she had "asked Jesus into her heart" when she was eight years old, but now she wasn't sure if she was a Christian. "I grew up in church, and I still go to church with my family when I'm home from school. I used to read my Bible and pray but haven't for several months now. I want to be a Christian, but I'm really confused."

It is essential to understand someone's salvation testimony because many professing Christians have not truly trusted in Christ and repented of their sins. Therefore, they do not have the proper motivations to change or the empowering presence of the Holy Spirit in their lives. At this point I didn't know Ashley well enough to discern her spiritual condition, but it was vital for me to hear her own take on her Christian experiences and the spiritual influences in her life.

I also knew that people with anorexia often struggle with perfectionism. "Do you think you might be a perfectionist?"

I asked. "Well, my family and friends think I am, but I'm not so sure," Ashley offered. "I think I just want to do my best, which is a good thing."

I asked Ashley how much she had weighed and what was going through her mind when she started on her initial diet prior to college. "I was a senior in high school, and I realized I was fat. I weighed 135 pounds, and I'm only 5 feet 3 inches. I just wanted to lose about 20 pounds and be little like my best friend. I did lots of research online, learned how to eat healthily, and then started working really hard at dieting and exercising. At the beginning I got a lot of compliments, so I doubled my efforts."

"Do you have rules about what you absolutely will not eat?" I asked (well aware that two of the most common expressions of anorexic drive are strict dieting and relentless exercise). "Yes, but they *are* all based on healthy eating," Ashley clarified. "I don't eat any sugar, fat, or bread. No red meat; only lean chicken and fish. No starchy vegetables like potatoes. I do eat some fruit and nonfat yogurt."

Ashley's confident, detailed answers revealed that she had really put some time into this endeavor. I asked how she learned what's healthy and what's not. "From doing research online," she answered. Her mother added, "She's spent countless hours on the computer doing research."

"And what about your exercise routine?" I asked. "Usually I fast-walk or jog about 45 minutes each day. Then I try to do 30 minutes of aerobic exercise and stomach crunches. Right now it's difficult for me since I don't have much energy, but I try."

Ashley was sinfully obsessed and driven. She had a goal, even if it had become a moving target, and she had a plan. She had made great effort and great sacrifices to whittle her body down to the scant 85 pounds that had collapsed on the library's floor.

Knowing that all of this had put a significant strain on their family, I gently asked Ashley about her relationship with her parents. "It used to be good," she started. "But now they harass me all the time about what I eat. I tell them if they'll just leave me alone, I'll be fine."

"What do you think would happen if you ate what your mom wanted you to eat?" I responded. "I'd be fat," Ashley exclaimed, "and I've already worked too hard to get the weight off. I'm not going back there!"

As we continued to talk, I gained more and more clarity regarding Ashley's thoughts, feelings, and motivations, along with the external factors, unique circumstances, and family dynamics that all contributed to the perfect storm of her drive to be thin and beautiful.

Knowing the enslaving nature of anorexia and the miserable bondage it promotes, I carefully asked Ashley if she had ever contemplated suicide or developed a plan for taking her own life. "Sometimes I've wished I were dead," she admitted in a courageous act of honesty. "But I've never thought about how I might actually take my life. I'd never do that." It was relieving to know that Ashley had never thought seriously about suicide, but that relief only freed me to focus my thinking about other items on my counseling agenda list.

A Path Sprinkled with Hope

As I continued listening to Ashley and her parents, I began mentally categorizing what I was hearing in order to clarify the many issues making up Ashley's physical and spiritual emergency. As the conversation transitioned, I prayed for wisdom and wrote up a list of topics to address in our upcoming conversations. My spontaneous list looked like this:

- hope
- parental involvement
- the gospel of Jesus Christ
- medical care
- restructuring eating/exercise habits
- the big picture (remembering Christ and the two greatest commandments)
- renewing the mind
- vanity
- perfectionism

Later I would go back and organize these topics into a logical order for subsequent sessions, but for now I just wanted Ashley and her parents to know some of the angles we would be taking and some of the conversations they could anticipate in coming weeks.

Sprinkled throughout my questioning and listening were nuggets of hope that I offered to both Ashley and her parents. They were afraid and desperate. They needed to hear repeatedly that the hope found in the life, death, and resurrection of Jesus Christ was as real as the air they breathed. Although the food Ashley feared and the weight she watched seemed to be in control, that control was an illusion. As long as she remained deluded, the bathroom scale and the bedroom mirror would rule her life. The illusion was not unbreakable. It could be (and would be) shattered by the good news of redemption.

I told Ashley that she was embarking on a difficult journey but not an insurmountable one. By faith she could expect to overcome her self-consumed mentality. She could even grow to experience a sense of joy and gratitude when she ate her meals.

I also reminded her that the bad news of sin, enslavement, and misery had been getting all the attention in her heart but that the good news of forgiveness, freedom, and renewal could take over the headlines as she learned to rewrite her thoughts with the truths of God's Word. Her self-centered, harmful desires were sinful, but God would give her the grace of forgiveness and the power of repentance. God would forgive, and Ashley could change.

"Ashley, I know you're probably afraid that I'm going to make you eat and eat until you're fat," I predicted. "The truth is that God doesn't want you to be uncontrolled or irresponsible in your eating. Instead, he wants you to exercise self-control, to have joy in what you eat, and to glorify him in all of it."

This process would be agonizing for Ashley, like an addict coming off a drug. I knew that the idea of altering her mentality, changing her perspective, and increasing her weight was petrifying to her. "We'll move slowly," I promised. "One of the things you'll slowly learn is how to 'trust in the LORD with all your heart, and do not rely on your own understanding'" (Prov 3:5). This would mean trusting in God's perfect Word and following the scriptural wisdom of others instead of following her own deceitful, enslaving thoughts that had led her so far astray.

A Book Filled with Hope

What specific Scriptures would saturate Ashley with the hope she desperately needed? I spent some time reading and explaining some of the biblical passages that were most relevant and powerful for Ashley's situation.

In the midst of this physical, spiritual, and emotional storm, Ashley needed a strong ballast at the bottom of her swaying ship. She needed to lay the rock-solid truths of Rom 8:28–30 at the foundation of her efforts to change. Paul wrote:

> We know that all things work together for the good of those who love God: those who are called according to His purpose. For those He foreknew He also predestined to be conformed to the image of His Son, so that He would be the firstborn among many brothers. And those He predestined, He also called; and those He called, He also justified; and those He justified, He also glorified.

Ashley needed to believe—truly believe—that she wasn't predestined to be conformed to the air-brushed image on the cover of *Vanity Fair* or the plasticized image of a Hollywood superstar or even the real-life image of her best friend. Instead, if Ashley was a Christian, her focus needed to turn her vanity to glorifying God. The perfect image of Jesus the Son of God was her destiny, and that's all that ultimately mattered. Before the universe had even existed, God had chosen Ashley, called Ashley, justified Ashley, and had made Ashley perfect in his sight. Now she only needed to learn how to grow into these established realities.

Ashley also needed to believe that every morning when she reached for the alarm clock, swung her legs out of bed, and placed her bare feet on the floor to face another day, God would show her mercy, Jesus would be her sympathetic high priest, and the

Holy Spirit would empower her to win the mental battle between lies and truth. By God's grace he would enable her to make the moment-by-moment choices that seemed utterly impossible in the present. Ashley needed to share in the ancient hope of the Jewish prophet Jeremiah, who suffered such constant and intense hardships that he was called "the weeping prophet":

> Yet I call this to mind, and therefore I have hope: Because of the LORD's faithful love we do not perish, for His mercies never end. They are new every morning; great is Your faithfulness! I say: The LORD is my portion, therefore I will put my hope in Him. The LORD is good to those who wait for Him, to the person who seeks Him. (Lam 3:21–25)

At every doctor's visit, at every weigh-in, and at every meal, Ashley could "call this to mind" and "therefore have hope." She could remember that God's faithful love would keep her from perishing, his mercies would never end, his graces were rising fresh every morning with the sun, and that his faithfulness was great—far greater than any of the diverse challenges that were threatening her.

Practically, Ashley also needed to know that in the moment of temptation, God would be faithful and would give her the help she needed, whatever that might look like on any given occasion. So I held out the hope of 1 Cor 10:13, which was written to Christians living in the midst of constant temptation in the cosmopolitan city of Corinth (a Las Vegas of the first-century Mediterranean world). Paul said, "No temptation has overtaken you except what is common to humanity. God is faithful, and He will not allow you to be tempted beyond what you are able, but with the temptation He will also provide a way of escape so that you are able to bear it."

Practical Guidance for the Physical

After spending some focused time reading and explaining the biblical passages above and giving her a list of relevant verses to take with her, I began turning her attention to physical issues. Because she was facing a physical emergency, I explained to her that she would need to be under the care of a medical doctor. She would need to undergo a complete physical exam coupled with a weekly weighing at the doctor's office. Her doctor would determine a healthy weight range for her height and weight.[3] Her mother would need to go with her to each visit in order to track the weekly weigh-ins and hear the doctor's advice.

Many people seeking help for anorexia panic when they gain even a single pound, leading some counselors to set up a process that keeps all weight changes secretive. However, I believed that it was essential for Ashley to know about each weight change so she could learn to face the facts and to reshape her beliefs and values in light of reality. Instead of shoving things into the closet of denial, Ashley needed to learn to respond with hope and trust in the Lord.

I asked that Ashley keep a food diary with her parents' oversight. She was to eat a minimum of 1,600 calories per day and record the specific foods and the amount eaten at each meal. Even though this calorie intake wasn't even enough for Ashley to maintain her current weight, I knew she would still panic over this increase in her daily food consumption. Therefore, I also assigned her to keep a "Self-Talk Log" where she would write down what she was thinking when she felt anxious, frustrated, or overwhelmed. This record would assist in evaluating how Ashley's mind needed to be renewed. I also instructed her to limit her exercise to 20 minutes per day and warned that she might need to stop exercising entirely if her weight did not stabilize. Each of these steps—knowing her weight increases, keeping a food diary, recording her thoughts and feelings, and limiting her exercise—would be an extreme challenge for Ashley. She could always remember, however, that this new path—no matter how difficult—was still sprinkled with hope.

---

[3] An eating problem like the one Ashley battled is a serious matter of life and death. It is absolutely critical for any counselor to consult with a physician who can provide medical advice about the struggling person. This is especially the case given the high level of deceit practiced by those struggling with such eating problems.

Practical Guidance for the Spiritual

Because Ashley was not just facing a physical emergency but also a spiritual emergency, she needed her eyes lifted up to the good news of Jesus Christ. I wanted to center her thoughts on the grace, forgiveness, acceptance, and power found in the message of the gospel. I assigned her the *Salvation Handbook* Bible study[4] and asked her to read daily in the Gospel of John. She was to read all of John's Gospel at least three times before our next meeting. I also asked her to record daily prayers in a prayer journal and to memorize Prov 3:5–8 and 1 Cor 10:13. I encouraged Ashley to read aloud to help herself concentrate since she might have difficulty thinking clearly due to her physical condition.

Even though I don't normally give out my contact information, I gave Ashley and her parents my phone number and e-mail address so they could contact me during the week if needed. This first week of adjustments was going to be difficult for both Ashley and her family, and they would need support.

Facing Reality

When Ashley and her mother arrived the next week, Ashley was clearly agitated. She was angry that the doctor had estimated her target weight at 115–120 pounds, meaning she needed to gain 30–35 pounds! She also felt like her parents were "on her case" about every bite of food she ate. Both Ashley and her mother began to cry in exasperation.

Ashley's food diary for this first week showed that she had eaten only raw or cooked vegetables, some fruit, and little meat. She had weighed in at 84 pounds at the doctor's office, and he had threatened to hospitalize her if she didn't start eating. Obviously, these were not good signs.

In spite of her struggles, it was encouraging that Ashley had done the mental and spiritual homework I had assigned her even though it had been difficult for her to concentrate. We spent most

---

[4] Martha Peace, *Salvation Handbook* (Bemidji, MN: Focus, 2005).

of this second session reviewing her *Salvation Handbook*. Ashley told me, "I do think I'm a Christian, and I really do want to honor God. I still think that if everyone will just leave me alone, I'll be all right." I asked her, "If you died today and the Lord asked you, 'Why should I let you into my heaven?' what would you say?" Ashley replied with precise accuracy: "I am trusting completely in your Son's death on the cross to save me—I am saved by your grace through faith."

Understandably, her thoughts and emotions were frightening and very emotionally painful for her. In her "Self-Talk Log," she had written:

- Everyone is watching me. Why can't they leave me alone?
- If I eat what my mother cooks, I will be fat!
- There is nothing wrong with wanting to be healthy.
- This makes me so angry!
- I hate being home!
- I don't feel like eating.

It was not surprising that Ashley refused to face reality. Her sinful, habitual obsession with food and her body was deeply entrenched in her heart. Her unopposed thoughts and unchecked actions had formed deep ruts. Her self-image had become her god, and she was willing to fight to the death to keep this destructive god at the center of her life and happiness. Her self-consuming pride was blinding her to the reality of her situation and even to the obvious love that her parents were showing her.

Remembering the Big Picture

During the second meeting with Ashley, I concentrated on two main biblical principles. First, I wanted Ashley to focus on the big picture. This meant cultivating an abiding sense of gratitude for Jesus Christ, who had sacrificed himself on the cross to suffer the punishment for her sins so that she could be forgiven by God. When her heart was filled with this gratitude, Ashley would find it much more natural to honor God by doing what was right regardless of her feelings. Remembering the big picture also meant turning to Jesus as a sympathetic high priest who had experienced temptation as a human being and who was eager and kind in helping everyone who would ask him. Hebrews 4:14–16 states:

> Therefore, since we have a great high priest who has passed through the heavens—Jesus the Son of God—let us hold fast to the confession. For we do not have a high priest who is unable to sympathize with our weaknesses, but One who has been tested in every way as we are, yet without sin. Therefore let us approach the throne of grace with boldness, so that we may receive mercy and find grace to help us at the proper time.

As Ashley grew in her willingness to seek Jesus for mercy, grace, and help in her struggles, she would also learn to let him shoulder her burdens instead of bearing them herself. "God resists the proud but gives grace to the humble. Humble yourselves, therefore, under the mighty hand of God, so that He may exalt you at the proper time, casting all your care on him, because He cares about you" (1 Pet 5:5–7).

Unlike the enslaving, burdensome, miserable bondage of anorexia and the condemning feeling that she could never be thin or pretty enough, Ashley needed to lift her eyes to the kind face of Jesus and open her ears to his gentle offer of grace. Instead of viewing every act of obedience as an impossible task, Ashley could grow into seeing Jesus' commands as gentle, kind, and helpful:

> "Come to Me, all of you who are weary and burdened, and I will give you rest. All of you, take up My yoke and learn from Me, because I am gentle and humble in heart, and you will find rest for yourselves. For My yoke is easy and My burden is light." (Matt 11:28–30)

Loving God and Loving People

Second, I wanted Ashley to focus on the two most important commands in the Bible: loving God and loving people. This had been Jesus' response to a question asked by an expert in the Old Testament law.

> "Teacher, which command in the law is the greatest?" [Jesus] said to him, "Love the Lord your God with all your heart, with all your soul, and with all your mind. This is the greatest and most important command. The second is like it: Love your neighbor as yourself." (Matt 22:36–39)

I explained that loving God would mean obeying his Word. Jesus had told his disciples, "If you love Me, you will keep My commands" (John 14:15). Loving God would mean believing and obeying specific commands in the Bible even though she might feel temporarily frightened or bewildered by the dramatic changes these commands required.

As she learned to value and trust the truths of the Bible over the entrenched lies of her own heart, Ashley would be following the exhortation of the apostle Paul: "Do not be conformed to this age, but be transformed by the renewing of your mind, so that you may discern what is the good, pleasing, and perfect will of God" (Rom 12:2). I encouraged her constantly to push away her sinful obsessions about weight and food. Instead, she needed to fill her mind with thoughts that were true, honorable, just, pure, lovely, commendable, morally excellent, and worthy of praise (Phil 4:8). Although she was surrounded by internal passions and external appeals tempting her to set her mind's eye on full-length mirrors, body measurements, weight loss, and passing compliments, God's faithful Word was telling her to contemplate only those things that were truly meaningful, valuable, and lasting.

As for loving those around her, Ashley's family was naturally the first group on the radar. I encouraged her to make her family's life easier (instead of more difficult) by gladly eating what was put before her instead of complaining or even rejecting it. She could also focus on spending time with her younger brothers and gladly sharing her life with her parents during this unexpected season of time that God had given them as a family.

The Battle of the Mind

We also spent time in this second meeting brainstorming together about how Ashley could renew her mind. The selfish, compulsive thoughts in her "Self-Talk Log" needed to be renounced and replaced by thoughts that centered on loving God and loving others. I wanted Ashley to see the stark comparison between the sinful, selfish, obsessive thoughts that were enslaving her and the biblical, selfless, reasonable thoughts that would free her.

Sinful, Obsessive Thoughts	Thoughts Centered on Loving God and Loving Others
"Everyone is watching me! Why can't they leave me alone!"	"Everyone is *not* watching me, and those who are love me very much. I don't blame them for being worried. Their worry is a sign of their care."
"If I ate what my mother cooked, I'd be fat!"	"If I gratefully eat what my mother cooks, I will be showing love to her by not being selfish" (cf. 1 Cor 13:5) "and showing love to God by not relying on my own understanding" (cf. Prov 3:5).
"There is nothing wrong with wanting to be healthy."	"There is nothing wrong with wanting to be healthy, but according to my doctor, my eating habits aren't healthy. I have to relearn what is healthy."
"This makes me so angry!"	"Thank you, Lord, for this trial, and thank you that I am still alive and that you have given me a family and a counselor to help me" (cf. 1 Thess 5:18).
"I hate being home!"	"It's God's special blessing to me that I can be home and receive the help I so desperately need. I'm glad to be at home."
"I don't feel like eating!"	"I'll eat whether I feel like it or not, and if I have to gain weight, I will just have to gain weight. I am going to honor the Lord. He will help me. I will remember that whether I'm eating or drinking, I should do everything to the glory of God" (cf. 1 Cor 10:31).

At this point in our meeting, Ashley's parents interjected: "What should we do when she just sits and stares at her food and starts to tremble and panic?" My advice was, "Talk to her calmly and give her hope. For example, you could say, 'I know this is difficult for you, but the Lord will help you. I want you to pick up your fork and take a bite of potatoes. Ask your heavenly Father to help you do what you know is right, good, and healthy. Let's seek his help right now, and then we'll keep eating.' After you pray, continue with the meal and turn the conversation to something besides this issue." I also reminded Ashley's parents that if they observed Ashley's physical state deteriorating, they should call her doctor or 911—it would be their judgment call.

Resetting Ashley's Diet

I carefully looked through Ashley's food diary for that initial week. One day she had managed to meet the target goal of 1,600 calories, but she promptly panicked and limited herself to 1,300 the next day. Most of those 1,300 calories were fresh fruit, which took almost more calories to digest than were contained in the fruit itself. Ashley had successfully avoided sugar, fat, juice, milk, and virtually all protein.

I considered sending Ashley and her mother to a nutritionist, but I decided to start by requiring that she add several specific items to her diet. Ashley was to drink eight ounces of orange juice and two eight-ounce glasses of whole milk per day. I also asked her to add two teaspoons of butter on wheat toast at breakfast, a serving of regular mayonnaise on her sandwich at lunch, and a serving of rice, potatoes, or pasta with butter at dinner. If she had not yet eaten 1,600 calories by the end of dinner, she needed to eat one serving of ice cream, a candy bar, or a brownie. Since she was scheduled for a weigh-in at the doctor's office the next day, I also let her know that if she had lost weight again, she would not be allowed to exercise until she had gained a few pounds back.

To the casual reader or to the person entangled in an anorexic lifestyle, these requirements may sound harsh or even physically unhealthy. Telling a radically self-conscious 20-year-old female that she must consume unwanted desserts if she has not eaten enough calories by the end of the day sounds uncaring at best. Yet this was exactly the point. Ashley was so entangled in a web of self-deception that she viewed the fundamentally life-giving act of eating as a threat to her well-being.

Practical Steps Toward Freedom

Because of this deep-seated self-deception, I knew it would not be enough simply for Ashley to hit the right calorie count each day or unwrap the after-dinner candy bar without a conflict with her parents. The ultimate battle was still in the heart, not at the dinner table. I asked Ashley to keep up her "Self-Talk Log," recording the thoughts racing through her mind when she was struggling. In addition, I asked her to memorize 1 Cor 10:31 and Heb 4:14–16, to read daily in the Psalms and the Gospel of John, to pray each day for herself and for others, and to keep a "Think These Thoughts" journal. This journal contained Bible verses, good quotes from a book, or specific thoughts that Ashley knew she should be thinking. I told her to add to that journal each week and to review it when she found herself struggling.

When Ashley and her mother left our second meeting, they still looked somewhat unhappy. At least they were no longer crying! Sometimes it's the smallest glimmers of light that remind us that dawn is coming.

It Takes Time

Over the next several weeks, Ashley managed barely to eat 1,600 calories per day. It was clear that she was still hanging onto her self-imposed eating rules. At our fifth meeting I increased her calorie total to 1,800 and gave Ashley and her mom specific ideas for increasing the calories.

She particularly objected to eating any kind of fat. I asked if she had been diagnosed with hyper-cholesterol disease.[5] She hadn't, of course. Therefore, despite her objections, her body was processing fat in a healthy way. So, instead of her preferred skim

---

[5] Since I have a medical background, I was able to talk with Ashley and her mother in more detail about these topics. Some counselors may be more comfortable referring people to a nutritionist for counsel on what to eat.

milk, I told her that she must drink whole milk. Instead of fat-free cheese, she was to eat regular cheese.

Far more than pushing these practical dietary steps, however, I kept reminding Ashley of the big picture: God had forgiven all of her sins and freed her from slavery to sin through the atoning death and victorious resurrection of Jesus Christ. If she continued to turn to him as her redeemer and helper, thanking him for his daily grace and strength and turning to his Word to uproot lies and implant truth, she would grow every day whether she could see the growth or not. I also encouraged Ashley to thank God that she could trust him regardless of how she might feel at any given moment.

Obviously it was difficult for Ashley to trust God over her own feelings and self-perceptions about her appearance. Very simply, she needed to know God better—who he is, what he's like, and how he works. I gave Ashley the book *The Attributes of God* by Arthur W. Pink.[6] She and her mother slowly worked their way through the book. I instructed Ashley to pray before and after reading each chapter and to record thoughts, quotes, and Scriptures from the book in her "Think These Thoughts" journal, looking up any Bible passages that were cited but not actually quoted in the book. After several weeks Ashley's attitude began to change. She openly confessed that she had lied several times to her mother and to me about what she'd been eating. She had been exercising secretly on days when she felt like she'd eaten too much.

Confessions of sin can seem negative, but they're actually positive. Ashley was beginning to comprehend the powerful impact of Eph 1:7–8 in her life: "We have redemption in [Christ] through his blood, the forgiveness of our trespasses, according to the riches of his grace that he lavished on us with all wisdom and understanding." She could confess her sin because she knew her sin was forgiven. Each week she continued to refine her thoughts even as she learned to renew her mind through the purifying power of God's Word.

[6] Arthur W. Pink, *The Attributes of God* (Grand Rapids: Baker, 2006).

At the same time, although I was experiencing more and more honesty from Ashley as her counselor, Ashley's mother was quite alarmed by the exposure of her daughter's sinful thoughts. I comforted her by telling her I was not surprised at the seemingly shocking perspectives that were being revealed week by week. After all, Ashley's temptations were "common to humanity" (1 Cor 10:13). Therefore, Ashley's mother could be confident that God was already helping her turn from her extreme self-focus to "set [her mind] on what is above, not on what is on the earth" (Col 3:2).

Becoming Who We Already Are in Christ: Justification, Sanctification, and Glorification

As Ashley grew to see and confess her sins and to grow in practical ways, what was her ultimate goal? To be like Jesus Christ—righteous in the sight of God. How would this happen? How would an emaciated 20-year-old lost in the vortex of her own sinful desires become a mature follower of Jesus fully devoted to his Word and his ways? If we zoom out for an aerial perspective (even a heavenly perspective) on this question, there are three major stages: justification, sanctification, and glorification. I made sure to concentrate on these stages in the early phases of my relationship with Ashley.

First, *justification* is a 100 percent work of God where he declares us to be perfectly righteous in his sight because the punishment for our sins has been completely paid by the sacrifice of Christ, and the perfect life of Jesus has been credited to our moral account. "For all have sinned and fall short of the glory of God. They are justified freely by his grace through the redemption that is in Christ Jesus" (Rom 3:23–24). Every true believer in Jesus is united with Christ in his death, burial, and resurrection. By God's grace, the believer actually is united in Jesus' death, which destroys the penalty and power of sin. The Christian is united in Jesus' burial, which leaves the old sinful person behind in the grave. The believer comes alive in Jesus' resurrection, which makes him a new person sharing in the new life of Christ. Because

Ashley was "in Christ," she was justified with Christ. Her justification happened at a moment in time when she fully trusted Jesus. It was a permanent, irreversible, invincible declaration. Ashley was justified—completely accepted by God.

Second, *sanctification* is the "continuing work of God in the life of the believer, making him or her actually holy."[7] Unlike the one-time divine act of justification, sanctification is progressive. Ashley's sanctification began the moment God saved her and would continue until the day she died or Christ returned. It would be a lifelong process of being transformed into the image of Jesus. Sanctification is simultaneously God's work and our work: God convicts us of sin and trains us in righteousness. We are responsible to "work out [our] own salvation with fear and trembling" (Phil 2:12). Paul exhorted his apprentice Timothy to "train yourself in godliness, for . . . godliness is beneficial in every way since it holds promise for the present life, and also for the life to come" (1 Tim 4:7–8). I explained to Ashley that this self-training would mean renewing her mind and, by God's grace, doing the right thing over and over again until it became a righteous habit. I also reminded her of the much-beloved promise in Rom 8:29: "For those He foreknew He also predestined to be conformed to the image of His Son." The sanctification process is also a promise.

Third, *glorification* is the final stage (both chronologically and conceptually) of our righteousness before God. Glorification is another 100 percent work of God where he transforms both soul and body into an immortal, righteous, sinless being. Ashley would finally be sinless when she went to heaven to be with the Lord. She could also hope in the glorious words of Paul that describe what our bodies will be like when we are raised from the dead at the end of time—we will be "raised in incorruption," "raised in glory," "raised in power," and "raised a spiritual body." Then we will "bear the image of the heavenly man [Jesus]" (see 1 Cor 15:42–49). On that final day, "He will transform the body of our humble condition into the likeness of His glorious body" (Phil 3:21). Ashley's body would one day be perfect but not the false

[7] Millard Erickson, *Christian Theology* (Grand Rapids: Baker, 1985), 967.

"perfect" she had envisioned for herself. Her version of "perfect" had led her into bondage and to the brink of death. God's version of "perfect" would be truly ideal, flawless, and free.

After I had explained these stages of justification, sanctification, and glorification, Ashley had a puzzled look on her face. "But I've always been taught that if I make any effort in my flesh, I'm 'out of fellowship' with God." Ashley had believed the well-meaning lies that she should "let go and let God" and that her fellowship with God had a whimsical on-off switch. She needed theological correction regarding the balance of trust and action as well as the stability of her relationship with God. "Actually, we *are* to make an effort to grow, and we're to ask the Lord to help us as he's promised," I replied. "But this 'all or nothing' idea of being in or out of fellowship is not true. A true believer is permanently justified in Christ, and nothing can change that, not even a believer's remaining sin." Of course, there are times when a professing believer needs to be warned that his constantly sinful patterns are demonstrating that he may never have been converted in the first place (Matt 7:21–23), but this was not what Ashley needed to hear at this time.

I gave her an example of how her spiritual effort could please the Lord instead of displeasing him, as she'd been taught: "You could say to yourself, 'I am going to eat this meal because I love the Lord, and it's my joy to please him. He will receive the glory because He will help me obey him.'" From Ashley's response it was clear that she was reconsidering what she had been taught in these areas. Her hope was slowly growing.

God's High and Holy Purpose in Hardship

Another essential perspective I wanted Ashley to understand was God's high and holy purpose behind his discipline of her. Even though she was experiencing the consequences of her own sin, she was not going through this process in vain. Hebrews 12 begins with an exhortation for Christians: "Let us lay aside every weight and the sin that so easily ensnares us. Let us run with endurance the race that lies before us, keeping our eyes on Jesus, the source and perfecter of our faith" (vv. 1–2). The supreme example of this perseverance is our Lord Jesus Christ who "endured a cross" and even "despised the shame," all because he saw "the joy that lay before Him" (v. 2).

I also encouraged Ashley with the next exhortation in Hebrews: to not "grow weary and lose heart" in the battle against sin (Heb 12:3–4). She could be confident that there *was* a high and holy purpose behind God's discipline of her. The author of Hebrews explains further:

> In struggling against sin, you have not yet resisted to the point of shedding your blood. And you have forgotten the exhortation that addresses you as sons:
>
> My son, do not take the Lord's discipline lightly or faint when you are reproved by him, for *the Lord disciplines the one He loves* and punishes every son He receives.
>
> Endure suffering as discipline: God is dealing with you as sons. For what son is there that a father does not discipline? But if you are without discipline—which all receive—then you are illegitimate children and not sons. Furthermore, we had natural fathers discipline us, and we respected them. Shouldn't we submit even more to the Father of spirits and live? For they disciplined us for a short time based on what seemed good to them, but he does it for our benefit, *so that we can share His holiness*. No discipline seems enjoyable at the time, but painful. Later on, however, it yields the fruit of peace and righteousness to those who have been trained by it. (Heb 12:4–11, emphasis added)

I continued emphasizing to Ashley that God did indeed have a high and holy purpose behind his discipline of her. His discipline was not meant to be destructive but constructive; purifying, not punitive. Even as I write this sentence, it is astounding to think that because of God's goodness and grace, we can actually share his holiness. The pruning is painful in the short term, but it ultimately glorifies God and results in supernatural peace and righteousness. God's graciousness toward us, in spite of our sin, is truly amazing!

Hollow Beauty and Holy Beauty

One major issue that God's gracious discipline had exposed in Ashley's life was vanity. Vanity is just as common as it is powerful. The word *vanity* refers to something that is "empty, futile, vain, or worthless."[8] In the sense of a love of beauty, it is an inordinate love of one's own beauty, an "inflated pride in one's appearance."[9]

When I listed some of the possible signs of vanity, Ashley admitted she struggled with many of them.[10] She was overly concerned about how she looked, and she almost constantly compared her appearance to others'. She was also unable to receive compliments. Instead of graciously saying "thank you," she would become embarrassed or angry at the person complimenting her. She was often depressed or anxious because she believed herself to be fat, and she was on a quest for thinness that led her to abuse her body through anorexia.

To cut through these deceitful desires, we embarked on a brief study through various Scriptures that address vanity. The Old Testament emphasis is summarized powerfully in Prov 31:30: "Charm is deceitful and beauty is fleeting, but a woman who fears the Lord will be praised." Later the New Testament emphasizes the true beauty that shines when a woman adorns herself with proper clothing, good works, and a gentle and quiet spirit: "The women are to dress themselves in modest clothing, with decency and good sense, not with elaborate hairstyles, gold, pearls, or expensive apparel, but with good works, as is proper for women who affirm that they worship God" (1 Tim 2:9–10).

Good works are done mostly behind the scenes. Few people, if any, know about them. Consider the woman who quietly works

---

[8] *The Merriam-Webster Dictionary* (Boston: G. K. Hall, 1977), 981.

[9] Ibid.

[10] For a more complete list see Martha Peace, *Damsels in Distress: Biblical Solutions for Problems Women Face* (Phillipsburg, NJ: P&R, 2006), 92.

in the kitchen to clean up after the church picnic or sits by the bed of a friend recovering from surgery. She takes meals to the sick or cleans the house of the woman whose husband is dying.

Together we explored possible good works Ashley could pursue in the coming week. After some brainstorming, Ashley decided to visit a woman from their church family who was in a nursing home. She would take her some flowers and read to her. After almost dying in her sin of hollow beauty, Ashley was beginning to learn what true beauty is in God's eyes.

We also talked about how she tended to surrender to her fear of not being thin, beautiful, and perfect by starving herself. We also explored the biblical alternative—trusting God, graciously accepting her natural appearance as a gift from him, and thanking God that although she could not attain her own "perfect" standard, by his grace she could be faithful.

That week I asked Ashley to read the chapter on vanity in the book *Damsels in Distress* and to answer the questions at the end of that chapter.[11] She learned that the world considers vanity a disease—a body image problem. In contrast, she learned that vanity is really an internal issue and that true holy beauty is on the inside—a godly heart. As she began to see that her sinful self-focus was truly ugly, she grew in gratitude for the grace and mercy Christ had shown her on the cross.

The next week, Ashley's "Self-Talk Log" reflected new attitudes—grief over her sin, confession to God, and a new softness toward those seeking to help her. She had gained only one pound since beginning counseling, so it was time to increase her calories to 2000 per day. I reviewed her food diary and gave her practical instructions such as how to add two more servings of fat, two more servings of bread, and two more servings of meat.

I continued to remind her of the big picture—turning to Christ for comfort and help, expressing gratitude to him, and showing love to him by obeying him even if she felt afraid or frustrated. In addition, I encouraged her to keep considering how to show love to others in the midst of her own difficult circumstances.

---

[11] Ibid, 89–102.

A Gentle and Quiet Spirit

The apostle Peter, a married fisherman who became one of Jesus' closest disciples, knew about true beauty. He exhorted the Christian women in his day:

> Your beauty should not consist of outward things like elaborate hairstyles and the wearing of gold ornaments or fine clothes. Instead, it should consist of what is inside the heart with the imperishable quality of a gentle and quiet spirit, which is very valuable in God's eyes. (1 Pet 3:3–4)

I knew I would need to explain what "a gentle and quiet spirit" really means. It did not mean Ashley needed to whisper when she talked or shift her eyes away from anyone who talked to her. It did not mean being passive or a pushover. It meant accepting that God's dealings with her were right and good, instead of giving in to anger, fear, or constant arguing. It also meant cultivating a sense of true humility and modesty that sought the best for others instead of attention for herself. This kind of "gentle and quiet spirit" is "very valuable in God's eyes."

The Flaw of Perfectionism

In our first conversation Ashley acknowledged that others saw her as a perfectionist, but she herself disagreed. She thought doing her best was a good thing. Now that God had been softening her heart, however, she was more ready to consider the possibility that she really was a perfectionist.

Perfectionism means striving for an impossibly high standard, usually for selfish ends.[12] In the case of those who are anorexic, the perfectionist drive centers on having the perfect body and eating perfectly; but the underlying issues are selfish motives and sinful desires. Their distorted mind-set descends into bizarre thinking and behaviors because they are actually worshipping themselves. Hardened by their own pride, they become willing to destroy their

---

[12] This section on perfectionism was adapted with permission from Amy Baker's workbook *Overcoming Perfectionism* (Lafayette, IN: Faith Resources, n.d.). Available at www.fbclafayette.org/store.

own body and sacrifice themselves in the pursuit of their ideal self-image. Blinded by their self-righteousness, they cannot see Christ as their righteousness.

I asked Ashley, "In light of eternity, just how important are your perfectionistic goals when it comes to your body?" Ashley thought for a while and said, "Obviously, it's not important at all, but I just can't stop thinking about food and my body!" Knowing that mental habits are incredibly stubborn, I assured her that altering her mind-set would take time, like all Christian growth. Yet God had given her several means of grace to help her. God had given her a new heart in place of the old, hard heart that spurns God and his ways. She possessed the indwelling Holy Spirit who would faithfully produce the fruits of the Spirit as she walked with him. She had God's perfect Word that was breathed out by God himself, making it profitable for "training in righteousness, so that the man of God may be complete, equipped for every good work" (2 Tim 3:16–17). She was surrounded by other believers who would help her stop her self-focused thinking by speaking the truth to her in love.

Ashley, along with her church family and the Christians who were helping her, would "grow in every way into Him who is the head—Christ" (Eph 4:15). "In other words," I explained, "we all help each other become more and more like Jesus Christ." With this hopeful aim in mind, I exhorted Ashley to persevere in renewing her mind by continuing to ask God to help her replace her old, sinful, habitual thinking with what the Bible calls the "new self, the one created according to God's likeness in righteousness and purity of the truth" (Eph 4:24).

I left her with three assignments for the coming week: (1) to memorize 2 Pet 3:18 and Heb 10:30, which would continually exhort her to grow in the grace and knowledge of Jesus Christ by persevering toward God's promised reward; (2) to continue recording her thoughts in her "Self-Talk Log," this time correcting her own thoughts instead of bringing them to me for correction; and (3) to keep working her way through *The Attributes of God* so her view of God would continue to grow into wholehearted admiration, trust, and devotion.

Lingering Sin

In coming days Ashley found herself continually badgered by her self-imposed rules about what she could and could not eat. She also found it difficult to shut out the running tally in her mind that tracked her calories and seemed to whisper ideas about how to make up for her food consumption by eating less at the next meal. This struggle intensified when I increased her calorie count or when she weighed in and saw that she had gained even as little as half a pound. After weeks of counsel, she finally admitted these rampant thoughts and began including them in her weekly "Self-Talk Log." She was soon eating 2,200 calories per day without exercising, and her weight increased from 85 to 92 pounds.

Even though she had gained weight, her sinful, habitual obsessions still tormented her mind. As we had discussed at the beginning of our relationship, we began talking about habits and how she would not be able to stop obsessing about food until she started being grateful to the Lord and setting her thoughts on pleasing him and showing love to others. This would require work on Ashley's part, and she needed God's grace to persevere. Here are some examples of what Ashley admitted to thinking, in contrast with the thoughts that I encouraged her to cultivate in order to renew her mind and honor God.

Sinful, Obsessive Thoughts	Grateful, God-Honoring Thoughts
"I'm not putting gravy on my rice—it's unhealthy and will make me fat!"	"Mom's gravy isn't unhealthy for me because I don't have a cholesterol problem. It's God's will that I gain weight and be grateful for this delicious gravy" (cf. 1 Thess 5:18).
"That serving of ice cream is 160 calories. . . . Tomorrow morning I'll skip breakfast but record some breakfast foods in my food diary."	"Heavenly Father, forgive me for planning to lie. Tomorrow morning please help me not only to eat breakfast but to be grateful for it" (cf. 1 John 1:9).
"Mom made us a chicken casserole, but I can't eat it because I don't know what ingredients she used."	"Love is not selfish. I can love my mom and influence my younger brothers by graciously eating what she's made for our family" (cf. 1 Cor 13:5).
"Any sugar, no matter what, is really bad for you. This is going to make me sick."	"Rejecting all sugar is nonsense. I have freedom in the Lord to enjoy sugar as long as I'm not gluttonous. Thank God for sugar!" (cf. Col 3:16).
"There's no way I'm eating that meatloaf. It's red meat and it's fatty. Everyone knows it's unhealthy. I can't believe my mom would do this to me!"	"The truth is that I'm healthy and don't have hyper-cholesterol disease, so I can eat a normal portion of meatloaf. It's fine! Only my religious anorexia tells me 'Don't handle, don't taste, don't touch'" (cf. Col 2:20–23), "but Scripture clearly tells me to enjoy the freedoms I have in the Lord and that God has declared even meatloaf good!" (cf. Acts 10:9–16).
"I'll eat some of this biscuit so that my parents will get off my back. But tonight I'll put in 20 more minutes of exercise to make up for it."	"Lord, please forgive me for making these deceptive plans. I'm going to eat this entire biscuit and be grateful to the Lord and to my mother for making it!"

The Everyday, Ordinary Christian

At this point I decided to walk Ashley through a brief study I've entitled "The Life of an Everyday, Ordinary Christian Who Is Maturing Towards Christlikeness and Thereby Glorifying God." In order to develop consistency in her Christian walk, she needed to remember her absolute need for God's supernatural grace to help her, and she needed to remember that God had not held back a single drop of grace that she needed in order to grow and blossom. She needed to hear the remarkable promise recorded by Peter:

> His divine power has given us *everything required for life and godliness* through the knowledge of Him who called us by His own glory and goodness. By these He has given us very great and precious promises, so that through them you may share in the divine nature, escaping the corruption that is in the world because of evil desires." (2 Pet 1:3–4, emphasis added)

Peter not only reminded us of our dependence on the Lord but also our responsibility to "make every effort" (2 Pet 1:5). What was Ashley to be pursuing? Faith, goodness, knowledge, self-control, endurance, godliness, brotherly affection, and love (vv. 5–7). As we briefly studied each of these characteristics together, we could clearly see that Ashley was putting diligent effort toward them. She was greatly encouraged by the promise that "if these qualities are yours and are increasing, they will keep you from being useless or unfruitful in the knowledge of our Lord Jesus Christ" (v. 8).

Bound for True Beauty

Ashley had come a long way from that day in the library when her heart had almost stopped beating. Her weight had continued to climb toward a healthy range as she passed the 100-pound mark. More importantly, she was learning to embrace the glorious "mercies of God" and to reclaim her body from the idolatrous altar of self-image and to lay it down each day "as a living sacrifice, holy and pleasing to God" (Rom 12:1).

She still struggled with her own false standards of healthy eating, and she still felt misplaced guilt about violating her previous dietary rules. As her "Think These Thoughts" journal continued to expand, so did her heart for the Lord. By God's grace and because of Christ's redemption, she persevered and gradually turned from her self-absorbed obsession with her body and her food to a healthy love for God and a strong desire to please him.

I continued spending time with Ashley, giving her hope, explaining the gospel, and reminding her of the big picture. We kept talking about renewing her mind, reclaiming true beauty, and seeing through the lies of perfectionism. I monitored her handwritten "Self-Talk Log" and "Think These Thoughts" journal, continuing to guide her through the process of correcting her own thoughts. We continued praying together as I exhorted her to trust God over her feelings.

I continued to work with Ashley, her mom, and their doctor for five months. The time came when Ashley no longer needed formal counseling every week, so we shifted to every other week for the next two months. Toward the end of our formal time together, we met only once a month for three months. I knew it was time to dismiss Ashley from formal counseling when we found ourselves spending most of our time together discussing how she could help her friends with their various problems. This once angry, depressed, self-consumed young lady had developed an obvious joy in the Lord, and he was now using her as a special blessing in my own life and in the lives of her struggling friends.

Ashley was one of my hardest cases—a legitimate double emergency with both her body and her soul threatened by the effects of sin. Once again, however, God's grace proved to be greater than even the most enslaving sins. He had revived Ashley—all of her. As I watched this truly healthy, spiritually fit young woman drive away from our last counseling session, my heart echoed the praise of the psalmist: "The instruction of the Lord is perfect, renewing one's life" (Ps 19:7).

Chapter 7

"Tony" and Bipolar Disorder

Garrett Higbee

A Vision for Biblical Soul Care

Sixteen years ago I made the difficult decision to leave my practice as a clinical psychologist, working in hospitals, residential organizations, and private practice in pursuit of a higher calling. After 15 years of counseling in a manner consistent with my clinical training, God showed me that true hope and help for man's most profound problems are found in Christ and his Word alone. Local churches must bear the responsibility of communicating that hope to hurting individuals by biblically caring for souls. Alongside my ministry at College Park Church in Indianapolis, this vision took shape in Twelve Stones Ministries (TS), an intensive biblical counseling retreat center.

Twelve Stones Ministries

The vision for TS was to transform the culture of the local church by inspiring and equipping both leaders and laity to regain confidence in the Word of God and his Spirit as his people learned to counsel competently. A primary strategy for accomplishing this vision would involve a retreat with counselees and those who walk alongside them ("advocates"). This retreat would facilitate a return to their church community with a growing love for the Lord and a desire to see others grow in Christ. In a sense our strategy was to send a benevolent virus back into local churches as we came alongside those in the greatest need of biblical soul care so that they might become the most infectious ministers of that same care to their church communities.

At times even the strongest families or individuals are caught in the midst of a situation so intense, a conflict so hurtful, or an emotional turmoil so overwhelming, that they need to turn somewhere for help. At the TS campus we sought to provide hope through biblically based and carefully tailored individual, couple, and family counseling. Our goal was to give real answers, lasting wisdom, and spiritual encouragement to those for whom life seemed hopeless and defeating. We believed in the power of the gospel—that is, the announcement of the way of salvation through Jesus Christ by grace through faith—to heal relationships by reconciling them to God and to one another. By working alongside local churches, their friends, and extended family, we aimed at a more personal support system, loving accountability, and follow-up. Since one-size-fits-all counseling does not change the heart, our approach included careful assessment and development of a biblical plan of action for couples, parents, youth, and—when appropriate—individuals who would be advocates, helping them transition back home after their stay at TS. There is a time to warn, a time to encourage, and a time to help; but in all cases patient care and love promote the goal of restoration that God planned for people struggling to find him in the trials of life.

The ministry invites people in extreme cases or crisis situations to a retreat (usually a weekend) of intensive counseling—without the distractions that battle for their daily attention. They are surrounded by the beauty and serenity of God's creation and the loving support of our staff. When I say intensive, I mean it. We pack about four to six months of counseling into two to three days. The people who accept our invitation often come with difficult issues to overcome: schizophrenia, bipolar disorder, suicide to name a few. At TS we do not think God and his Word need to take the backseat to a clinician when things get difficult. The hard cases are perhaps the greatest opportunities to see the power of God and his Word at work in changing lives.

The ministry's name is a reference to a story in the Old Testament book of Joshua. In obedience to God, Joshua has the leaders of the 12 tribes of Israel erect a monument made up of "12 stones" from the Jordan River. This monument was to be a symbol for the people to look on in time of doubt and confusion in order to remember God's awesome power, love, and faithfulness to them and future generations (Josh 4:1–9).

God's awesome power brought a man named Tony into my life at TS.[1] My prayer is that his story of change would also erect a monument to God's awesome power, love, and faithfulness in the heart of each reader.

Tony's Story

Tony was in his late thirties and married to Lisa. The couple had no children. He had been working hard at two part-time ministries—although both were actually full-time enterprises. The first ministry was as an associate pastor. The second was as the leader of a homeless ministry in a large city. On top of that, he also served in the apartment complex where they lived, caring specifically for elderly people in the building. Lisa also worked a full-time job and served alongside her husband when she could. They seemed like a couple gifted with a high capacity for work. To the observing world, Tony and Lisa had it all together; and they were beacons in their community. Things looked exactly the way Tony wanted. Secretly, however, their lives were falling apart.

Although their efforts for ministry seemed unparalleled, they had not grown in maturity or the understanding of the grace needed for highly effective ministry. Tony and Lisa claimed to be followers of Jesus Christ; however, Tony's life in particular showed signs that he had gone off course and was following worldly things. He

[1] The names and background information have been changed to honor confidentiality.

was often anxious and experienced periods of depression. There were clear signs he was physically neglecting his body, and he showed habits of poor time management. Indeed, Tony's life story revealed a long-standing pattern of self-sufficiency, feeling unappreciated, anger, and shame. Tony felt rejected by his father and was envious of his brother as the favored child. He had conflict with the senior pastor of his church, where he felt used and underrecognized. He was afraid of the dark, death, demons, and missing his purpose in life.

Lisa agreed that Tony was a mess. The two had drifted from a Christ-centered identity and sense of purpose. Though their commitment to Tony's ministries was astounding, their commitment to personal communion with God was shockingly absent—as shown by a slow decline in personal and family prayer, meditation on the Scripture, and pursuit of renewing their minds with God's Word and applying it specifically and practically to daily life. Instead, Tony and Lisa doubled, even tripled, their investments in performance-based faith. Tony especially had a desperate need to be self-sufficient, to prove himself to others, and to protect himself. His identity was caught up in many worldly definitions of success and importance; he had an insatiable desire for significance, security, and affirmation, especially by male authorities. The one bright spot was that Tony and Lisa's marriage was relatively stable. The house of cards that they had been building together, however, was beginning to totter. One night it finally collapsed.

Tony had continued living his high-stress life as usual, and he had not slept well for many days. One night he was overcome with extreme paranoia, fear, and delusions. He began yelling and screaming throughout the house and crying uncontrollably. Lisa was horrified. She had no idea what to do. She tried to calm him down, but the screaming and crying continued. Finally, scared out of her mind, and with no other idea about what to do, she called 911. Lisa pleaded, "He won't stop screaming! What do I do? I need help. . . . I need help; he keeps yelling and crying. Please, please; I need someone to help us." By the time the night was over, their home was full of police squads and medical personnel, and

Tony had been fitted with medical and physical restraints and was gone.

He spent 10 days in a psychiatric hospital where he was given the label "bipolar," placed on medication, and received education and counseling concerning this "debilitating disease." In response to all this new stress, he quit his ministry positions and began planning to move across the country. Tony and Lisa felt that they had been cared for by the hospital's supportive staff, but they could not help feeling empty as they returned home with the hope-destroying psychiatric label of bipolar disorder.

Both tried to make sense of everything. Tony felt he had pushed himself to some kind of emotional limit: "I worked myself into the ground, and now I am bipolar." He grieved over all the hours he had invested in serving God by helping people. For what? Look where *that* got him. Lisa was a bit more grounded. She seemed deeply concerned for her husband and made herself available to help. Their marriage appeared to be solid, but Lisa was worried. She wanted to know how to minister to her husband, but she was also afraid he might "lose it" again: "What has happened to the man I married? Will he ever get better? What will keep him from doing this again? I can't go through a night like that one again." She did not have much confidence that the hospitalization or medication provided any kind of lasting hope or cure for what led Tony to such an uncharacteristic episode of terror. She also struggled with thoughts of how this would affect her dreams for starting a family. Questions constantly flooded her mind: "Is it right to bring children into this type of environment? Could I ever count on Tony being a good father? Would I be able to mother a baby and a husband? Why would you take this away from me, Lord? Haven't I been serving you diligently?" Although she did not know how to articulate it, Lisa wanted a formula, a guaranteed approach to change. While they both appreciated the help they had received, it had not resulted in a clear plan or help in understanding how to prevent a future crisis.

At this point God directed Tony to TS through the recommendation of their pastor, who would ultimately support them as their advocate. At first they were skeptical about TS since they had received unhelpful counsel in the past from kind Christians who unskillfully attempted to provide biblical counsel. They gave general proof texts to help them feel better or solve the immediate anxiety. Unfortunately, they only addressed behavior, situational stress, and reactivity, instead of first addressing issues at a level of depth. Yet their pastor was hopeful that we could get to the heart of it from a biblical perspective, so they agreed to pursue TS for help. They believed that we could give them direction in understanding his "disorder." Although Lisa was fearful that this could be a life-dominating issue for Tony, she had genuine hope that this might be a wake-up call for both of them and that a new start could be beneficial in many ways. Tony and his wife were desperately in need of the hope of Christ and needed to be pointed back to Scripture to begin a journey toward genuine change. To better understand how we did this, we will walk through a step-by-step account of the counseling process.

The Counseling Process

Our ministry to individuals, couples, and families at TS begins with an initial contact either by phone or through an application submitted via our website. Before meeting Tony and Lisa in person, we gathered significant information through a Personal Data Inventory (PDI)—an element of the application—and a series of extensive phone interviews with the couple and their advocate.

In Tony and Lisa's case, we were eager to understand their hopes and fears as they entered counseling. We first sought to rule out medical or organic issues that may have contributed to their struggles. We asked for medical records to determine when Tony had a thorough medical checkup. It is important to determine if any medical issues such as a thyroid disorder or other physical problems could contribute to existing struggles. We often consult with a qualified Christian physician on the counselee's condition to better understand the impact of physical issues, medications, and factors such as sleep and diet. In Tony's case there were in fact both physical and circumstantial issues that contributed to his emotional breakdown. Someone manifesting bipolar symptoms or who comes in with the label has likely displayed both depressive and manic tendencies. There may be some complicating factors both physically and/or circumstantially that should be considered. For instance, sleeping habits, exercise, and diet can be a factor in mood swings. Multiple stressors or physical illness can also influence mood. A thorough investigation of all these potential factors is needed before counseling someone with this diagnosis. A medical evaluation and tests, however, showed that none of Tony's issues were conclusively caused by any medical condition. But lack of sleep and poor self-care were evident, and he was experiencing multiple stressors that were cumulatively weakening his resistance to the temptations in his life.

Subsequently, while there may not be an exact test to measure any physical issues complicating the mood swings with bipolar symptoms, there could still be organic factors that should be addressed with those coming in with significant clinical labels. Prescription and nonprescription drugs can be a primary factor in extreme moods. The issue of medication was indeed a concern for Tony. Should he be medicated for moods? What would happen if he took himself off these medicines? How long should he be on psychotropic medications? What do they do? Again, we work closely with physicians and in his case reviewed his hospital records to address these issues. It was not our place to undermine the medical regimen he was placed on or to overstep our role as pastoral counselors. Clearly, we could not act as physicians. We desired to be sensitive to the holistic nature of his symptoms and to develop a biblical action plan geared toward healing his entire person. We counseled them to wait until the end of our time to address these questions.

After ruling out any physical origin of his mood swings and determining the impact of other physical and/or situational factors influencing Tony's mental and emotional state, we began to listen for themes in his story that would point to heart issues. A careful assessment allowed us to connect with one another in a loving relationship, get accurate data, and begin to develop a clear direction for counseling. We cannot begin to reframe symptoms, behavior, heart issues, motives, and formative influences into biblical categories if we do not know what they are. It was clear after the initial interviews that Tony and Lisa were concerned we might be reductionists who would overly spiritualize his disorder and not address what they believed to be the physical side of this problem. They also feared condemnation for lack of faith or dependence on God for healing. As previously mentioned, Tony was only willing to come because his advocate, who heard about our work, was confident we could help. Our initial goals included providing comfort, structure, love, support, equipping the advocate, and identifying others who could be leaned on in the counselees' existing support system and community.

One month after the night of terror, Tony and his wife arrived at TS with their pastor/advocate, whom they trusted deeply. Their advocate had to be someone in their circle of influence who loves the Lord, trusts his Word, and loves them. Advocates are an important part of the intensive counseling ministry. They are asked to walk alongside the hurting counselee(s) both during and after the counseling session(s). Throughout the counseling process we left time for interaction and discussion with the advocate and even gave him permission to respectfully question and critique the homework if something did not resonate. This provided an additional opportunity to gain involvement and gather data on their worldview. The retreat setting in the company of an advocate creates a context that is particularly effective when someone is in a crisis or has experienced trauma where extended care, encouragement, and accountability are needed. The cumulative impact of multiple consecutive hours of counseling and care can help break through issues with those who have experienced bad counseling sessions or are resistant to change for various reasons. There are few times when a counselee is going to grow and change more than in a crisis. Issues of worship, idolatry, and identity are out in the open. This is a time to seek God and see what there is to learn in each trial. Tony and his wife were tired and apprehensive when they arrived at TS. Little did they know that they would later look back on the weekend as the turning point in their lives with each other and with God.

Friday Evening

Whenever possible we spend two to four hours gathering history in the initial meeting. The time required for a couple will often be closer to four hours; an individual usually needs two hours or less. The first challenge was to listen well and understand their worldviews individually and as a couple. It is important to create a context that says to the counselees, "We are not going to rush this. We care about you, and we want to understand your experience before applying God's Word." It is also crucial to provide structure and a safe atmosphere.

The first night at TS we assigned Tony, his wife, and the advocate the "Motives" pamphlet by Ed Welch.[2] This is a particularly good assignment for anyone who needs to reframe psychological diagnoses as heart issues. A large part of good counseling is helping counselees see that at the root of all psychological problems are theological errors. No one can have a proper view of self without a proper view of God. We also had them read chapter 4 in *Instruments in the Redeemer's Hands* by Paul Tripp.[3] They were to read both assignments and highlight meaningful sections. They were to have five key statements or revelations from each reading, discuss them together, and pray before going to bed. Last, they were given an assignment to review some Puritan prayers. Before ending for the night, we had an extended time of prayer together.

Saturday

In preparation for each day of counseling, we (the TS staff) pray with every individual, couple, or family each morning. We pray for their situation and share our prayer requests as well. Our day would consist of two three-hour segments: (1) listening to

---

[2] Ed Welch, *Motives: Why Do I Do the Things I Do?* (Phillipsburg, NJ: P&R, 2003).

[3] Paul David Tripp, *Instruments in the Redeemer's Hands: People in Need of Change Helping People in Need of Change* (Phillipsburg, NJ: P&R, 2002), 57–74.

Tony's life story in the morning, and (2) graphically illustrating his story on a whiteboard in the afternoon.

Segment 1: Tell Me Your Life Story

First, we had the advantage of several hours Saturday morning for data gathering through a guided life story from birth to the present day of counseling. Although this time was not focused on their marriage, Lisa also shared her life story, which greatly helped show how they interacted in their marriage. Why a whole life story to address an event that only happened in the last month? It is important for a variety of reasons. Proverbs 20:5 says, "Counsel in a man's heart is deep water; but a man of understanding draws it out." Slowly drawing out the heart will help you develop a sensitive and accurate biblical approach to the entirety of your counsel. Most likely it will save you time in the long run. We often waste energy on rabbit trails, focusing on problems that are not at the core of transformation and heart change.

Everyone has a past, a series of events and persons that have influenced him or provided a catalyst for him to make successive decisions in forming the way you now meet him. One's past—though influential—is not determinative (that is, it cannot determine who a person will be forever, without the ability for change). The past is also a crucial element of knowing a person. Attention to one's childhood, family dynamics, and long-term history can reveal significant insight into who a person has become. With Tony and Lisa, it was beneficial to listen carefully to their history, probing with questions intended to expose their hearts as opportunities arose. This allowed us to obtain valuable, heart-revealing information. By reflecting on the formative influences of the past and reframing the language Tony used, we could speak the truth in love much more clearly and sensitively into his life. Looking at the past is useful and important—not to place blame or excuse behavior but to learn themes of an individual's heart as he emerges through multiple stories. After questioning, Tony and Lisa gained a sense that we now knew them better and cared more deeply for them. Building this relational foundation provides the distinct advantage of planting a pivot foot in their story while keeping our other foot planted in a solid understanding of Scripture. This was helpful in moving from symptoms to core heart issues.

Having an advocate in the room was invaluable, both as an intercessor and for accuracy of perspective. He also took careful notes, capturing key truths to be shared in later application. Tony and Lisa depended on him many times for reassurance and to clarify points. He was able to walk through their life story, add context, laugh, cry, and pray at key times. It was helpful to get Lisa to participate and share as well before moving to a time of diagnosing the problem biblically.

As expected, Tony shared symptoms that included periods of depression and at least one manic episode. We wanted Tony and Lisa to see that while these symptoms of bipolar were real, the underlying cause might be different from what they were taught or believed. Notwithstanding some physical habits that needed attention, we wanted Tony to see that many of his symptoms were, in fact, *the result* of root issues of the heart. Scripture is rich with descriptive and prescriptive language for those coming in with psychiatric diagnoses. For instance, someone suffering with what the world calls bipolar would find that the Bible has profound wisdom for him. The heart issues would be seen and described throughout the stories and proverbs as a combination of despair and uncharacteristic periods of foolishness. In our afternoon segment together we sought to take a fresh look at Tony's story. Tony had openly offered his version of his life story; now it was time to let God's Word offer its version of the same characters and events as we walked through the details with Tony, Lisa, and their advocate, while looking to the Scripture for perspective.

Segment 2: Listen to Your Life Story

As stated earlier, Tony's life story revealed extensive patterns of self-sufficiency, bitterness over being unappreciated, anger, shame, feelings of rejection and envy towards his family, personal conflicts in his church, and other strange fears and behaviors. While we really wanted to help Tony with the practical problems resulting from his symptoms such as loss of income, management of his medications, or improving communication in his marriage, we were leery of jumping to conclusions or getting roped into unbiblical "behaviorism" that falls short of transformational change. Fear, especially the fear of man, was the most obvious heart issue throughout Tony's story. Fear drove his impulsivity, which led to consequences, which led to feelings of guilt and sadness. Another issue was Tony's performance-based faith, which could possibly be motivating him to perform for us. The more prominent motives or idolatrous lusts that became apparent as we walked through Tony's story graphically on the whiteboard were his insatiable desire for significance, security, and affirmation—by male authorities. These themes would be essential in helping him see he had a worship disorder, not simply or necessarily a medical condition. I began to see that what Tony believed about God and the world around him had influenced his symptomatic actions, feelings, and perspectives. This biblical understanding needed to be presented so that Tony, Lisa, and their advocate could also see clearly how God's Word diagnosed their problems more accurately than their psychological professionals had done.

The idea was to reframe their problems biblically, using their language and exposing heart themes to show them how God viewed their story. Tony had the wrong idea of why he did what he did. As biblical counselors, we have an opportunity to reframe the experiences of counselees like Tony. By giving a new interpretation to their present problems and by laying a biblical template over the psychiatric diagnostic labels, we can transform these categories of psychological syndromes into language Scripture uses.

While sin is clearly involved and at the core of any problem, legitimate suffering needs a compassionate ear. In Tony's case, as with most counselees, it was necessary to engage each of these themes. A focus on sin would encourage repenting of sinful fear, despair, or foolishness, spending more time in the Word, and stopping sinful worry. A much more balanced approach that combines truth and grace would bring conviction of sin, but it would also focus on the power of the gospel and living in relationship with

Christ. A biblical example would be the story of Christ talking with the woman at the well (John 4). In this case, Christ knew of her life and did not have to draw it out, but his words show deep conviction without condemnation. There was a call for the woman at the well to see herself honestly and to worship God for who he is. Our goal in counseling is threefold: (1) to get the counselee to see God's character and compassion through the lens of Scripture; (2) to get the counselee to see himself and his problems as God does; (3) to get the counselee to feel God's conviction and comfort as he peers intensely into the mirror of his Word.

Thus, the counselee needs to begin thinking theologically: how is God involved in all of this? Tony first had to correct some of his thinking about God, himself, and others, even as he renewed his mind based on the gospel and the redemptive story of the Scriptures—how God was sovereignly working from before the world began to deliver his people from sin and death unto eternal life with him to the praise of his glorious grace (Eph 1:3–14). He needed to see what God has declared for him in regard to his identity, and he needed God's grace to enable him before trying to work in God's strength to please him. The Bible is not an encyclopedia, and Tony's relationship with Christ cannot be reduced to a one-dimensional strategy to alleviate fear. Our goal was not to proof text every verse that directly deals with fear but to help Tony see that he could trust God, since he essentially showed by his words and actions that God's love was conditional, that God did not care for him, or that God would not come through in the end. By going vertical, Tony could see how far he had drifted (Heb 2:1).

Saturday Evening

That evening we asked Tony and Lisa to assess their predominant heart attitude. We used the "4 Hearts" worksheet (pp. 184–85) to help them reach their own conclusions from Scripture, see where their hearts were, and how their worldview shaped their perceptions and responses. In general, we helped them see what

FOUR COMMON HEART THEMES

FOUR HEARTS

Flesh Bent	Flesh Statement	Flesh Question	Renewed Statement	Renewed Question	Renewed Heart
ANGER *Torch lighter* Isa 50:10–11 Divisive Prov 29:22	"I deserve some ____________!" "My will be done."	"Is God really on my side?" "How do I get respect?"	"Christ is my Lord." "His will be done."	"Whom can I serve?" "How do I forgive?"	Yielding and Submissive Tender and Kind
FOOLISHNESS *Broken Cisterns* Jer 2:13 Self-reliant Prov 28:26	"I want it now." "I can't help myself."	"Is God really enough?" "How can I get more?"	"God is worthy and awesome." "God is enough."	"Whom can I bless?" "Can I wait on him?"	Reverent Fear, Seeking Wisdom, Self-control
DESPAIR *Vain Striver* Eccl. 2:20 Giving Up Isa 61:1–3 Rom 15:13	"I need to be understood." "No one knows my pain."	"Is God compassionate?" "Does anyone really care?"	"God is compassionate and near." "I am in his sovereign hands."	"Whom can I give to?" "Where is my hope?"	Hopeful Giving Praise and Worship of God
FEAR *Man Pleaser* Gal 1:10 Eyes on trial Matt 14:25–31 Forgetting God Deut 31:8	"I am unlovable." "I can't risk it." "I can't see a way out of this situation."	"Is God trustworthy?" "Does anyone love me?" "Does anyone really care about me?"	"I trust God with all my heart." "My esteem comes from Christ's love."	"Whom should I need less and love more?" "With Christ as my friend whom or what shall I fear?"	Trusting and Loving More Than Needing Gratitude for All Things

<u>Anger</u>—The person characterized by an angry heart has a propensity to make an idol of power, control, having his own way, or to be covetous. This person might find himself making conscious and/or unconscious statements like, "I want respect or peace!" or "I can't believe so and so!" A person who chooses not to deal with an angry heart may be characterized by bitterness, judgment toward others, discontentment, lack of joy, strained relationships, and/or continual conflict in relationships. Others might comment that his actions and attitude can be volatile, ungrateful, condemning, grouchy, intimidating, irritable, or difficult.

<u>Foolishness</u>—The person characterized by a foolish heart has a propensity to make an idol of escape, pleasure, self-sufficiency, or self-gratification. He may find himself constantly in pursuit of certain feelings, objects, or the accumulation of things. This person may find himself making conscious and/or unconscious statements like, "I want it now!" or "I just can't help myself!" The person who chooses not to deal with a foolish heart may be characterized by consuming addictions, blame-shifting, irresponsibility, and self-destruction. Others might comment that his actions and attitude are cavalier, irresponsible, lazy, selfish, or immature.

<u>Despair</u>—The person characterized by a despairing heart has a propensity to make an idol of easing pain, feeling good, and creating comforts. This person may find himself making conscious and/or unconscious statements like, "I deserve!" or "I'm totally helpless!" The person who chooses not to deal with a despairing heart may be characterized by a victim mentality, an inordinate need for security, self-pity, strained relationships, and a propensity to self-medicate or escape through fantasy or self-destructive behavior. Others might comment that his behavior or moods are melancholy or down in the dumps. When relating to others, he can be distant, isolating, draining, or self-absorbed.

<u>Fear</u>—The person characterized by a fearful heart has a propensity to make an idol of security, perfection, or looking better than he is. This person may find himself making conscious and/or unconscious statements like, "Will they reject me?" or "I can't risk it!" or "Where is God?" The person who chooses not to deal with a fearful heart may be characterized by false guilt and shame, social and/or spiritual paralysis, fear of man, and a shaken faith. Others might comment that his behavior or moods are up and down, nervous, tentative, and his social interactions are sometimes avoidant or even paranoid in nature.

lenses they viewed life through, how their pasts could skew truth, and how their feelings could influence their perspectives.

Sunday

In our first full day we focused on careful assessment and "going vertical with God." By focusing more on the relationship with Christ than temporal relationships, we helped Tony and Lisa align their priorities with what they say they value most.

Tony was visibly tired yet more relaxed in our second day of counseling. Lisa seemed at ease, and the advocate was smiling more. We (the TS staff) again prayed for them and shared our prayer requests as well. A unique approach at TS and many churches that practice biblical counseling is the nonclinical, nonprofessional environment of counseling. Indeed, pastoral care and biblical counseling can be a refreshing change from a more sterile or professional counseling atmosphere. For example, eating and fellowshipping with the counselees gives us the opportunity to gain more access into their lives and see them in a different light. We find by taking the attitude that the ground is level at the cross and the Holy Spirit is present in the counseling room, we are able to be ourselves, to share our family news and struggles, to use humor, and even to give a comforting arm around the shoulder to let them know we do not fear them or their "disorder."

We reviewed Tony and Lisa's homework to see if they could understand God's perspective on their issues and to give them some new language to reframe their experience. First Corinthians 2:13 contrasts human wisdom and things taught by the Spirit. Because we believed that both Tony and Lisa had evidence of fruit in their lives, we sought the mind of Christ together. Tony was struggling to see his motives behind the exhausting pace he had kept in ministry. Though resistant, he began talking to his wife and advocate about his performance-based faith. We reviewed his life story by pulling out themes and statements that seemed to reveal the orientation of his heart. We were able to see a number of places where he was shaped and influenced by the world and its wisdom. With help, Tony and Lisa were able to identify several key themes of his heart over the course of the day.

For example, Tony *looked* like a model servant, but he had been neglecting his personal relationship with Christ and had replaced service with true devotion to Christ. For years Tony had resented his father's failures, and now that resentment had morphed into hardened bitterness. Tony was terrified of failing at his ministry and was deeply frustrated with the pastor who was his boss. He was also unusually fearful of looking incompetent in front of others. Tony was focused on his own reputation, not on Christ's. Tony's heart was full of the fear of man instead of reverential respect for Christ.

Part of the process of orienting Tony back toward Christ was to help him see himself, God, and others from the lens of Scripture. We worked with a few key passages in Proverbs and sections of James 3–4 to anchor his thinking biblically. This is where we started to use different words to describe the same phenomena. For instance, we helped Tony replace "impulsivity or manic episodes" with "foolish thoughts and behavior" and "needs" with "desires or demands," depending on the intensity of his longing.

All of this understanding led to a tough second day. Tony was beginning to come to grips with the sin behind his symptoms. He was feeling ashamed for what was in his heart, and he did not want to take responsibility. Tony was defensive and seemed distant at times. Lisa was losing hope. The advocate was with us, but he wondered what it would take to get Tony engaged. Tony was wrestling with his perceived need for affirmation. He was recognizing an authority issue and slowly tracing things back to his relationship with God.

It is easy to get stuck in counseling. In team counseling we often remind one another that we cannot work any harder than the counselees, or we will become frustrated and hopeless. We need to place them at the foot of the cross in prayer and in action during the session, not just before and after. Sometimes we just need to give them some hope from Scripture, something tangible to think about and work on before calling it a day. In Tony's case it meant taking a break, going on a walk, and taking some time to pray. This type of work is draining, and we may need to go away to pray ourselves or get counsel from a trusted mentor to gain perspective before going back in. It is hypocritical to tell a counselee to trust God while you lean on your own skills, effort, and rehearsed Bible knowledge. Sometimes more Bible knowledge only beads up on a hard heart, and prayer is often the only way to furrow the soil so the Word can take root.

After some prayer time, Tony admitted he was feeling judged. We turned to the Scriptures and reviewed 2 Cor 7:10 to compare godly and worldly sorrow. This was a great opportunity to talk openly about the difference between conviction and condemnation. One of the most powerful things we can offer to a counselee in crisis is the hope that comes from knowing God's forgiveness and love. We also looked at Prov 28:13, which clearly says prosperity does not come from concealing transgressions but mercy comes to those who confess and forsake them. What Tony was doing was an exercise in pursuing mercy from God himself. Tony had confessed sin, but he needed to renounce it. We also looked at 1 John 1:9 to give Tony hope as he was reminded of God's faithfulness to forgive. Eventually Tony realized his difficulties stemmed from his guilt and not our judgment. He recognized that it was God's intent to bring conviction, not condemnation. After this he was able to repent and sensed tremendous relief in God's long-suffering, kindness, and love.

Tony was broken. We reminded Tony that "no temptation has overtaken you except what is common to humanity" (1 Cor 10:13), and we shared some of our own personal struggles. We wanted to make clear to Tony that he was not odd or of lesser spiritual stock than any of the rest of us. We wanted to be sure we did not get stuck in counseling because of our own arrogance and pride. God was gracious, and our openness was effective. Tony began to be open and trusting again. Through the kindness of God, Tony was disarmed by this time of prayer, the teaching from Scripture, and by our personal stories.

At this point in our time together, we began to investigate a biblical theology of suffering. The hardships Tony faced created natural and obvious questions concerning how a good God can use such difficulty in the lives of one of his own children. A great assignment for further detail on this point is Paul Tripp's *Suffering: Eternity Makes a Difference*.[4] We wanted to talk about this matter with Tony in our time together.

A discussion about suffering and trials versus suffering and consequences ensued. Tony realized that he did not see God clearly in his suffering and that his behavior and choices had led him down a path away from God. Lisa had been hesitant up to this point, but she then shared her perspective of a slow decline of their spiritual life and time of prayer together. Tony was familiar with the concept of being transformed by the renewing of your mind (Rom 12:1–2), but he had not been living it out and became susceptible to the world's trappings. He did not see his identity in Christ as his primary identity, nor did he fully embrace the redemptive power described in Gal 2:20. Though difficult, this was a breakthrough conversation about where they had wandered from the truth, how his life was no longer his own, and the need to refocus by spending time at the cross.

As God had forgiven him, Tony now had to forgive the "villains" he blamed for creating so much of his difficulty. This true need to grant forgiveness led to a great discussion on the fear of man, his father, and personal idols. Tony began to see beyond his father's sin to his own in their relationship. This was a critical turning point in our time together. There was an obvious countenance change in Tony. He had never seen so clearly the fear or the bitterness that kept him from maturing or communing with Christ. Of course, he hoped his father would receive him well, and he would confess his sin. Regardless of his father's response, Tony was committed to keep peace (Rom 12:18). His advocate volunteered to facilitate a meeting between Tony and his father.

[4] Paul David Tripp, *Suffering: Eternity Makes a Difference* (Phillipsburg, NJ: P&R, 2001).

Tony and Lisa came alive as we talked about being in Christ. We assigned more meditation than memorization, with the goal being to see them apply what they already knew. We also helped Tony see the need to respond to God as his holy Father. In Ps 27:10 the Lord declares that even if our own father and mother forsake us, God will not deny us. In Prov 23:26, the father appeals to the son to "give me your heart." Tony needed to forgive his earthly father and put his hope in the Father who will not leave or forsake him.

Sunday Evening

Tony, Lisa, and his mentor had a good evening of reading and prayer. They had turned the corner and were seeing their problems in the light of Scripture. They read chapter 4 in *Seeing with New Eyes* by David Powlison.[5] The chapter is entitled "Peace, Be Still: Psalm 131." This book's emphasis on abiding in Christ and the sufficiency of Christ reframed the performance issues and bipolar symptoms as Tony saw his foolishness and despair as part of a desperate need to be self-sufficient, to prove himself to others, and to protect himself.

One of the most meaningful assignments we often give to counselees involves their direct relationship with God. Both counselees and advocates are asked to write their own psalm to God. This psalm is obviously not inspired as are the ones in the Bible, but it is effective in trying to understand where the counselees are with regard to their view of God. They are asked to review two or three psalms related to their heart condition before outlining their own. In the case of someone like Tony, we might ask him to read and model his psalm after Psalm 22. In that passage the psalmist is afflicted but is ultimately aware of the comforting presence of his faithful God. Tony would write his psalm and, if willing, share it with everyone in the counseling process. (We specifically ask the advocates to participate in assignments for their own edification, to show we are all in need of change, and to help them better relate

[5] David Powlison, *Seeing with New Eyes* (Phillipsburg, NJ: P&R, 2003), 75–90.

to the counselee as they go through the time together.) The reading of the Psalms and each of their individual psalms gave great hope and glory to God.

As we concluded our time, we discussed the importance of two critical realities. First, we looked at John 15:1–8 and the critical need for Christians to abide with Christ (see circles diagram). In our time with our counselees, we want to do more than merely give them a biblical understanding of their problems and principles to help. We want them to learn how to have a dramatic and daily relationship with Christ through prayer and Bible study. Many counselees who are spiritually dry and exhausted have benefited from reading Andrew Murray's book on abiding, especially chapter 1, which is a masterful weaving of John 15:1–8 and Matt 11:28–30.[6]

Second, we discussed the crucial issue of forgiveness. We asked Tony to consider three questions. First, what are some of the things for which God has forgiven you? Second, where are some areas where you need to forgive others? Third, where do you still need the forgiveness of others? Such questions encouraged Tony

[6] Andrew Murray, *Abiding in Christ* (Bloomington, MN: Bethany House, 2003), 13.

to consider God's grace toward him and to look at others with more mercy as he considered sins they had committed against him. Finally, he should look at areas where he had not asked for forgiveness or fully repented of sin. Tony needed to see all three of these areas to be able to move forward in a way that would please God. He was able to see significant categories where God had forgiven him all the way back to childhood. He was then able to identify some bitterness and hurt that needed to be addressed. He realized his bitterness was, in fact, a sin against his father. He broke down, and we were able to comfort him. Mourning over being sinned against as well as our own sin is a huge part of brokenness and repentance: "Blessed are those who mourn, because they will be comforted" (Matt 5:4).

Going Home

Tony's problems were not solved over the weekend, but by the grace of Jesus we had made some significant strides. Knowing that to put down competing desires in their hearts and old patterns of living much work still lay before Tony and Lisa, we wanted to send them home with clear direction. We developed a spiritual action plan with the following elements that included the feedback of both the couple and the advocate:

- *Prioritizing abiding in Christ.* Tony and Lisa were to establish a regular pattern of reading God's Word with application in mind, daily prayer, times of meditation, and fellowship. Several key Scriptures were assigned for meditation and memorization: John 15:1–8 on the centrality of our abiding relationship (see circles diagram, p. 191), and Phil 4:6–9 and Matt 13:22 to address worry and fear.
- *Marriage commitment.* We suggested that Tony and Lisa take time to walk together, to pray together two or three times per week, to have sex regularly (two times per week for them), and to ask themselves honestly, "Who is in between us figuratively in the marriage bed? Is anyone competing for our affections?" The leaving-and-cleaving issues were not so much literal interference as family of

origin issues they both carried into the marriage. Finally, we also discussed the supremacy of Christ over the world's philosophies and labels based on 1 Cor 2:13 and Col 2:8. We challenged Tony to see marriage and family as his first ministry opportunity. He saw how he had neglected his marriage, and he was thankful for his wife's forbearance.

- *Financial provision.* We spent some time discussing how Tony should choose a job in light of his performance issues. A big revelation was his understanding of his felt need for the approval of men in authority. He acknowledged his need to love people more and fear them less. He has spent a lot of time trying to please people instead of God (see Gal 1:10). Some practical concerns were addressed related to how to budget their resources for the transition to the new area to which they would move.
- *Advocate relationship.* Tony and Lisa's relationship with their advocate was to continue on after leaving TS. We wanted them to read Ed Welch's book, *When People Are Big and God Is Small.*[7] They were to read this as a couple and to review three key takeaways from each chapter with their advocate weekly.
- *Local church membership.* We strongly emphasized to Tony and Lisa the role of community and being more intentional in going deeper with a small group of people (see again circles diagram on community). This necessitated that they first aggressively pursue a church and small group on arrival in their new community. They were also encouraged to look up a biblical counselor in their area. The place for long-term healing and support for individuals and families is the local church. The body of Christ is absolutely necessary in providing deep, long-term transformation.
- *Seeking reconciliation.* Tony agreed to meet with his father with the assignment of confessing bitterness and dishonor toward him. Tony's father had also sinned against him, but

[7] Ed Welch, *When People Are Big and God Is Small* (Phillipsburg, NJ: P&R, 1997).

he could not go in good conscience and confront his father without first owning his own sin.

Weekend in Review

The counselees received 16 hours of biblical counseling over a three-day period, and our time ended well. Tony and Lisa had significant hope. One of the most encouraging things coming out of our time was Tony and Lisa's confidence in God's Word and their desire to get godly counsel going forward. They now felt they knew what to look for in a counselor. The seriousness of Tony's diagnosis had made them leery that "Christian counseling" could really help. Seeing God's perspective on his problems, Tony now felt that any more secular counseling would only be confusing. While staying under the care of a physician to consider the long-term medical regimen was wise, they were committed to approaching their problems from a biblical worldview. Tony saw his difficulty as rooted in a pervasive heart attitude that he could overcome with the help of God's Word, his Spirit, and the community of Christ. Tony was no longer focusing on a *diagnosis* but on his *heart*. Lisa was much less fearful of a lifelong "curse" or sickness that she would have to learn to live with in her husband. They saw a long road ahead but had direction. Incidentally, there had been some fear of having children after Tony was diagnosed, but this fear was decreased significantly as they saw their struggles through new eyes.

It was neither Tony's diagnosis nor even his resistance to counseling that proved to be the most difficult problem. Tony's problems were—at their core—theological. Tony was seeing that his worst problem had to do with a worship disorder. His odd behavior was symptomatic of a deeper heart issue. His stress and anxiety were due to a history of unforgiveness, fear of man, and unbiblical responses to conflict, especially interpersonal problems. Ultimately, Tony had never fully embraced the gospel or lived it out consistently. It really came down to a need Tony and Lisa had—to have an encounter with Christ who could engage their problems in a unique way. God knew they had been disappointed with previous counseling, that their issues had them exhausted and doubtful, and that they had been exposed to worldly wisdom that had them confused. The bipolar label left them feeling stigmatized and hopeless. The blend of grace and truth pierced their hearts and gave them new hope. Understanding that their problems were spiritual in nature and grew out of human sinfulness brought them hope. How can this be hopeful? Because sin has a cure. His name is Jesus.

What of the bipolar diagnosis? The symptoms that such a label point to were never ignored in our time with Tony and Lisa. We never minimized the seriousness of the problems that a bipolar diagnosis signifies. Instead, we listened carefully, gave them hours more of our time than they had received in other counseling, and provided an understanding that was superior to the secular one because it reflected God's truth. Tony and Lisa each reported that it was a turning point in their lives with God and each other.

A Monument to God's Power, Love, and Faithfulness

Tony and Lisa both decided it was best to follow through with plans to move to a new area. They had relatives in the community where they planned to move, and they were going to stay with them as they looked for new jobs and for a place to rent. For the time being they also chose a job with less stress for Tony. Lisa was capable of helping with income and was prepared to pursue employment until they had children. Tony had repented of his performance-based faith and fear of man. He was excited to spend time pursuing his relationship with Christ and serving others in ways that were less formal than vocational ministry. The advocate was committed to weekly phone calls and even accompanied Tony as he sought reconciliation with relatives. Tony went and asked his father's forgiveness. He also granted forgiveness. By God's grace Tony claims that his days of being stuck in a past full of fear, bitterness, and shame are behind him.

It is important to mention here how critical it was that Tony and Lisa were diligent to pursue deep involvement in their church community within a few months. Though counselees can take many positive steps toward biblical change, problems do not disappear after a few intense days. Because we know this to be true, we spend time discussing the importance of community and how to participate in it. Counselors must be careful not to overlook the importance of engagement with the larger Christian community outside of counseling.

As we prepared Tony and Lisa to engage in community, we asked them to realize that the interaction we had together was deeper than the kind to which most Christians are accustomed. Most of their peers will not have had this experience and may be less inclined to be as serious about a biblical worldview and doing the serious work of pursuing Christ in a daily way. Advocates can be helpful in assisting counselees to stay on track.

In the last three years Tony and Lisa have continued to make significant progress. They stayed in close touch with their advocate for the first year as they transitioned to the new area. Tony reported that the first six months were the hardest. He believed what we said about his identity and hope in Christ was true, but he continued to look back in fear and times of unbelief, wondering if he could ever really be "normal" after what they went through in their worst days. He cited a few things that were most helpful from our time together. First, the balance of truth and grace was extremely helpful. Tony and Lisa heard the truth, but they heard it spoken kindly from people they knew cared for them. Second, Tony and Lisa appreciated the reframing of his problem away from the "disease model" and toward the spiritual. Tony was not *sick*—he was *sanctified and justified in the name of the Lord Jesus* (1 Cor 6:11). Finally, Tony was gripped by Gal 2:20, "I no longer live, but Christ lives in me. The life I now live in the body, I live by faith in the Son of God, who loved me and gave Himself for me." Tony's life was no longer his own. He was identified and defined by the work of Jesus for him. Such an understanding was freeing for both Tony and Lisa.

Tony decided to see a doctor as soon as he was settled in their new area to discuss phasing-out the medication, trusting his wife and advocate to help him be discerning in this matter. He knew in his heart that the psychiatrist's claim that he would always need medication was not necessarily true. Incidentally, he eventually chose to stop taking his medications against medical advice, which was not our recommendation, but he has been off his medications for over two years. It has not always been easy, but he has never experienced a "breakdown" or severe mood swings since discontinuing them. He credits the Lord's working through his time in Scripture, his small group, and his family as the reasons he has been able to progress in his walk with Christ. Though difficult, he literally forced himself to memorize and meditate on significant passages like Psalm 139—a breakthrough for him from his perspective. He stated that Christ became very real and present as he encountered him in his Word.

Tony took a few part-time jobs, but he is now a full-time teacher in a public school and reports being content and doing well. The testimony of his advocate is that "God snatched them out of that dark period." He said that the way we did not condemn or make light of the secular counsel but brought to light the superiority of the Word of God was life changing to him, and to Tony, and Lisa. Although he was primarily there for Tony, he told us he reviews the notes he took for himself and his family periodically to this day. He felt that if we had been less gracious and patient that we would have lost Tony to unbelief, and Tony would have fallen for the distortions of a secular system. Not every case ends so well, but this case was a monument to God's faithfulness: someone with a serious psychiatric label and a history of poor counsel can experience a dramatic turnaround by God's grace.

Another sign of the growth and stability in this couple's life subsequent to counseling was their response to a miscarriage a few months back. They handled it well with appropriate grief and leaning on support from their community. When a counselee weathers significant trials with grace and dependence on God after counseling, that is a great sign of growth and change. Tony and Lisa are not the same. Tony is not stuck with a new identity as a psychiatric case or damaged goods. Lisa has been helped by the process to trust God more as well. Involving her and the mentor changed them all and drew them closer to God and each other. May God continue to get the glory for what he has done in this couple and now in the community around them. Tony is writing a book about this journey, and I pray and hope it will help many who are struggling to find God's Word, his Spirit, and his community when life gets hard.

Chapter 8

"Jackie" and Dissociative Identity Disorder

Stuart Scott

An Unexpected Reunion

God has a way of giving his people lifelong Christian friends who grow as close as family. But these gifts often develop in the least expected ways. Nothing brings lives together more meaningfully than walking together through a storm of sin and suffering toward the peaceful tranquility of God's grace. Jackie is one such family friend who joined us long ago for one such amazing journey. To this day she is a trophy of God's grace, whose own personal reflections are sprinkled throughout this chapter; and she has long been a sister fully capable of encouraging our family when we need it most. But our relationship did not begin this way at all.

One Sunday evening in the church where I first pastored as a young man, I saw a new yet familiar face enter the back of the sanctuary as the service began. Jackie slipped in and sat down alone. As I glanced at my wife who normally met the eye of any visitor with a warm smile, I first noticed a surprised expression as she seemed to slump down into her seat. Something was up.

As it turns out, Jackie was as surprised as my wife to find herself providentially sitting in our little church. After the service my wife kindly greeted Jackie and reintroduced me to her college friend, whom I had first met at our wedding. Jackie looked different. The past five years had taken their toll on her. We exchanged brief updates on our lives and commented that we should have her over soon.

Later, with a painful look on her face, my wife asked me to pray for her inner struggle about getting involved in Jackie's life again. Even though Jackie was dear to her, everything within her said that she was not ready for another difficult journey with her. However, because she recognized God's patience in her own life and knew that his grace would enable her, there was nothing to do but trust God and exhibit the love of Christ to her old friend.

Days Gone By

I had forgotten all about Jackie. Not long after my marriage to Zondra, she had received an unexpected call from Jackie. They were close friends. Zondra had been the floor leader in Jackie's dorm and had helped her through a number of troubling situations, including a horrible drug addiction withdrawal. Jackie was calling to ask Zondra's forgiveness for maintaining a life of habitual, compulsive lying while in college. She communicated that she had recently been saved and wanted to confess that the drug problem and other crises she had shared with Zondra were total fabrications, including her claim of being violently raped. Zondra was shocked. At this point in her life, my young wife had no idea how to trust or help someone with such deep problems. As she reflected on Jackie's admission of her bizarre deceit, Zondra was secretly relieved that she and Jackie were separated by many miles and that someone else was now involved in Jackie's life. In reflecting back on this particular time in her life, Jackie wrote:[1]

---

[1] In preparation for writing this chapter, I had Jackie reflect on her experiences and lessons. She contributed to this chapter in her own words, which I have quoted several times.

> I became very legalistic trying to ease my guilt. . . . When I went off to college, I met someone who would eventually be a catalyst for God's amazing mercy and grace being revealed to me. It was once again an authority figure, and I again used her and lied to her. . . . She left school before I did. . . . God began to work in my heart and bring me to the point of realizing that I did not really know him. Then the guilt was even greater, so I tried confessing to God and others, . . . but I still did not realize that I needed to truly and personally trust the gospel and give my life to Christ. I really didn't know what either meant.
>
> The next six years were the worst of my life. A failed engagement led me to a life of isolation and despair—even wanting to die. I blamed God for many things and left the Church. . . . For five years I denied the truth of Scripture. . . . I lived life for me! My thinking became futile and my foolish heart darkened. I believe that at this time God gave me up to the lusts of my heart, and I dishonored my body . . . and as Romans 1 says I exchanged natural relations for those that are contrary to nature. I had a three-year relationship with another woman. More guilt! More lies! More double life . . . this dishonoring relationship brought me to even greater despair. I was just miserable.

Coming for Counseling

Zondra wasn't sure Jackie would return, but once again she was surprised when Jackie began regularly attending our little church and spending time in our home. It was soon obvious that Jackie had many doubts and questions about who God really is and whether she could be forgiven and know him personally. She expressed a desire and a commitment not to make things up about herself anymore, but she continued to be very private, had difficulty relating to people, and still tended to manipulate others in various ways for attention.

As Jackie attended church and heard the Word of God, the Spirit began to work in her life. The gospel became more personal. She would later reflect on this time, after many conversations and sermons which clarified for her the true gospel and the transformative nature of the new birth:

> My [faith] professions over the years were just that—professions. They were not true conversion. [When I was] twenty-five however, God literally brought me to my knees and broke my heart and saved me. The first thing I did was end the sinful relationship I was in. And I began a discipleship Bible study with a woman at church, but there was so much garbage in my life from years of living in sin.

We slowly got reacquainted with Jackie, but we were still woefully ignorant of her past as well as all that was going on in her life at present.

Jackie manifested an understandable tension that commonly plagues those who are saved out of years of secret sin. She had a fresh hope based on her secure, eternal, grace-based standing with God, but she also had trouble getting out of long-standing sin patterns and developing new righteous habits. This tension can produce a deeply strained Christian experience, and people like Jackie often find themselves in desperate need of the interpersonal ministry of God's Word. Jackie needed the light of God's Word to shine on her daily desires and thoughts. She needed to understand the divine and human dynamics of change. Most of all Jackie needed the glories of Christ and his gospel to explode with fresh relevance for her current challenges.

Still plagued at times with guilt and shame over her past, she regularly struggled with depression and anxiety. She was still experiencing difficulty deciphering reality and telling the truth. Her emotions were unstable, and she was uncomfortable giving or receiving expressions of affection. These serious and legitimate issues were outweighed by a greater concern on Jackie's part as she came to me for help. She was aware that she could not account for substantial blocks of her time, and she actually thought that she was (in her own words) "catching glimpses of Christ or someone while at home."

Unfortunately, at this point in my ministry, I had no idea how to help someone like Jackie. In fact, my seminary training had taught me to refer such troubled individuals to a Christian psychologist or psychiatrist. I chose to recommend Jackie to a local Christian psychiatrist, assuming she would receive some secret psychological or medical key from a biblical perspective and be prescribed the medications she likely needed.

Because of Jackie's arrival and two other difficult counseling cases in our church, I simultaneously began to seek further training that might help me in my counseling ministry as a pastor. A past ministry colleague told me about a biblical counseling program, but I was skeptical. Could it be true that the Word of God was sufficient for handling complex psychological problems?

As I followed the progress of both Jackie and the other two members with their counselors, I grew increasingly concerned. The methods their counselors were using were anything but biblical, and I realized that virtually no biblical truth was being offered. All of them were getting worse, becoming more self-focused and troubled. In fact, Jackie was now having panic attacks. *How can this be right?* I thought. How could this be reconciled with the sanctification claims of the Bible? As I investigated further, I learned that even with a signed release form it was difficult to obtain any kind of substantial explanation of Jackie's troubles or a basic summary of the help she was and would be receiving. I eventually received this from her psychiatrist:

> I saw "Jackie." . . . At that time she complained of symptoms of depression and anxiety and also some dissociative episodes. I believe diagnostically Jackie suffers from dysthymic disorder (chronic depression) and possibly from an identity disorder. . . . She has an extreme amount of difficulty integrating her feelings and her thoughts. . . . The memory lapses she experiences

probably serve the defensive function protecting her from unacceptable emotions.

Dissociative Identity Disorder

I later learned that Jackie had been diagnosed with multiple personality disorder, or what is now called dissociative identity disorder (DID). Her therapist held to the perspective (common even among Christian psychiatrists) that multiple personalities were responsible for conflicting behaviors and memory loss. A number of factors led Jackie's psychiatrist to give her the DID label. First, Jackie could have won an acting award for her habitual pattern of lying, which led to a great deal of confusion about the truth and who she actually was. Second, she had a traumatic childhood experience. Third, she was engaging in bizarre behaviors such as walking aimlessly down the middle of the street in a rainstorm at night, not knowing what she was doing or why she was doing it. Fourth, Jackie had great trouble now managing her emotions. Fifth, as mentioned, she was losing blocks of time. A final, critical piece in the diagnosis was her sexual confusion and inability to explain it.

The popular Christian Survivors website states:

> The process of healing for people with DID is a long and complex one, with very different outcomes for different people . . . Some systems will come to a place where they are actually able and willing to integrate, [or blend] their alternate personalities into one whole person; whereas others will reach a place of high function, with the alters happy to remain separate, but co-conscious (able to communicate) with one-another.[2]

These perspectives are built on and follow the presuppositions and theories of secular psychology divorced from biblical truth.[3]

---

[2] Susannah Brown, "Explaining DID," Christian Survivors [online], November 11, 2005, accessed June 1, 2010, http://www.christiansurvivors.com/forums/showthread.php?t=15226.

[3] Many licensed Christian counselors refer to the *DSM-IV-TR* (Diagnostic Statistical Manual) definition and treatment guidelines when diagnosing and treating DID patients. Another Christian Counseling practice in Sacramento

Such theories are merely derived through human interpretation of the observation of troubled individuals. *The Diagnostic and Statistical Manual of Mental Disorders* (then the *DSM-III-R*) encompasses the prevailing psychiatric thought about DID:

> The essential feature of Dissociative Identity Disorder is the presence of two or more distinct identities or personality states (criteria A) that recurrently take control of behavior (criteria B). There is an inability to recall important personal information, the extent of which is too great to be explained by ordinary forgetfulness (criteria C). . . . Dissociative Identity Disorder reflects a failure to integrate various aspects of identity, memory and consciousness.[4]

The Psych Central website states:

> Approaches vary widely, but generally take an individual modality (as opposed to family, group or couples therapy) and emphasize the integration of the various personality states into one, cohesive whole personality. It should be noted that while it's convenient to talk of people who suffer from this disorder as having "multiple personalities," this is just a theoretical construct. People who suffer from this disorder *believe* they have multiple personalities which then take on a life of their own within the individual (perhaps reinforced by the belief). The new term for this disorder in the DSM-IV more accurately reflects the problem—the individual suffers from dissociative identities. Their personality is the sum of these identities, which have been split off at some point in the past. The split is usually due to some individual or multiple traumatic events.[5]

---

summarizes the DSM-IV on their website: "Patients with this Dissociative Disorder suffer from alternation of two or more distinct personality states with impaired recall among personality states of important information"(Bob Parkins, "Diagnostic Criteria for 300.14 Dissociative Identity Disorder" [online] 2009, accessed June 1, 2010, http://www.bobparkinslmft.com/info/did.html).

[4] *Diagnostic and Statistical Manual of Mental Disorders: DSM-IV-TR* (Washington, DC: American Psychiatric Association, 2000), 386.

[5] John M. Grohol, Mayo Clinic Staff, "Dissociative Disorders: Treatment and Drugs," Mayo Clinic [online] March 3, 2011, accessed October 17, 2011,

The Mayo Clinic, a resource highly regarded by most, has this to say about dissociative disorders:

> Psychotherapy is the primary treatment for dissociative disorders. This form of therapy, also known as talk therapy, counseling or psychosocial therapy, involves talking about your disorder and related issues with a mental health provider. . . . Psychotherapy for dissociative disorders often involves techniques, such as hypnosis, that help you remember and work through the trauma that triggered your dissociative symptoms. The course of your psychotherapy may be long and painful. . . . Although there are no medications that specifically treat dissociative disorders, your doctor may prescribe antidepressants, anti-anxiety medications or tranquilizers to help control the mental health symptoms associated with dissociative disorders.[6]

Jackie grew concerned that the results of her therapy did not justify the expense. She believed all she was doing was talking about her feelings and was seriously considering discontinuing her sessions. In our conversations I also voiced my own concern about how she was doing. During this period my wife and I received a call from the police in the middle of the night. Jackie was found distraught, in the middle of a busy street, running barefoot in the rain. Clearly she was not improving, and she was now endangering herself.

Eventually Jackie did stop attending therapy. At the urging of my colleague and friend, I began to counsel Jackie. I decided to try the biblical counseling program. Within a relatively short time, I was assured that I could offer Jackie better help with the Word of God, the supernatural work of the Holy Spirit, and the involvement of the church. What Jackie needed was to understand her problems biblically and to apply God's truth specifically to her life.

---

http://mayoclinic.com/health/dissociativedisorders/DS00574/DSECTION=treatments-and-drugs.

[6] Mayo Clinic Staff, "Dissociative Disorders: Treatment and Drugs," Mayo Clinic [online] March 3, 2011, accessed October 17, 2011, http://mayoclinic.com/health/dissociativedisorders/DS00574/DSECTION=treatments-and-drugs.

Giving Hope and Getting to Know the Real Jackie

As I began my new counseling training, I began meeting with Jackie more consistently (often with Zondra present). My situation allowed me to consult with other biblical counselors regarding her case. Because Zondra and I already had a trusted relationship with Jackie, my first priority was to shine some hope into the situation. I explained to Jackie that we were going to trust God's promise to sanctify her by his Word (John 17:17). We were going to depend on his faithfulness to provide a way out of her present struggles and lead her to a walk with Christ that would bring him glory (1 Cor 10:13; 1 Pet 1:3–4). Through our discussions we established that her old sin-enslaved self was dead and buried with Christ and that her new nature was invincibly alive with Christ. In certain ways, since her conversion she was a completely new person, never to be the same again (2 Cor 5:17). Jackie was alive from the dead, inhabited by the Holy Spirit, and empowered to love and obey God. Through Christ she had a new heart and new power to appropriate biblical truth in new ways. She had a new relationship with God, and even with all her current struggles, Zondra and I had seen a difference in Jackie's life and desires.

My second priority was to learn all I could about Jackie's life. What was her story? Wisdom speaks clearly in Prov 18:13: "The one who gives an answer before he listens—this is foolishness and disgrace for him." I needed to listen well before I could counsel well. Here is Jackie's own lengthy personal account of the information I gained through the early data-gathering process and subsequent conversations.

> Growing up in a Christian home, I always knew about God and his Son Jesus Christ. There was not a time (that I can remember in my formative years) in which I did not think that Jesus was who the Bible said he was. I believed the basic facts: that Jesus was the only way to heaven, that everyone was a sinner, and that everyone needed a Savior. As a very young child, I lived in a home full of love and security. My mother held weekly Bible clubs for the

neighbor kids, we were all involved in the Bible Memory Association, and I memorized quite a lot of Scripture. My life seemed perfect at age four. I had wonderful parents and two brothers, and my mom was expecting another baby. I was so excited.

We had two boys, so I asked my mom for a girl (not realizing there wasn't a choice). When the baby came, it was not a girl; it was another boy. I remember being very angry and hurt because my mom didn't listen to me. Resentment settled in my heart over this and was compounded by the fact that when he came home from the hospital I had to share my room and my mother's attention with him! I did not like him. Sometimes I even wished he were never born. I was confused and upset at my mom for not giving me what I wanted; it seemed only fair to me.

I turned five years old just a few weeks after my baby brother was born. And my near perfect life was about to change again. When my baby brother was about four months old something happened that would play a major role in the development of my emotions for many years to come.

I was staying with my aunt for a little visit. My parents and three brothers were at home. It came time to come and pick me up, so they all piled in the car to come and get me. Not too far from home, they were involved in a traffic accident. A policeman came to my aunt's house to notify us of the situation. I heard them talking and knew that my family was in real trouble. This is when it began—the guilt, the fear, the detachment from painful emotions. It turned out to be a horrific accident.

Everyone was injured to some degree, but the two people who were hurt the worst were the two people that I had wished were no longer in my life, my mom and my baby brother, Ryan. And oh, the guilt! I was sure it was my fault. I never told anyone this. I was too ashamed and hid the guilt that was always in my heart. This apparently was not something I could cope with on my own at five years old. I suppose I was too young to realize initially I could verbalize my guilt, fears, and confusion to God or anyone else.

My mother and brother almost died. Their injuries were severe. They both still suffer with some of the effects of the accident some 45 years later. We, the children, stayed with my aunt. We weren't allowed to see my mom and brother, as they were in the hospital for a long time. I missed my mother and was scared I would never see her again. Dad would visit us at my aunt's.

Eventually Mom came home, and then Ryan, and relatives or people from church came to care for us there. I began to do everything I could for my mom and Ryan to make up for all the bad thoughts and wishes—to try and soothe my guilt. My baby brother became my favorite, and from then on, I was his protector. Sometime during age five I was attending revival meetings at our church and the preacher, who was the "fire and brimstone" type, scared me half to death. I just about ran down the aisle to profess Christ and obtain my fire insurance (a pass to get into heaven and most importantly to stay out of hell!). Soon after this I was baptized, and life went on as I knew it before; except now, I was "saved from hell," so I thought.

The traffic accident changed our entire family. From my perspective nothing was ever the same again. I continued on the path of resentment and private guilt, rather than being honest with anyone. Not too long after my mother's recovery, my parents felt the Lord was leading them into full-time missionary work. So by age seven there was yet another huge change. We relocated and began our missionary training. I clearly recall that during this time I was fantasizing, making up stories and pretending for relief. It seemed to me that in my pretend world, I was getting the attention I once had, and my "new world" was much more fun than my real one. I had no idea where this would lead me.

The next three years we moved every year to further our training, but we finally ended up where I lived from age nine and for many years. At this time we were very involved in the work of the mission, church, and youth groups. It was then that I really began to make things up. I would lie to myself about who I was or what was going on around me.

Most of the time there was a great dichotomy between what was going on in the inside of me and what I was portraying. On the outside I was the good girl who never got into trouble, the dutiful Christian daughter. On the inside I was afraid, miserable, and pretending. Then my life of nonreality and deceit took the next step down. I don't know all the reasons why, but a huge one was for attention. I began to lie to others (mostly those in positions of authority) and make up things that would cause them to have sympathy for me and want to spend time with me—to counsel me and "help the poor child." I was for the most part doing great (I had a good and stable life and was doing what was right). But with these people I pretended to be a rebellious, wayward teen. I fabricated that I was fooling around with guys, into drugs, enveloped by sadness, and having confusion about spiritual things that I really understood. I thrived on the attention I gained while being "taught," when I really understood all along.

This life of lying went on for years. When I exhausted one person's help, I would move on to another and another, draining them of their time and love for very unnecessary reasons. My life of deceit and guilt and confusion led to turning inward and clamming up. I was a very "shy" person. I stayed in the background mostly. I really lived life in my head. Well, I lived two lives: the real one (in a sense) where I acted the part of a model Christian girl, going to Bible clubs and being the award winner; I was the missionary kid who never did anything wrong. And a false one about which I lied to select people and regularly lived in a fantasy world in my head. Whom I was around would dictate the life that was presented. I knew that I was deceiving others but felt compelled to do so. I was a slave to my sin and addicted to attention. This lust would breed manipulation and jealousy in any relationship of significance.

I did gain a lot of attention and loved it for the moment. But it was never real, never enough, never lasting. So I had to continue to use people, to go to the next person I could exhaust. I was looking for satisfaction. It never came in people or the attention I gained. I was still a miserable person.

As far as my spiritual life went, I believed I was a Christian on the basis of my profession and baptism at age five. I strove to perform like the Christian of the Bible in many respects. But I knew I miserably failed. I was always feeling I couldn't follow "the rules." Of course, the guilt of my double life and all the sin that was there were playing a more major role than I realized.

My "life with Christ" was pretty much duty, nothing personal for sure. I was simply growing in my knowledge of Scripture, and my days were either good or bad according to what kind of deeds I had or had not done. As time went on, I became more and more legalistic in my dutiful life, trying to ease my guilt. I believed I could sometimes talk to God and ask him for things, depending on my performance.

My life was about to take another turn. When I was 19, I went off to college. I continued my fabrications and my use of people, but, as mentioned, I met someone there that would eventually be an instrument in God's hand toward my true conversion. . . . [But first,] after two more years of lying and another empty profession of faith to appease my guilt, I left school over my first serious relationship with a guy . . .

When my failed engagement led to isolation, despair, and even wanting to die, I turned my back on God and spiraled into all kinds of degradation, just like what is pictured in Romans 1. From early childhood I knew God existed, but I did not honor him as God, nor did I give thanks to him. My thinking became futile, and my foolish heart was indeed darkened. I exchanged the truth about God for a lie, and I did not worship God. During this time I saw so much evil coming from my life [including the earlier mentioned sexual relationship with another woman]. The things that came out of my mouth and life showed that there was more sin in my heart than I ever thought possible. This time brought me to new levels of low. Finally, I knew God was far from me and inaccessible. Then God began to work in my heart, drawing me to himself.

At this time I began to desire returning to church—to try and somehow clean up my life and seek God again. I was still in a relationship with a woman, which continued to bring guilt and shame; but I began to seek out a church. I did find a church, and by God's providence the wife of the pastor (Zondra) was the college friend I had lied and confessed to years earlier. The relationship needed much repair. But I was willing to overlook

> Zondra's disappearance from my life, and God gave her grace to open her life to me again.
>
> Under the ministry of Stuart and Zondra, I finally and personally recognized my great sin, my need for a personal Savior, and God's genuine offer of grace to me. And for the first time I received his forgiveness. Although I was no longer purposefully making things up about who I was, I did still lie a lot about things that really didn't matter. I had gotten into such a habit of lying that I lied without even thinking about it. And the guilt and shame still engulfed my heart at times.
>
> Several months after my salvation, I went to Stuart (my pastor) for help for the problems I was still having. . . . He sent me to see a psychiatrist but eventually began to counsel me himself.

In our early sessions together, Jackie and I discussed most of the dynamics surrounding her life story. I investigated her family relationships more deeply. I explored her interaction with the trials in her life, including how the tragic car accident changed her life so dramatically. We talked about her understanding of God and the spiritual steps she tried to take along her path. I looked for evidence of her goals in life and took note of the sins in which she was currently engaged. I questioned her more carefully about exactly how she related to others in her life, and I began to ask myself what God says about each of the key discoveries learned.

Where Do We Go with Jackie?

During my time gathering information about Jackie, I also learned that she had not been sleeping much at all. It was important for me to minister to her as a whole person since spiritual and physical components do affect each other (1 Kgs 9:1–18; 2 Cor 4:16–18). One of my first steps was sending Jackie for a physical checkup, and her physician prescribed a few nights of sleeping pills. It was crucial that Jackie get some good sleep to stabilize her overall physical and emotional state, to increase her ability to concentrate, and to help her benefit from counseling.[7]

Over time we dealt with the issues in Jackie's life one by one. Following the initial promise of hope in Christ, we started with (and often returned to) her recent conversion and its implications for her daily life. We unpacked 1 Cor 6:11 and 2 Cor 5:17 as we discussed the gospel and especially her identity in Christ. Whether Jackie's old identity was viewed as multiple confused personalities or a singular enslaved personality, her past identity as a whole was just that—old and dead. "Such *were* some of you," Paul wrote to the converted sinners of Corinth (1 Cor 6:11 NASB, emphasis added). Now, along with these redeemed saints, Jackie was, in a real sense, a new creation (2 Cor 5:17). We also pondered Phil 2:12–13 as we examined her role and God's role in the process of change. God desired Jackie to work hard at growth and tend the garden of her own thought life. He also promised that her labors would be fueled and fertilized by his own energizing and cultivating work within her. This blend of serious responsibility and energizing power was designed by God to amplify Jackie's commitment to apply God's truth personally to her life (Jas 1:22) for the right reasons (Rom 12:1–2). Even in the face of great difficulty, it was wonderful to watch Jackie work at the assignments I gave her with prayer and zeal. Ultimately she had a true desire to honor the Lord and submit to Scripture. This commitment went a long way in facilitating the Spirit's supernatural work in her life (Eph 4:30).

Idolatrous and Destructive Life Agendas

Jackie's heart was genuinely arrested by God's grace. Therefore, she was ready and eager to consider the practical issue of what her heart was worshipping in her everyday living. After talking through certain Scriptures that deal with one's heart

[7] Edward Welch discussed the relationship between body and soul in *Blame It on the Brain* (Phillipsburg, NJ: P&R, 1998).

(Romans 1; Ezekiel 14; Jas 1:12–15; 4:1–4), Jackie was motivated to contemplate some questions I gave her: "What am I willing to sin to get, or sin if I don't get?" "For me, to really live is what?" (see Phil 1:21). "What have I habitually sought and set my heart on in this life?"

With compassion for what Jackie had been through as a child, we traced patterns of sinful worship which she had been pursuing throughout her life. Her eyes were opened to certain lusts she had developed—for attention; for a personal, all-satisfying relationship; for the approval of others; and for control over her situations. It was essential for Jackie to understand that every human heart always fixates on some object of worship because we are created to worship (Deut 11:16; John 4:23; Rom 1:18–32; Col 1:16).

She learned that prior to salvation her heart was enslaved to false worship and engaged in it constantly. It also made sense to her that while life's circumstances may have influenced the direction of her affections and her false worship, such external factors were not the ultimate cause of her idolatry. Rather, her sinful idolatry must be attributed to her fallen condition and the lustful bent of her own heart (Jer 17:9; Titus 3:3). It was helpful for her to understand that because she did not know God she would have found something to worship instead of him—even if her family's car accident had never happened. Without Christ, Jackie became increasingly convinced that other *things* would bring her meaning and happiness. Her pursuits, choices, and responses had all flowed from the true objects of her affections and her hope or loss of hope in them.

Exchanging the worship of God for the worship of her idols, Jackie spiraled down into new sins. A lesbian relationship followed her complete and decisive rejection of God's truth and a full pursuit of what she desired most. She was given over to her lust for a personal, all-satisfying relationship and was willing to fulfill it any way she could. Unlike some, Jackie did not struggle with a desire for women throughout her life, nor did she have a problem with it following her salvation.[8] It was driven by her false worship and by her outright rejection of God. With the embracing of God's grace came also a decisive rejection of this particular sexual sin. Still, while Jackie was no longer a full-time idol worshipper and didn't fulfill her basic relational lust in that way, it showed up in other ways at various times until it was recognized, repented of, and replaced with a deeper and more united pursuit of Christ.

In contrast to Jackie's idolatrous lusts, we discussed the supreme worth and value of Christ along with the saints' profound experience of knowing and worshipping him alone (Ps 73:25–28; Phil 1:21). Jackie was deeply affected by this revelation about her daily heart's desires and passions. She confessed her sin to God and asked him to remind her of his value and his call to undivided worship if and when she began to resurrect these idolatrous lusts. In the coming months she would have many opportunities to practice this repentance. Over the next few weeks, we continued to paint a picture of undivided worship in her daily life while emphasizing the possibility and importance of being satisfied in God alone. Honing in on the heart (her affections, beliefs, and thoughts) was vital for her growth.

In order to give God the worship he deserved, Jackie would need to pursue several significant new mind-sets: appropriating the gospel daily and embracing God's love for her (Eph 3:17–19), learning to give love rather than seek it from others (Acts 20:35; Phil 2:3–4), and cultivating a trusting and submissive spirit, yielded to a good God's control rather than trying to control her own life and the lives of others (Ps 138:8; Prov 16:9; Jas 4:13–15). In the coming months and years, several of these passages would become precious to Jackie.

Practically Working at Change

God's Word teaches that in the disordered soul, it is natural for sin to flow from the affections, to the thoughts, to the emotions,

[8] Because of the sexual pleasure to which Jackie had become accustomed, she did have to work through the temptation to satisfy sexual desires in other ways. An older woman in our church provided her godly counsel.

and to the behavior. The flow of righteousness within even a new and changed heart, however, faces active and powerful obstacles—the flesh, the world, and Satan (Gal 5:16–17; Rom 12:2; 1 Pet 5:8–9). Therefore, I needed to help Jackie work on both the heart and behavioral aspects of her life. It was vital that thankfulness and worship of God remain her motivations and that she learn to depend on Christ's power so that her new pursuits would actually please God. She also needed to learn the principle of *exercising* herself toward godliness in tangible and specific ways (1 Tim 4:7–8). Her application of the put-off/put-on principle from Eph 4:22–32 needed to differ entirely from her past efforts to staple good fruit onto a dead tree (her dead heart) and from the toxic legalism that once reigned in her life.[9] As expected, learning these lessons was not a one-time event but rather came in successive seasons of life in which she grew by increasing degrees.

Addressing Her Guilt and Shame

A significant theme and substantial problem throughout Jackie's life was her pronounced guilt and shame over her sins, including her bitterness as a child. The guilt of her sin was still playing a central role in her depression and anxiety, and it often hindered her relationship with God. It was obvious that even as a five-year-old, Jackie had been aware that her angry, simmering thoughts toward her mother and brother were wrong. At such a young age, she was naturally confused about her seeming responsibility for their accident and about what to do with her guilt. Her guilt, stemming from both the violation of God's Word and her own rules, needed to be confessed and/or forsaken.

We discussed the extent of God's forgiveness through Christ, how to deal biblically with all of her past sins, and how to clear her conscience.[10] On the basis of John's merciful promise that God responds to sincere confession with full forgiveness (1 John 1:9),

---

[9] Paul Tripp expounded on this analogy in *Instruments in the Redeemer's Hands* (Phillipsburg, NJ: P&R, 2002), 63–65.

[10] Steve Viars has done a great job addressing these principles and many more in *Putting the Past in Its Place* (Eugene, OR: Harvest House, 2011).

I gave Jackie the opportunity to confess to the Lord anything she had not already confessed. Emphasizing Christ's work for her again (2 Cor 5:21), I pointed out her lack of genuine trust in his atonement at times and encouraged her to confess this as well. Jackie then returned often to the shadow of the cross. This particular session and her continued application of its truth to her familiar patterns of thinking brought a level of peace and freedom to Jackie she had never known before. She learned to bask in God's forgiveness and its implications declared by the apostle Paul: "Therefore, no condemnation now exists for those in Christ Jesus" (Rom 8:1).

Confronting Dissociation and False Refuges

From an early age Jackie had found ways to dissociate herself from feelings of guilt and pain, escape into nonreality, and dichotomize her "spiritual" life and speech from her personal practice and inner thoughts. There were significant ramifications of this repeated choice. Her ability to relate personally to God's truth or to relate meaningfully to others was severely hindered. She possessed little emotional capacity to face her own thoughts and feelings honestly. Over time she grew largely out of touch even with good emotions and became fearful or devastated when negative ones emerged. The false refuge of her mental fantasies cornered her into isolation, and she began to voice her fantasies to others as though such ideas were real. She would sometimes get confused about certain aspects of her two lives (made-up versus real), wondering which one was real. Jackie was so personally detached that parts of her memory were affected more than what is typical for those sharing her struggle. She was a small step away from completely compartmentalizing aspects of her person, fully retreating into other "realities," and being subject to the suggestion of multiple personalities.[11] Thankfully,

[11] "MPD may be created through the power of suggestion. . . . Sociocognitive explanation: MPD is an extreme form of the ability we all have to present different aspects of our personalities. . . . MPD allows troubled people to make sense of their problems. . . . Therapists 'reward' patients by paying attention to these specific symptoms which helps patients organize their memories to make them *more* consistent with the diagnosis. . . . Little empirical support for the existence

the Spirit of God broke through with the gospel and led her to discontinue her secular-based therapy.[12]

Jackie needed to know God as her sufficient refuge in reality (Ps 46:1–3). Obviously, focusing on God's character and his faithfulness to her was foundational for her reliance on him. For this purpose, I asked her to read Psalms and see how the psalmist related to God. She recognized how he experienced difficult emotions at times yet poured out his heart to God (Pss 62:8; 142:1–2), returned to God's character and truth (Pss 31:9–24; 40:1–5), and trusted God for the grace to get through his painful situation and emotions (Ps 73:23–28). My wife remembers clearly how Jackie pushed through her fears and began imitating this mind-set. Once she began to be honest with God about her thoughts and emotions, the floodgates seemed to open. During this time her emotions were more heightened than she would have liked, but the process was essential.

It was extremely helpful at this time for Jackie to learn how renewing beliefs (embedded ideas of thought) and specific thoughts

---

of MPD," Charles M. Slem, "Psychological Disorders," California Polytechnic State University College of Liberal Arts [online], 2000, accessed January 2012, http://www.cla.calpoly.edu/~cslem/101/10-E.html.

[12] There have been claims that DID is a therapy-induced phenomena. "Many biological psychiatrists who base their practices around medication management will tell you the condition doesn't exist, or that if it exists it is 'iatrogenic,' meaning it is caused by therapists training their patients to interpret their symptoms as if they have a whole set of distinct personalities. On the other hand, there are clinicians who specialize in the condition and they take the presence of multiple personalities so seriously that they will separate therapeutic meetings with each of a patient's 'alters' (i.e. individual personalities). True believers will point to data that different personalities have different electroencephalogram tracings. Cynics will point out that actors can generate different EEG tracings when they switch characters. . . . Does this mean that dissociative identity disorder exists? In my opinion it depends on what we mean by 'exists.' Yes, dissociative identity disorder exists if by exists we mean there are people who complain of its symptoms and suffer its consequences. Do I think that some people have many biologically distinct entities packed into their heads? No. I think that some people dissociate so badly that either on their own or as a result of therapeutic experiences it becomes the case that the most convincing way for them to see their own experience is as if it is happening to multiple people," Charles Raison, "Is dissociative disorder real? [An] expert answer," CNN Health [online], February 23, 2010, accessed January 2012, http://www.cnn.com/2010/HEALTH/expert.q.a/02/23/dissociative.identity.disorder.raison/index.html.

could affect and help manage her emotions. She needed to confront her anxiety with truth in a personal way. I encouraged her to ask God for the help she needed to face her thoughts and feelings honestly. She found him faithful to give her the help she needed. She was able to learn to take her thoughts captive regarding some longstanding beliefs, her fearful and anxious episodes, and her memories about her past (Rom 12:2; 2 Cor 10:5; Col 2:8).[13] This was another huge step in her walk with Christ and her overall growth.

God's Control Versus Her Control

In addition to the guilt over her sin, not trusting God's good control over her life had contributed to Jackie's anxieties and panic attacks. As we continued talking about the love of God for her through Christ, we also began pinpointing evidences of God's common grace, ways he had worked in her life, and what he had been doing in times of trouble (Ps 145:9; Lam 3:19–28, 31–33; Rom 8:28–29). Seeing his love demonstrated in this way was an important motivation for embracing the sovereignty of God and viewing her past differently. It also encouraged her to trust God's control in both the present and the future. Seeing afresh God's sovereign love and learning to repent of the false control she had learned to practice concerning her own life and the lives of others helped her lingering anxiety to subside. Reading *Trusting God* by Jerry Bridges led to even greater strides in trust.[14]

Untangling the Web of Deceit

Jackie had practiced the sin of lying for so long and in so many ways that dishonesty had become second nature for her. From the time she began hiding her guilt and shame as a child, deceit had become a way of life. It helped Jackie to know that deceit is a natural, sinful outflow from any unredeemed heart (Jer 17:9). Many years of false worship and turning to other refuges had developed this strong habit that would not be easily broken. It

---

[13] Jackie learned to use the general pattern found in Phil 4:6–9 for handling her thoughts.

[14] Jerry Bridges, *Trusting God* (Colorado Springs: NavPress, 1990).

would take a full offensive and relentless accountability. We spent time going over deceit from a biblical perspective (Prov 12:22), examining the various forms of deceit illustrated in Scripture—from purposefully giving wrong impressions to telling a complete untruth.[15] Jackie was learning to value and worship Christ above all else. She was committed to confession and repentance any time she was deceitful, no matter how painful. I had her track specific instances of deceit in a weekly calendar so that we could gain insight into any patterns, facilitators, or motivators.[16] Evaluating this information while continuing to examine Jackie's tendencies toward idolatry helped her make regular progress. Though her temptation to deceive seemed to linger the longest, she did eventually become a truth-teller. Jackie later wrote: "There came a day when I HATED to lie about ANYTHING, and I would go back and correct so many little 'white' lies. Truth is now a very precious thing to me. Knowing *God's* truth (his Word) is the *most* precious of all."

Learning to Love

One of Jackie's greatest needs was to learn to love others in a Christlike way. Rather than work on her self-esteem, self-image, or self-confidence, she needed to consider and revel in the love of God and forsake her inordinate focus on herself in her thoughts and relationships. Because of her inward focus, isolation, and preoccupation with fantasies and attention, she did not know the first thing about typical relationships, much less biblical ones. Learning to give unselfishly and sacrificially—rather than using, manipulating, and desperately needing others—would bring glory to God, which was her new goal in life. Doing this would also liberate her from the bottomless pit of self (Phil 2:3–4). Only as she sought to love others just as Christ loves her would Jackie find joy in relationships.

---

[15] Lou Priolo did a great job discussing these various forms of dishonesty and handling the issue of deception as a whole in *Deception: Letting Go of Lying* (Phillipsburg, NJ: P&R, 2008).

[16] See Jay Adams, *The Christian Counselor's Manual* (Grand Rapids: Zondervan, 1973), 280.

We studied pride and humility and how these opposing mind-sets related to her preoccupation with self or her desire to be approved by God and others based on her own merit. I had Jackie study 1 Corinthians 13 and envision how she could specifically apply love's various characteristics to her own life. She was then to make concrete plans for loving and serving others. As Christlike love for others became a driving motivation, behaviors like responding to others, communicating more, expressing emotion, and displaying appropriate affection were much easier to work through. I helped her formulate thoughts on how to develop godly relationships from a biblical perspective and to outline practical plans for growth. With Christ's help Jackie began to experience joy and liberty in relationships in addition to the greater joy she was finding in Christ's love and her increasingly undivided devotion to him. Her own reflections reveal how pivotal it was for her to learn to love like Christ:

> I discovered the joy of loving others and being expressive in that love was one of the highlights! When I gave my life away to others, my heart was filled with a peace and joy like I had never known. . . . Many deep and long-lasting relationships were opened up to me, and I wasn't seeking them or trying to manipulate them into existence! . . . I went from someone who hid from others and held back my feelings to someone who opened their home and filled it with people to love.

The Importance of the Body of Christ

Our small church community was also an integral part of Jackie's growth and change (see Gal 6:1–3; 2 Corinthians 12; Eph 4:1–13). In many ways it was the catalyst for the public and private ministry of God's Word to her. It was a spiritual family like she had never known, and it was her training ground where she could apply what she was learning. Through several women who ministered to her, Jackie discovered and began using her own spiritual gifts. In the words of the Christian Counseling and Education

Foundation (CCEF), floundering people are "best able to image the triune God as they live and grow in community. Therefore we embed personal change within God's community—the church, with all its rich resources of corporate and interpersonal means of grace."[17] After all, "change is a community project."[18] Jackie's transformation brightly illustrated this truth as the church served as the crucial communal environment of truth, care, encouragement, service, and accountability. My work with Jackie was not private by any means.

Reflections

Jackie's hope grew incrementally from day one. It was small and weak at first, but as she learned about God's character and commitment to her she began personally and practically interacting with the Word of God. Changes began to take place in her life, and her meager hope blossomed into a strong faith. Through our counseling sessions, family conversations in our home, and Bible study, a biblical understanding of the dynamics of nonorganic depression along with God's answers for it began to emerge. Her problem of mysticism and subjectivity in her relationship with God and her decision-making as well as how to handle anger, bitterness, and resentment biblically became a focus of work. Jackie began to conquer impure thoughts, developed a proper view of dating, set clear vocational goals, and began to put in place biblical financial principles.[19]

It was an awesome thing to watch God work in her life. She became one of the greatest servants in our church and one of the most contented single women we have ever known. It wasn't that Jackie never wanted to marry. She just became more and more

[17] David Powlison and Tim Lane, "CCEF History, Theological Foundations and Counseling Model," CCEF [online], November 10, 2009, accessed January 2012, http://www.ccef.org/ccef-history-theological-foundations-and-counseling-model.

[18] Tim Lane and Paul Tripp, *How People Change* (Winston-Salem, NC: Punch, 2006), 73.

[19] I had Jackie do Bible studies on many of these topics. See Wayne Mack's *A Homework Manual for Biblical Living: Personal and Interpersonal Problems*, vol. 1 (Phillipsburg, NJ: P&R, 1979).

focused on loving, serving, and becoming more like the God who had graciously forgiven her and continued to change her. She ministered to our own family in a myriad of ways, particularly to my wife and children in key times of need.

This case is still particularly meaningful to me for many reasons. First, it was my earliest experience of seeing such drastic transformation in a life fraught with difficulties. I saw the personal ministry of the gospel working through God's revealed truth. Second, it was a personal lesson of trusting God's wisdom and ability in the face of my own inexperience. Third, it was a major catalyst for the invaluable training I received in how to minister the Word in counseling. Fourth, I have been able to follow God's continued work of grace in Jackie's life and to see the ongoing fruit of his Word.

Jackie's experiences and responses would have led to greater dissociation, more severe emotional upsets, and deeper escapes into nonreality had she stayed her course. To clarify if Jackie had evidenced stronger expressions when I was counseling her, I would have needed to stay *my* course of speaking the truth to her in any way possible. It would also have taken more perseverance in the personal application of the gospel and the patient explanation of biblical principles. I likely would have asked for greater accountability and involvement from the church. It may even have taken a stay at a residential biblical counseling facility.[20] If Jackie's problems had been even more amplified and contorted than they already were, God's Word remains true: "His divine power has given us everything required for life and godliness" (2 Pet 1:3), and "Sanctify them by the truth; Your word is truth" (John 17:17).

Jackie married 10 years later. At just the right time God brought her a godly man whom she loves and supports with joy. Their marriage itself is another story of God's grace. Today Jackie is a devoted mother of three children and also ministers faithfully

[20] Examples of biblical counseling facilities include Vision of Hope (http://www.fbcmlafayette.org), Twelve Stones Ministry (http://www.twelvestones.org), and His Steps Ministries (http://www.hisstepsministries.org).

to women in her church. Now, 27 years after the fact, Jackie reflected on her time in counseling:

> It quickly gave me great hope for "today" and the future ahead. There was a purpose for my life. It was the person of Jesus Christ and all that he wanted to do in me, for me, and through me. Where once I was fearful of other people, unable to even approach someone for a need or question, now I can stand and teach crowds of ladies and just love it! It showed me that as I depend on Christ, the truth of God is definitely all I need for life and godliness. Through his Word, the Lord directs, corrects, encourages, and shows his great love for me, who was once His enemy.
>
> There are many trophies of God's grace in my life. It is hard to choose one I value most. But if I had to choose, it would be that I understand what it means to be a Christian. It is not about do's and don'ts, lists to check off, feeling good about myself when I do right, or condemning myself when I do wrong. It is about a personal relationship with the God of the universe. It is about coming to understand how deeply and thoroughly I am undeservedly loved by this amazing God. In one of my favorite books, *Because He Loves Me*, Elyse Fitzpatrick quotes Tim Keller: "We are, each one, more sinful and flawed than we ever dared believe, but more loved and welcomed than we ever dared hope."[21] What joy that I am seen by the Father through Christ! This means that all glory belongs to him, not me. And that the one who deserves all the focus is Christ—my life, my joy, my all.

---

[21] Elyse Fitzpatrick, *Because He Loves Me* (Wheaton: Crossway, 2008), 57.

CHAPTER 9

"JASON" and Homosexuality

Kevin Carson

WHEN JASON ARRIVED FOR COUNSELING, he looked like any other single, career-minded 25-year-old. At first glance he would fit in almost any church. But as he began his story, Jason made clear that what brought him to Sonrise for counseling was also what made him feel alone, scared, and rejected by the church. A friend had heard about our counseling ministry and convinced him at least to try it. Although Jason was still fearful, he decided to come. He began, "I love God, and I believe he loves me and wants me to be happy. I just don't know how my life fits together. I struggle with same-sex attraction. I spend time with other guys." Jason's struggle was with the sin of homosexuality.

As he told his story, Jason's demeanor varied greatly: quivering lips, tear-filled eyes, awkward smiles, and intense scowls. He described how he grew up in the church and knew early on what the Bible teaches about homosexuality. He also explained his goal for counseling: "Since it's a sin and God doesn't like it, I don't want to struggle with this anymore. I want to be happy and to feel good, but I don't want to sin or to think about what God doesn't want me to think about." Although he described his struggle as a sin, he continued: "I enjoy the company of other guys, and it makes me happy. I know God wants me to be happy and have joy—and this is just one of the things that makes me happy." Jason continued, "I wonder, though, how it fits together. I'm told—and I see it when I read the Bible—it's not good in the Bible. Yet it seems good in my life."

What do you do with Jason? His testimony is that he loves God and that he desires not to sin. Yet he is happy when he is with other guys and is sure God wants him to be happy.

Before you whip out your Bible and begin to wax eloquent regarding the wickedness of homosexuality, its hurtful consequences, its reckless health risks, and the overall disgust you may feel toward Jason's life choices, there are several key issues to consider. As a counselor, your decisions *prior* to counseling Jason are as critical as your decisions *when* you counsel him. Who *you* are, how *you* live, and what *you* think about those whose lives are filled with sexual sin are critical questions to ponder. Every time a new Jason comes to you for help, your preparation for these initial moments of counseling matters greatly.

Getting Priorities Straight: Jason's Counselor

Counselors in training often hear the adage, "A good counselor is first a good counselee." If you hope to please God as you minister the gospel to others, it is important that the gospel first be at work in your own heart. This is sometimes referred to as self-counsel. The mature counselor considers his own thoughts, attitudes, desires, and behaviors, pursuing the Spirit's refining ministry in his life as he seeks to develop the thoughts, attitudes, desires, and behaviors manifested by Christ when he ministered on earth (Eph 4:1; Phil 2:5). This process requires a lifelong commitment by the counselor and is essential before counseling those embroiled in sexual sin or any other sin.

In addition, with regard to homosexuality and other sexual sins, the counselor must carefully consider which potential authority is influencing his counsel. There are a number of options for an authority that could be influencing a counselor. The authority could take the form of his professed belief system (formal), or it could take the form of his practical beliefs that exercise real-time control over his thinking and counseling (functional), even though these practical beliefs differ from his professed belief system. Typically, the counselor operates from some combination of both formal and functional authorities. There are at least three potential authorities that influence a counselor's approach to Jason: contemporary culture, previous experience, and scriptural knowledge.

Counseling from Contemporary Culture

Jason's story presents almost a perfect case study demonstrating how easy it is for cultural perspectives to control one's counseling. His parents divorced when he was four years old, and he lived with his mom who remarried almost immediately. Jason's mom and stepdad went to church, but his father did not. Jason describes his mom as "very, very strict—I had to do everything by the book when I was living with her." However, when he would go to his dad's house every other weekend, things were different: "It was a release. It was an escape. I could do whatever I wanted." Jason's dad was uninterested in spending time with him (Jason described his father as "passive"), so he spent time primarily with "bad friends at my dad's house." The contrast was significant. "It was a different life, but I never let my mom know I was hanging out with those friends because she wouldn't have liked any of them."

At the age of seven he was first introduced to sexually explicit material through one of these friends. While upstairs in a friend's house, they discovered magazines that included both heterosexual and homosexual pictures. Jason said, "Every time we had free time, we would go back to that same spot. We'd make sure no one knew we were there, and we'd put the pictures back just like we found them." This launched a lifelong battle with the desire to view pornography. Over time curiosity and lust drove Jason to view primarily homosexual pornography.

While in junior high he realized that he enjoyed hanging out with his male friends as they were talking about girls. "I would talk to my guy friends about girls, and that was fine because I liked spending time with the guys. Plus, I didn't want them to think I didn't like girls." As he moved into high school, Jason even dated a few girls. "I had several that I was really close to, but it was more of a cover to make sure nobody knew that what I really wanted was my guy friends and spending time with them."

Jason never remembered a time when he chose homosexual behavior. "I just never liked girls," he recalled. "In fact, I find that I'm often most interested in what people would call 'girly' things." He used his image as an example: "My appearance is important to me, and I believe it's important to God, too." A typical week for Jason included a couple of trips to the gym, a haircut, getting his nails done, and going shopping. "It's really important that when I go out, people notice that I take care of myself," Jason explained. "I don't want them to think otherwise, and I think God cares about it too."

Over the years Jason's desire for friendships dominated his behavior. He lived a life full of deception. Just as he hid his secret passions from his guy and girl friends, he believed he could not share his struggle with either his parents or anyone at church. "I would always think, *If people figure out who I really am, I'll lose all my friends*." He went on to describe his predicament: "I never shared my struggle. I thought a lot of people would stop talking to me, and I would lose all the friends I had . . . so I didn't want to tell anybody at the church about this." Therefore, he often found himself living with various levels of deception at home, around friends, at school, and at church. It was not until after high school that he began active homosexual practices.

You can see how Jason's story contains key elements often identified with male homosexuality: a dominant mother, a passive father, early exposure to sexually explicit pictures or acts, and an inclination toward homosexual tendencies. It is certainly true that there are many potential factors contributing to a person's struggle with same-sex attraction.[1] People are complex, and their

---

[1] In this case, I counseled a male dealing with same-sex attraction. Factors contributing to same-sex attraction in females are often somewhat different. Some helpful resources regarding homosexuality (including potential

responses to their diverse life circumstances can be complex. The critical issue is how I consider Jason: Do I see him as the product of his biological makeup or his genetic code, the result of a poor relationship with his same-sex parent, the outcome of early sexual stimuli, or one fearing rejection by others due to low self-esteem? If I accept contemporary secular explanations for homosexuality as part of the cause, then I am ultimately accepting culture as the authority for understanding and helping Jason. *Or* I can take the perspective that the ultimate cause of Jason's homosexual behavior is his sinful heart and that all of these important pieces of data make up various significant influences or pressures to which his sinful heart responded.[2]

Counseling from Previous Experience

A second potential authority for the counselor is his own previous life experience. When a person hears Jason's story, similar stories may come to mind. Many personal experiences can cloud one's ability to counsel Jason, such as your own past—whether you have committed sexual sins or you have been sinned against sexually; whether others you know were engaged in sexual sin but never changed, such as counselees who said they were changed but then returned to their original sexual sins, and so on. If you are not aware of this potential authority, then you might counsel Jason from your own experience rather than from what the Bible

---

contributing factors to homosexual tendencies) include Kerby Anderson, *A Biblical Point of View on Homosexuality* (Eugene, OR: Harvest House, 2008); Joe Dallas, *When Homosexuality Hits Home: What to Do When a Loved One Says They're Gay* (Eugene, OR: Harvest House, 2004); David Powlison, "Sexual Sin and the Wider, Deeper Battle," *The Journal of Biblical Counseling* 24, no. 3 (Spring 2006): 30–36; and Edward T. Welch, "Homosexuality: Current Thinking and Biblical Guidelines," *The Journal of Biblical Counseling* 13, no. 3 (Spring 1995): 19–29. For additional material regarding the biblical view of sex and how to handle sexual temptation, see Joshua Harris, *Sex Is Not the Problem (Lust Is): Sexual Purity in a Lust-Saturated World* (Colorado Springs, CO: Multnomah, 2003); John Piper and Justin Taylor, eds., *Sex and the Supremacy of Christ* (Wheaton: Crossway, 2005).

[2] Homosexuality is always condemned in the Bible as sin. It is impossible to review the biblical data in this chapter, but using normal hermeneutical practices, each of the following verses declare homosexuality as a sin: Gen 19:1–27; Lev 18:22; 20:13; Judg 19:22–23; Rom 1:26–27; 1 Cor 6:9–10; 1 Tim 1:9–10; Jude 7.

presents as the true authority in his situation. Again, the goal is to catch any differences between your formal and functional authority or theology.

Counseling from Scriptural Knowledge

A third potential authority is scriptural knowledge. Obviously, considering the convictions of this book, Scripture must serve as the foundation and source of the counsel offered to Jason. However, beyond the issue of right and wrong, the answers are not always simple when it comes to homosexuality and the Bible. You may never have considered what the Bible teaches about homosexuality or sexual sins in general, especially regarding the potential for and process of change. It is important not to allow a lack of knowledge to influence your opportunity with Jason and to create a wrong functional authority in this situation. I would want any counselor to consider a few key passages and their implications before counseling Jason.

Your Opportunity—Ministry (Hebrews 13:17). This verse says, "Obey your leaders and submit to them, *for they keep watch over your souls* as those who will give an account, so that they can do this with joy and not with grief, for that would be unprofitable for you" (emphasis added). First, as a counselor (functioning as an extension of the local church and under the authority of its leadership), you must recognize that God has called you to be a guardian of Jason's soul. You have a great and weighty responsibility before God due to the spiritual direction you offer and the ministry decisions you make on behalf of those you counsel. What incredible accountability! God pays attention to the decisions made by Christians engaged in personal ministry! Think of it this way: God's wonderful plan for you always includes the person in front of you, whether Jason or someone else. He has given you the opportunity to speak into this person's life in a wise and godly way. Therefore, it is essential that you as a counselor carefully examine your heart to evaluate your attitude toward any individual God places in your ministry path. You are responsible for your response and advice to Jason.

Your Attitude—Humility (1 Corinthians 10:12–13). Each counselor is also wise to consider Paul's explanation of temptation: "No temptation has overtaken you except what is common to humanity. God is faithful, and He will not allow you to be tempted beyond what you are able, but with the temptation He will also provide a way of escape so that you are able to bear it." Paul declared that *no* temptation falls outside of the biblical category of *common* human experience. This is an essential reminder because, when faced with someone like Jason engaged in homosexual sin, it is easier to see his issues as *different* rather than *common*. In fact, the cultural perspective on many life problems (especially when mixed with our own personal experiences) tempts us to believe that many issues fall outside of this biblical category of "common to humanity." Paul helps us overturn our preconceived ideas regarding the problem or circumstance facing us. No matter how much I am tempted to believe that the person in front of me or the situation calling for my attention is *different* or *abnormal*, the Bible calls me back to a clear, biblical, and hopeful perspective. Paul reminds me that no matter how uncommon someone's story may sound to me, I must draw my conclusions within the biblical boundaries of *common human experience*.

Paul chose the term *peirasmos* in this text, which is translated "temptation." However, *peirasmos* is a neutral term, meaning either "temptation" or "trial." The context determines its emphasis. As a trial, this term may refer to any pressured situation one may face where ultimately the person chooses to glorify God (Jas 1:2–12). As a temptation, it means that one's heart has responded to any pressured situation in a way that involves temptation to sin (Jas 1:13–15). In either case the situation itself is the same. The difference is the individual's heart response. One individual responds by enduring the trial and glorifying God; the other individual responds by being lured and drawn away to sin. Here in 1 Cor 10:13, Paul used the general sense of the term. He emphasized that there is no pressured situation (which would also include the temptation to sexual sin or homosexuality) that falls outside the category of typical human experience (*anthropinos,* translated "common to humanity").

So how do you apply this biblical category of common temptation as well as the larger context of this passage to Jason's situation? You ought to view Jason as a person who faces temptations, just like every other individual. Jason definitely has responded in ungodly ways to his temptations—he has chosen sin. Yet we must guard against our own temptation to focus primarily on the nature of the sexual sin and thereby miss seeing it as the untamed result of a heart full of sexual lust. The greater context of 1 Cor 10 suggests that from God's vantage point committing sexual immorality is no more immoral than complaining (v. 10). For many of us, those guilty of sexual sin rank much differently from the average complainer in our church. Yet both sins fit within the biblical category of "common."

Further, when we fail to recognize the common thread running through Jason's sin and our own, we set ourselves up for failure: "So, whoever thinks he stands must be careful not to fall" (1 Cor 10:12). Counselors often respond poorly to those seeking help when we forget, even for a few moments, that we are equally susceptible to sin and that we must remain continually aware of our own hearts. The root of Jason's sexual sin is the same fundamental root threatening to sprout in every counselor's heart. Lingering too long on a revealing TV show, looking at an immodest picture online, imagining an inappropriate relationship, or taking a second look at an attractive guy or girl on the street are temptations for us all. Every single person engaged in personal ministry must heed this warning.

Your Hope—Change (1 Corinthians 6:9–11). Paul warns, "Don't you know that the unrighteous will not inherit God's kingdom? Do not be deceived: No sexually immoral people, idolaters, adulterers, or anyone practicing homosexuality [literally: *passive homosexual partners*, *active homosexual partners*], no thieves, greedy people, drunkards, verbally abusive people, or swindlers will inherit God's kingdom" (vv. 9–10). Paul highlighted the general behavior of unbelievers in order to emphasize how believers should act consistently with our position in Christ (see Rom 6:1–10). He gave a lengthy laundry list of sins that generally characterize an unbeliever rather than a believer. Although his was not an exhaustive list, Paul clearly declared these sins as he dealt with a great majority of the moral issues a counselor typically faces. Notice that Paul included sexually immoral people, adulterers, or anyone practicing homosexuality.

Paul does not finish his discussion here. He said, "And some of you *used* to be like this. But you were washed, you were sanctified, you were justified in the name of the Lord Jesus Christ and by the Spirit of our God" (v. 11, emphasis added). Paul understood the "common" element of sin and temptation. He knew that all kinds of sinners have been saved. Jason has hope because God's grace is powerful enough to take someone from being dead in sin to alive in Christ (Eph 2:1–10). It is this same powerful grace that gives any person enslaved to homosexual sin the hope of change. God's grace is grace unto change (Titus 2:11–15).

Your Approach—Kindness (2 Timothy 2:24–26). These verses say, "The Lord's slave must not quarrel, but must be gentle to everyone, able to teach, and patient, instructing his opponents with gentleness. Perhaps God will grant them repentance leading them to the knowledge of the truth. Then they may come to their senses and escape the Devil's trap, having been captured by him to do his will." Paul wrote these words to Timothy, his ministry protégé who was facing various ministry pressures. Paul instructed Timothy on how to minister well in the midst of these challenges. Notice the attitudes necessary for the Lord's servants (including counselors): not argumentative but rather patient, kind to everyone, striving to teach, and offering correction with humility. When dealing with the sin of homosexuality and navigating the great cultural and moral debates in society, it is easy for a counselor to judge Jason inaccurately and harshly. Instead, with self-control and kindness, we should desire to communicate the truths of the Bible with the love and grace the Bible itself requires.

In our first session Jason shared about the struggle he had with his church. He reported that his pastor "talks about homosexuals as perverts and people who are lovers of themselves." He later said, "Really, he [the pastor] just didn't care for them [homosexuals] and it sounded as though he would just kick me out of the church if he knew how I was struggling." Jason's experience is similar to another man I counseled, who said of his church, "The pastors handed me off and passed me on to other people as if I were a baton. They didn't seem comfortable with helping me and maybe not even comfortable talking to me." Of course, the counselor often hears only one side of the story, and someone struggling with homosexual desires will certainly be extremely sensitive to any remarks about homosexuality coming from the church. Nevertheless, why do Jason and many others who share his struggle perceive that they are being treated with such disdain? Often it is because some Christians make thoughtless remarks and use sarcasm to address this hot-button sin, never considering the impact of their remarks on those who may be embroiled in an intense battle. Many Christians are repulsed by homosexuality and see the sinner not only as broken but also disgusting and dismissible. The reaction of society at large has often shared this disgust—picking on homosexuals, mocking homosexual characteristics, and generally rejecting the homosexual as a "sissy," "mama's boy," "dyke," "faggot," and "queer." Jason and others like him find themselves with nowhere to go—they are as rejected in the church as they are in the locker room—so they turn to other homosexuals for love and acceptance. But Paul reminded us that ministers of the gospel are not qualified to serve as ministers of the gospel if we contribute to this harsh and unloving approach toward those who most need our message and our counsel.

Your Calling—Restoration (Galatians 6:1–5, 10). This is the final passage a counselor should consider before counseling Jason because this is where Paul presented the Christian community with a clear vision of the goal of counseling:

> Brothers, if someone is caught in any wrongdoing, you who are spiritual should restore such a person with a gentle spirit, watching out for yourselves so you also

> won't be tempted. Carry one another's burdens; in this way you will fulfill the law of Christ. For if anyone considers himself to be something when he is nothing, he deceives himself. But each person should examine his own work, and then he will have a reason for boasting in himself alone, and not in respect to someone else. For each person will have to carry his own load. . . . Therefore, as we have opportunity, we must work for the good of all, especially for those who belong to the household of faith.

The goal in counseling is always to work for the good of the counselee, and Paul declared that what is good is restoration, which refers to bringing a fellow believer back to a place of usefulness. It was a common word for fixing something that was broken or torn. This kind of restoration takes place when the counselor, with a gentle spirit, comes alongside the one in sin and helps carry the overwhelming baggage that we take on when we choose temporarily to enslave ourselves to sin and its consequences. At the same time the counselor must humbly evaluate his own heart to determine how he himself is doing in his efforts to live consistently with the gospel.

Galatians 6 orients the counselor toward the right goal: restoration. Restoration means that Jason would learn to live life with the ultimate purpose of pleasing God through the power of the gospel (2 Cor 5:9). This ultimate purpose is vital because, if the counselor is not careful, both he and Jason can end up with the sole functional goal of eradicating homosexual desires and cultivating heterosexual desires. However, the counselor should begin the counseling process with the understanding that God's goal is that Jason return to a place of usefulness for God's purposes, which means living life in the Spirit (Gal 5:13–26) and learning to say no to the temptations of the crucified flesh with its passions and desires (Gal 5:24). This means that both the formal and functional goal of counseling (in any situation) is for the believer to glorify God regardless of the *type* of temptation that needs to be overcome.

Once again the counselor must carefully consider his own attitude toward homosexuality and similar sins before beginning the counseling process. As I began with Jason, I could not let contemporary culture, personal experiences with others, a limited knowledge of Scripture, a lack of understanding about Jason's specific sins, failure to see my own susceptibility to sin, or an underestimating of the possibility of real change keep me from ministering God's Word effectively to this struggling soul.

Jason's Struggle

You already know most of Jason's story. He was a churchgoing 25-year-old from a divorced family where dad was passive, mom was dominant, and stepdad was absent. He stumbled across homosexual pornography at age seven and spent his junior high and high school years hiding his homosexual desires from everyone around him. After high school he began expressing his homosexuality in physical immorality, yet he maintained his secrecy, afraid that he would be rejected by his church community if the darkness of his heart were ever exposed. He came to me scared and confused, and only at the urging of a friend.

As I got to know Jason, he began explaining more of his current struggles. He shared that he often fantasized about guys he saw when he was in public places. "I struggle with fantasizing and thinking about friends I know or even just people I see at the coffee shop or at the mall." He further explained that the more he visited certain public places, the easier it was for him to quickly survey a room and "know" who was or was not "like" him. "When I go somewhere, I know that I can just take a glimpse around the room and kind of see who's who and potentially spot the people who are just like me—and I can tell if they're looking at me. Usually they smile. It happens a lot at the gym and the coffee shop, and particular places at the mall." Jason continued to explain that this kind of self-trained intuition was one way he would often meet people. Another method was through the Internet in chat rooms (or similar places). Often these conversations would end with an agreement to meet somewhere in public and talk about their history, backgrounds, likes and dislikes, and how they came to this point in life. This process of meeting other potential partners through surveying the crowd at specific public spots or surfing the Internet (in particular chat rooms) is often referred to as "cruising." In Jason's case he was looking for long-term relationships of acceptance and love. In many cases, though, it was just a one-day or multiple-day experience. Jason explained his desires: "I feel loved when other guys are around me and pay attention to me, and we talk with each other about things that we both care about. I just love being around people who are just like me."

Jason also described a life driven by feelings. Even as he helped me understand his concept of God, his conceptualization was a colorful illustration of his feeling-orientation:

> One thing that really perplexes me is the way God is talked about in church, and he is willing to do so much for us in sending Christ and he cares about us so much. I feel like I care for my friends and the guys I am attracted to because I care for them like God cares for me. I wonder why my feelings are wrong. If God loves us and I feel loved when I am around another guy and we spend time together and I enjoy their company and it makes me happy, then why is it wrong if God wants me to be happy and have joy?

Jason understood how he felt and was allowing those feelings to guide his decision-making process. However, he did not know how to evaluate those feelings and ideas about God biblically.

The longer I talked with Jason, the more I recognized that his most powerful temptations arose on nights when he had spent the day alone. Returning home after a long day, he would sit alone and become angry, then down, and then he would stop caring about what happened next. To feel better he might choose a trip to the mall or a visit to an online chatroom; but either way he would go searching for some kind of connection with another guy to make himself feel better.

Like any other human being, Jason had a blend of thoughts, feelings, desires, and behaviors that needed to be considered in light of the gospel. If I were to focus solely on his homosexual desires, I would miss the greater whole. The temptation when counseling someone like Jason is to see the blinking neon light of homosexuality as *the* issue and to miss the *many* issues seething in his heart. But Jason's fundamental problem was much bigger than an attraction to guys.

As I began to listen, I started making a list of issues to address as I sought to minister the gospel to this professed brother in Christ. Among other issues, I wrote:

- lives for his feelings
- craves attention from others
- longs for affection, affirmation, relationship, acceptance
- some rebellion against the legalism of his church and against his parents
- anger

As you scan this initial list, you will notice a striking absence: the sin of homosexuality is not even on the list yet. This is because it is one issue among many. Although it will be necessary to pay particular attention to it, the issue of homosexuality is no different from any of the other issues in Jason's life. Therefore, counsel to Jason must be able to address his experience of life as he knows it—dealing honestly about current research, the culture, his past, his behaviors; moreover, counsel must also in grace recognize that Jason needs a spiritual friend full of compassion and biblically sound advice who can help reorient Jason to understand his life through the lens of the gospel.

Jason's Process

Jason was involved in high-handed and persistent sin. It is good and right to question whether Jason was a true believer—not because he struggled with homosexual behavior but because often his behavior (whether homosexual or not) was willful and persistent. In the first session I had asked Jason about his relationship with Jesus Christ. He professed to be a believer in Christ and could articulate the reasons. Therefore, I took him at his word and assumed that he was a struggling believer like so many other Christians. Ultimately his growth in Christlikeness proved this assumption to be correct, though there were bumps and questions along the way.

Counseling someone like Jason is not an event but a process. Jason had heard plenty of platitudes, and he had heard the law of God his entire life. He needed counsel (and a counselor) that reflected the thoughtful sensitivity of 1 Thess 5:14: "And we exhort you, brothers: warn those who are irresponsible, comfort the discouraged, help the weak, be patient with everyone." A main goal of mine was to be patient throughout the process. There would be times to warn and admonish, times to comfort and encourage, and times simply to help Jason through a particularly long day of struggle. Regardless, the road with Jason would require patience as we sought together to strengthen his ability to honor God in the midst of his daily battles. As you read about the process we walked through, keep in mind that these are only the big-picture steps we took together. Each primary concept or passage does not reflect a particular exchange or an individual session but lengthy conversations and multiple sessions. This long-term approach is mandatory in the long walk toward godliness because the road of leaving homosexual behavior is not a nine-to-twelve-week road.

Normalizing the Abnormal

My first session with Jason was tense. My goal was to demonstrate that I was genuinely interested in him as a professing believer, and I respected his courageous step to seek help. Jason expected to be dismissed by me as having a sin that was gross. I wanted him to know that I viewed him as a fellow struggler who needed God's grace to change. The primary question in my mind was this: What is Jason's experience of his current problem?

There were many angles from which to approach Jason, but my hope was to address the broader battle of what was currently gripping his heart. Finding an accurate aerial perspective would require many questions and extended listening; developing the details of someone's story and how he is currently responding to life pressures always takes time. As I listened to Jason's story, it became apparent that he did not believe his experiences fit within the broader category of a Christian's typical life experience. So before we ended our first session, I reviewed 1 Cor 10:13 with him in an effort to help him make sense of these things. Jason was aware that something was broken in his life—and it was him! I wanted him to have hope in the fact that although he felt so broken, he was actually no more broken than anyone else. His sinfulness did not relegate him to the fringes and the margins of humanity. Rather, his experience was part of common human experience. The good news for Jason was that God desires to demonstrate the glories of his marvelous grace and his never-ending faithfulness by redeeming and restoring broken people.

As I sought to normalize what Jason considered abnormal, two particular emphases seemed to resonate with him. First, he could appreciate Paul's encouraging words offered to those facing seemingly inescapable pressures: God would be faithful to help Jason by providing "a way of escape" so that Jason would be "able to *bear* it" (1 Cor 10:13, emphasis added). The idea of bearing a burden emphasizes a process of perseverance. I wanted Jason to know that we were not looking for God to work some kind of magic that would make his significant pressures disappear overnight. Instead, God promised that throughout the long journey of growth, he would provide grace equal to every challenge. So if Jason were willing, I was committing to walk the path with him and to help him through the process of bearing this burden.

The second truth that resonated with Jason was the realization that God does not promise to alleviate our pressures. Instead, God promises to be faithful in the midst of our pressures. This truth is significant because it enables us to define counseling "success" in light of reality. Certainly, it was natural for Jason to set his sights on eradicating his struggle with same-sex attraction. Yet whether or not his temptation completely disappeared, by God's grace Jason could obtain the necessary tools for making it through the temptation. Whenever and however he was tempted, Jason would have the strong help of a faithful God and the undying power of the gospel of Christ.

Jason was willing to walk this journey with me and also agreed to take some practical steps to cultivate growth between sessions.[3] I gave him some purposeful assignments for the first week. (1) Memorize 1 Cor 10:13 by writing it on a card and reviewing it five times each day. (2) Fill your mind with the statement "God's grace is up to the challenge" by writing it down and reviewing it 20 times each day. (3) Begin reading 2 Corinthians 5 and write down preliminary thoughts about what it means and how it applies to your situation.[4] (4) Begin a temptation journal where you record each instance when you are tempted so that you can begin to discern bigger themes in your life and struggle.

For his temptation journal I wanted Jason to become a good journalist, observing and investigating his own heart so that we could use his recorded insights in a strategic battle against his sin and temptation. I asked him to answer questions like these:

- What was going on when you struggled?
- When did you struggle?
- Where were you?
- What were you thinking?
- What were you feeling?
- How did you respond?
- Did you resist?

---

[3] Not all of the homework I gave Jason appears in this chapter. In a message titled "Homework That Changes Lives," presented at the NANC Annual Conference, 2006, Randy Patton teaches that the counselor should begin counseling with the end in mind and suggests the following six categories of homework for each session. These helpful biblical disciplines should be cultivated as long-term commitments in the counselee's life: (1) daily Scripture reading, (2) Scripture memory, (3) theological reading, (4) regular church attendance and involvement, (5) serving others, and (6) consistent prayer.

[4] The counselor could assign a passage the week before and then discuss it at the next session (like I did with Jason) or assign the passage *after* discussing it in a session. I often assign the passage prior to discussing it in order to get a person thinking on their own. In our review the following week, I make sure the person understands the context of the passage and the specific meaning of the verses in question before having him share what he learned and asking him to unpack its implications for his particular situation.

- If you resisted, what were you thinking about?
- How did you resist?
- If you did not resist, what were you thinking about?
- How did you respond to your failure?

The Gospel and the Love of Christ

After hearing Jason's story in our first session, the topic for our second session was clear: the love of Christ seen in the gospel. We began to consider the implications of this good news for Jason and his struggle. He had read 2 Corinthians 5 during the previous week, and we discussed what he thought it meant along with its implications for his circumstances. After putting the passage in its larger context and sharing with Jason its specific meaning, I focused our attention on three key verses. I hoped to help him begin to grasp a much bigger context for his life—the specific purpose of pleasing and honoring God. The only way this would happen was for Jason to understand the centrality of God's love, seen through the work of Christ in the gospel.

2 Corinthians 5:21. This verse says, "He made the One who did not know sin to be sin for us, so that we might become the righteousness of God in Him." Paul explained the heart of the gospel message: God placed the sin of mankind on Jesus (including Jason's homosexual sins) so that mankind could be forgiven (including Jason) and could enjoy a restored relationship with God. God treated Jesus as if he had sinned Jason's sins, and God treats Jason as if he had lived Jesus' perfect life of righteousness. I went on to explain how God imputes the righteousness of Christ to the believer. I wanted Jason to begin to comprehend the incredible love of God demonstrated by Jesus on the cross.

Jason and I also discussed his previous week's homework. He had more questions about 1 Cor 10:13 and had been encouraged by the constant reminder of God's grace and faithfulness throughout the week. He had also begun his temptation journal which we took some time to review. His journal was specific for a few days and then trailed off toward the weekend when he had embraced temptation and gone cruising on the Internet. He visited the coffee shop and met with a man with whom he had previously interacted with online, but by God's grace they did not go anywhere together. The weekend's struggle provided a great opportunity to discuss the other two key verses from 2 Corinthians 5.

2 Corinthians 5:9. This verse says, "Therefore, whether we are at home or away, we make it our aim to be pleasing to Him." The goal for Paul and for every believer is to aim at pleasing God. Jason's temptation journal was helpful at this point because it allowed us to hone in on his specific temptations and to review whether his guiding purpose in those moments was to please God or to please himself. For Paul, the compelling motivation to please God came from embracing the love of Christ in the gospel. "For Christ's love compels us, since we have reached this conclusion: If One died for all, then all died. And He died for all so that those who live should no longer live for themselves, but for the One who died for them and was raised" (2 Cor 5:14–15). As Jason learned to consider Christ's love for him, such recognition would serve as a strong motivator for a life of obedience to this One who died for him. Clearly, Jason's weekend struggle came not from a desire to please Christ out of grateful obedience; rather, his desire to please himself dominated his thoughts and actions.

Nevertheless, Jason's sin over the weekend reestablished his need to live in recognition of the gospel. He desperately needed to adopt Paul's life purpose as his own—to conduct himself in a manner well-pleasing to God. I tried to communicate to Jason that this restored lifestyle would not result from simple teeth-gritting efforts but would arise from his recognition of his righteous status in Christ due to Christ's sacrifice on the cross.

Before he left our second session, I gave Jason some more practical steps to take during the week. I wanted him to continue his helpful temptation journal and to go deeper into 2 Corinthians 5, recording his observations and thoughts as he read. I also had him start reading *A Gospel Primer for Christians* by Milton Vincent,[5] which would continue to saturate his mind and heart in

[5] Milton Vincent, *A Gospel Primer for Christians: Learning to See the Glories of God's Love* (Bemidji, MN: Focus, 2008).

the glories of Christ's work on his behalf. Jason also needed to make a serious structural change. From his temptation journal we had discerned that the coffee shop, the gym, and the Internet were all places where Jason was tempted most severely. We determined together that it would be wisest for him to quit going to the gym or the coffee shop and to install an Internet filter. I explained that these structural changes were not designed to please God simply by Jason performing them; instead, such changes would function as guardrails helping him keep his new commitments.

2 Corinthians 5:17. When Jason showed up for week three, he was visibly down. Although he had just committed to avoiding the coffee shop, the gym, and the Internet, he had done all three. "I wanted to do what was right," he confessed, "but I felt like I couldn't." Early in the week he had been contacted by an old friend who was visiting from out of town. Jason had shared a relationship with this friend in the past. He wanted to go out. One thing led to another, with Jason failing to follow through on his commitments. Again, Jason's sovereign God was allowing these circumstances in order to highlight the remaining key verse in our gospel-saturated chapter of Scripture: "Therefore, if anyone is in Christ, he is a new creation; old things have passed away, and look, new things have come" (2 Cor 5:17). This verse helped Jason realize that God had given him a new heart at salvation, and he could please God with this new heart. We once again discussed how God desired to change him from the inside out, and God had already started that process when Jason was born again. The difficulty Jason was facing was not the impossibility of earning God's gracious salvation but the challenge of living consistently with the salvation God had already worked in his heart.

It was a joy to help Jason recognize that God was changing him one step at a time and that God's grace had actually been up to the challenge, even though he did not feel like it in the midst of his temptation. It was necessary to remind Jason that his goal was Christlikeness and that his life direction was to please God—to live like the "new" had really come. Despite his setback, if he would continue the journey of growth as a believer clothed in the righteousness of Christ, progress would come. Although Jason and I were both disappointed, it was essential that we not become discouraged with his failure. Rather, we needed to remember that Jesus had paid for Jason's sin the previous week, and Jason still stood forgiven in Christ. Because Jason could see that growth would be slow, I also wanted him to remember that on some days being pointed in the right direction is as important as actual progress.

For homework following this third session, I asked Jason to continue reading Milton Vincent's *A Gospel Primer* because resetting his mind's orientation toward the gospel would require a lengthy process. I also encouraged him to read 1 Cor 6:9–11 and to write down his initial thoughts about its meaning and application. We also created a stronger practical plan to keep him from getting online or visiting the coffee shop and the gym. Finally, Jason would also begin participating in a specific small group at church and would discuss his need of accountability with the group mentors.

Identity

When Jason initially came to me, he was wondering why his life felt so disconnected and disordered. He was afraid to share his story because he feared rejection and saw himself as broken. He did not identify with Christ or with the church, the body of Christ. He primarily identified with the guys he met online or while cruising his favorite public places. Even in his speech Jason often used terms like "us," "we," and "them." He said, "In a sense we are outsiders to the public since we share a common bond in that we like other men." He later said, "I just love being around these types of people who are just like me." These are just a few of the instances where Jason identified strongly with others who practiced homosexuality. His self-perception is not uncommon. Often those wrestling with same-sex attraction or who have chosen a homosexual lifestyle see themselves as categorically different from family, childhood friends, coworkers, and church members. In many ways Jason is right. When he told his family about his struggle several years ago, his dad began viewing him as strange and different, and his mom wondered how she failed him. Early on his church also made clear through hurtful statements in sermons and insinuations in casual talk just how disgusting and unwelcome a homosexual was in the church community.

It was important for me to replant Jason's self-perceived identity in Jesus where it belongs. In this replanting process, 1 Cor 6:9–10 became helpful to Jason: "Don't you know that the unrighteous will not inherit God's kingdom? Do not be deceived: No sexually immoral people, idolaters, adulterers, or anyone practicing homosexuality, no thieves, greedy people, drunkards, verbally abusive people, or swindlers will inherit God's kingdom. And some of you *used to be like this*. But you were washed, you were sanctified, you were justified in the name of the Lord Jesus Christ and by the Spirit of our God" (emphasis added). Jason took a major step forward when he recognized the massive shift Paul highlighted in the passage. Although Jason may have been associated with practicing homosexuals as an unbeliever, now his identity was in Christ as a washed, sanctified, justified person.

It was exciting to hear Jason express how he understood and was encouraged by this new concept and determinative identity: "Just like I used to watch other guys who were like me and figured out how they looked, what they did, how they smiled, and how they carried themselves, you're basically telling me that now I do the same thing as I look at Christ and see myself primarily as a follower of Christ." *Yes*. God was constructing a critical foundation for growth in Jason's life. Although Jason needed to change his actions significantly, he needed much more than behavior modification. Jason needed to learn about and embrace his justified and sanctified position in Christ. With this in mind, we spent some time in Romans 6 and 8 to clarify his spiritual position in Christ and how that union changed everything for him with regard to the power of sin (broken) and the penalty of sin (paid). We also considered the power of the Spirit which would enable him to change as a result of his position in Christ (Eph 1:19–23; 2:10; 3:16). To continue marinating his mind in these groundbreaking truths, I also asked Jason to begin reading *Living the Cross Centered Life* by C. J. Mahaney.[6]

Heart and Desires

From our first meeting, Jason and I began discussing the biblical concept of the heart. I had intentionally introduced the concept to him as early as possible because it is such an essential human element in his long-term ability to grow in Christ. Jason also had behaviors that needed a radical transformation from day one, but altering his behaviors alone would produce a hypocrite as long as Jason did not comprehend the heart and its central role in living for God's glory. He did not know that changing behavior alone is *behavior modification*, yet heart change leading to behavior change is *sanctification*. When we finally reached verses that specifically unpack the inner workings of the heart, Jason was excited since I had been leading him along this path. He had several questions ready for me. I had assigned him to reflect on Mark 7:20–23 where Jesus said, "What comes out of a person—that defiles him. For from within, out of people's hearts, come evil thoughts, sexual immoralities, thefts, murders, adulteries, greed, evil actions, deceit, promiscuity, stinginess, blasphemy, pride, and foolishness. All these evil things come from within and defile a person." Jason asked, "Is this why you told me in the first week that in many ways, you and I are the same?" I agreed and explained to him that the pressures that are common to humanity intersect with the heart—every person's heart—and expose it.

Jason was beginning to understand why I had so often referred to his behavior and then referenced his heart. He left this particular week of counseling greatly encouraged and full of hope that he was finally getting it. He even mentioned a separate issue at work: his reaction to a coworker demonstrated what was going on in his heart at the time. I was also encouraged and pleased with his temptation journal, which he was still completing carefully

---

[6] C. J. Mahaney, *Living the Cross Centered Life: Keeping the Gospel the Main Thing* (Colorado Springs: Multnomah, 2006).

and honestly. Moving forward, I asked him to begin reading and contemplating Jas 1:1–18.

A Setback

The following week we had to skip our regular counseling session because of a work conflict. Because we were now weeks into the counseling process, I thought the missed week might be difficult for Jason but that the many truths invested in his mind would still have an opportunity to bear fruit. Through a text message, I let him know that I was available if something came up.

When Jason returned the following week, it seemed like the wheels had come off. He arrived discouraged and with a poor attitude. When I greeted him and asked how it was going, he started crying and said that it was no use trying to change. As I asked some probing questions, it came to light that when he had left our previous session two weeks before, he thought everything was going so well that it couldn't hurt to visit one of his favorite stores in the mall. As he walked in, he was immediately checked out by another guy. Jason pretended not to see him looking, but inside he burned with excitement over the attention he was receiving. He went about his business in the mall, but he could not stop thinking about the attention he had received. Eventually he created a reason to go back through the same area. This time he got closer just to see if he would receive the same kind of treatment. He did, and this time the night ended in physical sin. What was worse, Jason was concerned that he may have picked up an STD in the process.

We both wept together as we considered the devastation of sin and how easy it is to be ensnared. Yet once again, in the providence of God, Jason's sin provided the perfect opportunity to discuss the passage he had just been considering. His circumstances over the past several weeks allowed for an excellent illustration of the principle laid out in James: "No one undergoing a trial should say, 'I am being tempted by God.' For God is not tempted by evil, and He himself doesn't tempt anyone. But each person is tempted when he is drawn away and enticed by his own evil desires. Then after desire has conceived, it gives birth to sin, and when sin is fully grown, it gives birth to death" (1:13–15). I had already told Jason that the term James uses for "trials/temptations" was the same term that appeared in 1 Cor 10:13 regarding the trials/temptations "common to humanity." Now I explained to him that his experience in the mall was a significant pressure, though one that he had brought on himself. James teaches that when we are in a pressure-packed circumstance, we have a choice to make: either we can glorify God in the temptation, or we can succumb to our desires and sin. James makes clear that the determining factor in this decision is always one's controlling desire.

To clarify further, we looked back in chapter 1 where James has already taught these trial-laden Jewish Christians that God allows them to face pressure in order to grow in them the pieces of character which God knows they are missing (1:2–4). In the same way, God would provide the best possible situation (like the man who made eyes with Jason) to help Jason grow in godliness. If Jason was controlled by a desire to please God, then he would respond to the moment of temptation with self-control. But if his controlling desire was for the attention and affection of other guys, he would respond with lustful pursuits. Choices are determined by the heart's treasure (Luke 6:45). Whatever Jason desired most and therefore worshipped in the moment would be the person or the object that would influence his decision to resist temptation and grow or to embrace temptation and suffer the consequences.[7]

This lesson was relevant for so many different issues in Jason's life. It helped Jason see that his sexual sin was just that—sin. In God's eyes it was a desire exercising control that it should not exercise, no different from any other desire that exercises control of someone's heart. Desires for attention, affection, influence, or relationship could be just as sinfully controlling. Where Jason

[7] This perspective differs greatly from the world system. If Jason were to accept the world's view of the heart and homosexuality, then it would be his biology/genetics, his family background, and his early exposure to pornography that would be cast as the controlling factors in his homosexual tendencies. But the Bible presents these same events not as the final determiners of Jason's actions but only as factors that exercise influence (temptation). The final determiner is Jason's ruling desire, or whatever exercises functional control in his life.

should have been controlled by the love of Christ that would then motivate him to love God and his neighbor, he instead used his time and his energy to satisfy his sinful lust.

Casting this next week as a week of growth, I asked Jason to spend time considering Jas 4:1–10, which teaches that competing desires are at war within the believer. Since Jason's desires (whether good or evil) would end up holding functional control over his heart, it was essential for him to recognize this battle. When someone does not get what he wants, that person has a choice either to accept what God has given as better (see Jas 1:17) or to fight to get what he wants (Jas 4:1–2). The choice is an issue of control, as well as an issue of worship. Jesus is clear that a person can only serve one sovereign at a time: "No one can be a slave of two masters, since either he will hate one and love the other, or be devoted to one and despise the other. You cannot be slaves of God and of money" (Matt 6:24).

However, Jason could find good news in the book of James: "'God resists the proud, but gives grace to the humble.' Therefore, submit to God" (Jas 4:6–7). The proud want their own way and are unwilling to accept God's plan as best in any difficult circumstance. They are unwilling to rejoice in the pressures that are designed to grow them into Christlikeness (1:2–4), rather than choosing to believe that God should give them exactly what they want. When he does not, they do whatever it takes to get it (4:2–6). Instead, James implored believers to be humble and to let God's grace provide strength in the midst of trials. I encouraged Jason to recognize his dependence on God's grace and to ensure that what was ruling him was nothing less than "Your will be done" (just like Christ). As he left this latest counseling session (after his hard fall into sexual sin), Jason seemed encouraged. This had been a difficult lesson about the deceitfulness of his heart, and it would not be the last. Amazingly, however, Jason's gracious God was using even his sin to help him learn and grow in Christ.

Other Key Areas of Growth

With each new piece of the puzzle, Jason was learning not just about same-sex attraction and homosexuality but about embracing the gospel and its implications and living life to God's glory, regardless of the particular desires that warred for control in his heart. As time went on, I addressed several additional areas of needed growth.

Love. Love was no small issue for Jason. He deeply desired to feel loved. He longed for affection and a true sense of belonging. Early on as we discussed 2 Corinthians 5, we had worked on understanding and appreciating the love of Christ. As counseling progressed, we further unpacked the true meaning of love as reflected in the person of Jesus in 1 John 3 and Eph 3:14–21. Jason then began to see how the love of Christ served as the model which should dictate his own love for others. I urged him to find ways to selflessly serve others in and through his church small group.

Walk. The Christian life is a walk. Paul makes clear that God desires the believer to walk worthy in unity, in love, in light, and in wisdom (Ephesians 4–5). Jason did not initially understand the dichotomy between what he wanted and what God wanted. He had been appropriately disappointed by many professing followers of Christ and needed to reconsider his everyday conduct as a proclaimed disciple of Jesus. He needed to reevaluate (1) the temptations around him, (2) his response to loving accountability, (3) his patterns of self-deception, and (4) his opportunities to love and serve others. As we worked on the daily discipline of living for God's glory, we carefully unpacked how to recognize and flee temptation (Rom 13:11–14; Proverbs 4). During this time Jason also read and considered *The Joy of Fearing God* by Jerry Bridges.[8]

Past. Up to this point in his life, Jason had not only sinned against many others but had also been sinned against by many—including many in the church. As part of the counseling process, Jason learned to view his past in light of Rom 8:28–29. Together we drew up a list of people he needed to forgive and people from

---

[8] Jerry Bridges, *The Joy of Fearing God* (Colorado Springs: WaterBrook, 1997).

whom he needed to seek forgiveness. If I were counseling Jason today, I would use Steve Viars's book *Putting Your Past in Its Place: Moving Forward in Freedom and Forgiveness*.[9] This book provides much-needed teaching for believers to view their past rightly—both in areas where we have sinned against others and where we have been sinned against. The book also contains a helpful chart to help strugglers see what kind of steps they should take to please God.

Jason's Progress

I still have the privilege of working with Jason but now as a brother and friend in Christ more than as a counselee. I wish I could say that my friend has never struggled since the occasions recounted in this chapter, but that is not the case. Yet I do rejoice in the fact that he has not fallen into any physical relationships (temporary or permanent), and I remind myself that true progress in this life is not final victory but steady gains.

When Jason's struggles reappear, they usually follow a period of long, hard days at work without much interaction with other believers. The evening times can still catch him off guard if he is not careful. He does go to the mall occasionally and will visit a different coffee shop from time to time. But where and when he struggles, he shares it with his small group. He has found loving acceptance that does not compromise and a joy-filled life as he has connected more personally with his church. His deceitful life has been replaced with an open and vulnerable relationship with his small group, which keeps him accountable as he shares his temptations; the accountability even extends to *how* he shares his temptations.

Jason has also grown in his understanding of the gospel and in his love for Christ. In a recent conversation I asked him how his struggle was going. To my delight we talked for 30 minutes as he expressed many different pressured-filled situations, but same-sex

---

[9] Stephen Viars, *Putting Your Past in Its Place: Moving Forward in Freedom and Forgiveness* (Eugene, OR: Harvest House, 2011).

attraction never came up. It was not even on his mind as one of his most pressing struggles, and I sensed no need to bring it up either.

Once again, homosexual desires were just one issue among many for Jason. Yes, the practice of homosexuality is wretched, destructive, hurtful to others, and filled with health risks. I am not minimizing either the sin or its devastating effects on the sinner and those he sins against. What I want you to hear is not that homosexuality is *less* of a sin but that homosexuality is *another* sin—one among many. Jesus Christ died on the cross for those who engage in homosexual sins, just as he died to pay the penalty for gossips, complainers, and speeders.

When we stop to minister to someone like Jason, we must be vigilant to see his sin for what it really is—not what culture teaches, not what our previous life experience suggests, and not what a limited scriptural understanding tempts us to believe. Jason is a fellow struggler in need of the powerful message of the gospel, just like his counselor who desperately needs the power of the gospel. The reality is that every one of the issues surrounding Jason's life could be equally true of heterosexuals. Do you think the average heterosexual has ever been sinned against? Lives for his feelings? Craves attention from others? Longs for attention, affirmation, relationship, and acceptance? Reacts against the legalism of his church or his parents? Wrestles with anger? Of course—all our temptations are common to humanity.

Both the homosexual and the heterosexual are worshippers whose most fundamental need is humbly to embrace and serve the only true, real, merciful, loving God and Savior, instead of serving the false gods that war for our affections. May God give you and me the wisdom to grow in the midst of our own struggles and so be equipped to minister well to the next Jason.

Chapter 10

"Julie" and Addictions and Adultery

Robert D. Jones

What did I fear most when I became a lead pastor at age 26? It was not the fear of speaking before a crowd, shepherding people 40 years older than me, sharing the gospel, or leading an elder or deacon meeting. While these tasks challenged me as a young man, they produced no major consternation. Instead, what I feared most was facing a difficult counseling situation, the kind addressed by the biblical counseling contributors in this book.

In one sense my concern was unavoidable. Based on Scripture, I believed that my pastoral calling included counseling—that a shepherd must shepherd his members through their fears, conflicts, despair, sinful habits, and a host of other problems. I did not believe that God freed me simply to refer my struggling sheep to others, especially if their counsel would not center on Jesus and arise from Scripture. I could not dodge my duties to shepherd my people biblically. So I entered my pastorate with both a God-given command to counsel and a lingering fear about counseling the hard cases.

Hard cases, of course, come in many shapes and sizes. Some counseling scenarios are difficult due to the presence of bizarre behavior. Pastors may be perplexed by people acting in seemingly indecipherable ways—like manic or schizophrenic behaviors. The pastor's response can range from curiosity to discomfort to feeling downright spooked. Other cases are tough because they come with a psychiatric label attached, one with medical-sounding language that seems too technical or mysterious for the average pastor. From his seminary days he might remember the Greek aorist tense or Jesus' hypostatic union, but "bipolar" or "borderline personality" disorders appear to go beyond his training. Ministers unaccustomed to such jargon can feel stymied. Still other cases scare pastors because they feature entrenched sin patterns like pornography, complex relational dynamics like adultery, or life-dominating addictions like alcohol abuse.

The counseling case I want to share with you was hard for a number of reasons. First, the situation combined a host of these taxing components in one case. Second, I encountered it relatively early in my ministry when I was not accustomed to dealing with the kind of complex problems exhibited in the case. Third, the case was full of surprising developments. As I began, I believed it would be a fairly straightforward instance of marriage counseling. As the weeks and months progressed, however, I was shocked to discover how this seemingly straightforward situation quickly spun into the complexities of alcohol addiction, adultery, and persistent patterns of rebellion on the part of a wife and mother. These layered complexities created another complicating factor—a prolonged period of counseling. The case took over two years from start to finish.

Throughout the length and intricacy of this case, my own learning curve was steep. The story still stands out in my mind as a testimony to God's grace because I learned so much as I saw God use my imperfect counsel, and I observed the power of God in the lives of one of his daughters who changed in spite of her own efforts to run from his grace.

Julie's Background

A job transfer led Nate and Julie[1] to our area from the Midwest. Both were college educated and in their early thirties.

[1] All names and identifying details have been changed, and many components in this story are composites from other cases. Further, while much of my

They had been married for eight years when I met them. Traveling with two young children and one on the way had made the move itself stressful, but now their greater problem was homesickness. They both greatly missed their friends and family and longed to return home.

Nate and Julie were committed Christians, and their search for a faithful church led them to our congregation where they quickly joined and found a home. Since they had no relationships in the area, the fellowship of Christian brothers and sisters proved indispensable in their lives—and would later prove indispensable in counseling. Earlier in their marriage they had suffered a serious church split which left them cautious about church participation but also hungry for caring, authentic fellowship. Their most recent church experience had been legalistic and theologically shallow, so they came to our church lacking doctrinal depth without an understanding of the deep riches of God's grace.

My relationship with Nate and Julie began through informal church activities. My wife, Lauren, and others provided meals and babysitting when their third child was born. As we got to know them, Lauren and I began to sense some marital tension between them. Julie was also struggling in her relationship with the Lord and in her role as a wife, mother, and homemaker. Because of these concerns, I offered to spend some time with them in an effort to help. Nate was immediately receptive. Julie was cautious but willing.

The Initial Stage: "Normal" Counseling with Little Success

We first met for counseling in October of that year. In setting up the session, both had expressed a desire for biblical counseling. They wanted to grow spiritually and strengthen their marriage. Following my typical pattern for marriage counseling, I asked

---

counseling with Nate and Julie focused on their marriage, this chapter focuses mostly on my work with Julie, both in joint sessions (with Nate) and individual sessions (without Nate). Even the joint sessions were focused mainly on Julie. It was chiefly her behavior that made this case so difficult.

Nate and Julie to allow Lauren to join us along with their small group leader, Todd, and his wife, Jan. In our opening sessions we spent substantial time getting to know Nate and Julie, learning their backgrounds and asking about their present struggles.

As we talked together, Julie revealed a broad spectrum of spiritual, physical, marital, and family issues. She indicated that these were "lifelong" problems, though the marriage issues had begun about five years ago after their first three years of marriage. Julie shared a long list of stressors: "life, anxiety, depression, perfectionism, being in control of situations." She described herself as "overwhelmingly stressed out." Julie also had a history of psychiatric diagnoses and was taking several different psychoactive medications to treat depression, anxiety, and bipolar disorder. To summarize, four key categories of information arose from both our first session and a precounseling form Julie filled out.

Julie's Relationship with God and Her Neglect of Spiritual Disciplines

Unfortunately these two were virtually synonymous for Julie. She measured her spiritual status by the number of "quiet times" she observed. She spoke clearly about wanting to "develop spiritual disciplines" in her life—especially "daily time in the Word." She had enjoyed more consistent Bible reading years ago. The deterioration of her zeal for God's Word and the decline in her devotional habits greatly troubled her. She attended church regularly, but she usually failed to spend time alone with the Lord. Perhaps her most troubling comment was her admission that she was "afraid to be alone with God." I immediately recalled an insight from one of my biblical counseling professors: Most counseling problems reflect a distorted view of God and a deficient relationship with Christ.

I talked with both Julie and Nate at length about their commitment to Christ, and I determined they were followers of Jesus, though with opposite personalities and differing levels of zeal and maturity. Nate was disciplined, steady, and zealous in his faith. At times he could be unaccommodating, critical, and intimidating.

Julie ultimately manifested evidence of faith in Christ and submission to his Word, but her Christian life was random, sporadic, and fearful. Nate was rationalistic, thought in black-and-white categories, and could argue skillfully. Julie was emotionally driven and sought to avoid arguments with her husband. These differences exacerbated their marital conflicts. Nate's forcefulness intimidated Julie; Julie's cowering frustrated Nate. Nate's ability to accomplish tasks shamed Julie; Julie's underperformance irritated Nate.

Julie's Psychological/Psychiatric Problems

Julie also reported problems with "depression and anxiety even before high school." She wanted to be weaned off of her psychiatric medications which had been prescribed by different physicians. She also acknowledged being a perfectionist who nitpicked her own work and the work of others, maintaining unrealistic standards that led to a sense of failure and guilt. "When I fail, I usually dwell on it, feel guilty, and/or quit. I see myself as a failure as a Christian woman, wife, and mother. I want to be out of the bondage of guilt, failure, and anger toward my husband. I want to live in God's promises." She further described herself as someone with "low self-esteem," a "people pleaser," and one who constantly compared herself to others.

Julie's Physical Problems

Four years earlier Julie was diagnosed with fibromyalgia and chronic fatigue syndrome. Then, a year before their move to our town, a car accident produced a serious back injury resulting in surgery, chronic pain, and ongoing acute flare-ups. Her doctor prescribed pain medication as well as an antidepressant, both of which Julie continued to take in her new town under the care of several physicians.

Julie's Marriage and Family

Nate and Julie's relationship problems began about five years prior to our meetings after three years of marriage. Julie rated their marriage as terrible—zero on a scale of zero to five. She cited better communication and more joint spiritual activities as the main ways to improve their relationship. In our first session Julie focused more on her personal struggles than her marriage problems, but it was still evident that both were highly problematic. She accurately pinpointed a major need when she expressed her desire to learn to "fear God more than my husband," though her confused view of God made this honorable goal a difficult and distorted task. Early in our work together, she mentioned little about parenting struggles, but Nate made plain that Julie's failure to discipline their children was producing household chaos.

What had Julie done so far about all of these problems? "I take medicines for anxiety and depression. As for everything else, I've done little or nothing." The language of failure spoke loudly at every point.

Addressing the Issues

We first addressed Julie's relationship with God, helping her learn to read and apply Scripture on her own. We also focused on issues we believed were necessary to bring immediate relief to their marriage: communication, roles, and parenting. Given the amount of spiritual, physical, marital, and parenting pressures she felt, we opened to Psalm 46 and surveyed the psalmist's portrayals of God as our refuge and strength—on-site and mighty—amid an earthquaking world. We then helped Julie start a devotional plan where she would read a psalm every day (or every other day) in Psalms 120–134, a section of the Psalter with brief psalms and memorable images that help fix our eyes on the Lord. I also taught Nate and Julie my biblical peacemaking model involving a recommitment to please God and a willingness to examine, to confess, and to repent of heart and behavioral sins. I also shared some practical steps to love, forgive, and serve each other.[2] During the upcoming week they were to read chapters 1–2 in Ken Sande's

---

[2] This model is summarized in my book *Pursuing Peace: A Christian Guide to Handling Our Conflicts* (Wheaton: Crossway, 2012).

book *Peacemaking for Families*,[3] study and memorize some key Bible passages,[4] and keep a journal of their conflicts so we could work through them in upcoming sessions.

Around this time we took a break for several weeks so that Nate and Julie could visit their family over the Christmas holidays. When Julie returned, she was not doing well in any area of her life, and her demeanor reflected total indifference. As we continued to learn about her, we found a woman overwhelmed with parenting, homemaking, and marital problems. "I feel pressured to perform. Then I fail. And I just want to give up." Further, Julie felt that God was "very far away—he is still there and he loves me, but I feel overwhelmed; and I feel guilty when I don't run to him." Julie went on to describe her frustration that God was watching her fail in so many areas. The notion that God could ever say, "Well done, good and faithful slave!" (Matt 25:21), was far from her. She also repeated her previous admission that she was more afraid of her husband's standard than God's standard, even though she expressed confusion about what those standards might be.

First, in light of Julie's difficulty grasping God's grace, we began discussing a biblical view of performance. I explained to her, "God is not primarily looking at your performance, but the performance of Jesus your Savior for you, in your place." Given her physical, marital, and homemaking pressures, we considered together Jesus' temptations in Matt 4:1–11, but only in light of the broader context of Matthew. Julie was tempted to read this account exclusively as an example of how to fight temptation by quoting Scripture. Jesus' method of fighting temptation here is certainly exemplary, but Julie needed to see that the point of the story was not for Scripture memorization. Jesus is not mainly our example for how to handle temptation by citing and following Scripture; he is first and foremost our Redeemer and Substitute.

---

[3] Ken Sande with Tom Raabe, *Peacemaking for Families: A Biblical Guide to Managing Conflict in Your Home* (Carol Stream, IL: Tyndale, 2002).

[4] The early passages I had them memorize were Jas 4:1–2, which roots our conflicts in our selfish desires; Mark 10:45, where Jesus serves as the ultimate example of service; and Eph 4:32, which calls Christians to forgive as they have been forgiven in Christ.

As the son of Abraham and the son of David (Matt 1:1–17), Jesus fulfilled the Old Testament covenant promises, and he comes to us as our Savior (Matt 1:21) and our Immanuel, God with Us (Matt 1:23). As the true Son of God (Matt 2:15), Jesus succeeded where God's Old Testament son, Israel (Exod 4:22; see Hos 11:1) had failed. Jesus fulfilled the Old Testament, completing in his 40 days of temptation what Israel failed to do in 40 years of desert wandering—to perfectly trust and obey God amid overwhelming pressures. As the Son who always pleases his Father (Matt 3:17), Jesus is our righteousness. I reminded her, "Yes, Julie, you have failed. So have Lauren and I, and Todd and Jan, but Jesus never did. His perfect obedience there in the desert has been credited to you in the gospel of Christ. So, Julie, own the guilt for your failures, but hear the grace of God: 'Julie, I love you. You are my daughter. My Son Jesus has perfectly succeeded. At the end of the day, his performance and not yours matters most.'"

Second, I reminded Julie of a sermon she recently heard from Romans 8 on God's unconditional love for her in Jesus Christ. We encouraged her to cry out to God, "I do believe! Help my unbelief!" (Mark 9:24). Julie needed to preach the gospel to herself daily—to apply the truths about her finished justification, her definitional sanctification, and her unchangeable adoption.[5] She needed to learn that she is loved and owned by God, her Father. Since her previous church experience had not been gospel driven, we spent subsequent sessions addressing and applying various facets of the gospel to her life as she read C. J. Mahaney's *The Cross Centered Life: Keeping the Gospel the Main Thing*.[6]

Third, we continued to help Julie develop biblical direction for becoming a godly wife, mother, and homemaker, depending on and appropriating God's promises, power, and presence in her daily life. We returned to the refuge of Psalm 46 along with the Psalms of Ascent (120–134). We then unpacked Isa 41:8–10 where

---

[5] The truth of definitional sanctification—also known as definitive sanctification, positional sanctification (though this term can be understood too narrowly), or initial sanctification—is underplayed in too many evangelical churches.

[6] C. J. Mahaney, *The Cross Centered Life: Keeping the Gospel the Main Thing* (Colorado Springs: Multnomah, 2002).

God promises his chosen people that he will always be powerful and present to help them; Phil 4:11–13 where God promises to enable believers to live with contentment even amid hard circumstances; and 2 Tim 4:17 where Paul declares that "the Lord stood with [him] and strengthened [him]" in the midst of loneliness and opposition. Practically, Lauren and Jan proved invaluable as mentors and accountability partners helping Julie prioritize and carry out her homemaking duties.

Nevertheless, when we reconvened the following week, Julie seemed to be in the exact same place. She had not been reading her Bible, and she had gotten into another major fight with Nate. When asked about God, she was full of qualifications: "God loves me, but I cannot please God, so what's the use of trying?" she replied. Horizontal thinking dominated her. I once again reminded her of the gospel:

> On the one hand, Julie, you cannot please God. Our sins will always mar us. But the good news of the gospel is that God is already pleased with you because you stand in Jesus his beloved Son, our substitute. The starting point for you, Julie, is to cry out to God, "God, have mercy on me, a sinner" (Luke 18:13 NIV), and then, in light of Jesus' accomplishment on the cross, to thank God for that mercy. Julie, if you could get right with God through prayer and Bible reading, then why do you need a Savior? Reading your Bible is not a way to get right with God but to know the God who has mercifully saved and adopted you and to learn how he wants you to live in light of his grace.

We asked Julie and Nate to memorize and meditate on Col 3:12: "Therefore, God's chosen ones, holy and loved, put on heartfelt compassion, kindness, humility, gentleness, and patience." We longed for Julie to encounter her true identity in Christ as "chosen," "holy," and "loved." In the same vein we also directed her to spend some time studying Ephesians 1 to deepen her grasp of her identity in Jesus as the foundation for God-pleasing obedience.

These twin themes—God's forgiving, justifying, and adopting grace and God's sustaining, invigorating, and enabling grace—marked our ongoing counseling. Whether we were talking with Julie alone or together with Nate, or whether we were discussing marriage, parenting, or homemaking, we repeatedly stressed the pardoning and empowering grace of God. Little did we know that these emphases would be foundational for what we were about to face. I mentioned earlier that this case had unforeseen elements. We were about to turn the corner into our first big surprise.

The Crisis Stage Begins: Julie's Addictions Surface

Although we had been working with Nate[7] and Julie for several months, their marriage had remained troubled, with little growth seen either in Julie or in their relationship. Instead, her anger toward Nate had increased, and she was beginning to voice desires to get out of the marriage. At the same time Julie knew that she was hurting Nate and the children. This added to her fears and guilt. Parenting problems continued over how to discipline the children, whether and when the children should sleep in Mom and Dad's bed, and whether they should have more children. On the one hand Julie wanted to be a better Christian wife and mother. On the other hand she resented what she called Nate's legalism, perfectionist demands, and condemnation of her: "He is just looking for ways to condemn me all the time." While my counseling team did not view Nate's standards to be excessive, a woman lacking discipline and seeking to escape from pressures found even reasonable standards of homemaking burdensome.

Then, in a counseling session in February (we had begun counseling in October), Julie admitted that she had begun

---

[7] For the sake of space and focus, I am not documenting the conversations we had with Nate in both joint and individual sessions. In these important conversations we challenged him about his own anger and frustrations over Julie's failures and about his selfish demands that she change. His dreams of a strong, growing, exemplary Christian marriage too often controlled his heart and kept him from tenderly and patiently loving his troubled wife. He too needed the pardoning and empowering grace of God shown in Jesus. Over time we did see the Lord transform him.

drinking daily—resuming patterns of alcohol addiction that had been dormant for several years. She had grown up in a troubled home with two alcoholic parents and developed serious problems herself. Her drunkenness was doubly damaging—the problem of the alcohol itself was compounded by her mixing it with prescription medications.[8] We spent time addressing her drinking, seeking to expose the blend of feel-good and escapist motives fueling this sin. It was essential to deal not just with the choice to drink or the dangers of drunkenness but also with the heart motivations driving her resurgent habits. We identified Julie's sinful lust for alcohol as a worship disorder and an enslaving power (Rom 6:16),[9] while presenting Jesus as the One who could set her free from all bondage (John 8:31–36). At the same time her choices and behaviors could not go untouched. As we labored to help Julie change from the inside out, we also examined ways she should avoid access to alcohol, and we laid down some practical boundaries as well as some strong accountability measures to help control this access.

Meanwhile, the marital strife and parenting struggles continued, and despair marked Julie's mind-set: *I feel useless, I feel lost, I can't cope, I'm alone*. In addition to her disillusionment, Julie continued to express her desire to leave the marriage. At this point Lauren and Jan began to spend more time with Julie between sessions.

Once again, however, things worsened when Julie had a minor car accident the following week. Not only were the children in the vehicle, but Julie had also been drinking and had fled the scene. Soon she was cited by the police and given a court date. I reported

---

[8] At this point Julie was taking a shelf of prescribed medications including Lexepro, Klonopin, Wellbutrin, and Trazadone for anxiety, depression, and insomnia. She also took methadone for back pain, a Clonidine patch for nicotine withdrawal, and Synthroid for hypothyroidism, as well as over-the-counter Excedrin for occasional migraines. This diverse intake also meant that two or three different prescribing physicians were involved. Changing doctors—always seeking a new source of hope (and a new prescription)—frequently marked Julie's path. This revolving door also produced further marriage problems because Nate saw Julie as both fleeing life's pressures and overspending their money on office visits and medications that she would not need if she were truly seeking the Lord.

[9] See Edward T. Welch, *Addictions: A Banquet in the Grave* (Phillipsburg, NJ: P&R, 2001).

the situation to the elders of our church, one of whom joined us for the next counseling session. In this session Julie admitted that her use of alcohol was increasing as a means of dulling her depression, guilt, and fear while coping with the pressures of being a stay-at-home mom. She acknowledged that she was turning to alternatives other than God to relieve her pressures. Meanwhile Nate's patience had grown thin, and he too acknowledged his sinful tendency to shortcut the Holy Spirit in his rush to change Julie. Out of concern for her and the children's safety, our counseling team supported Nate's decision to take away her car keys so she could not steal away to the liquor store during the day. Yet Julie's reluctant acceptance of this reasonable decision demonstrated that her heart was not sufficiently humbled. We did provide her with the names and phone numbers of other stay-at-home moms in the area who could transport her and the children in case of medical emergencies or other needs.

During these sessions we continued to call Julie to a deepening repentance in light of Jesus' atoning cross and victorious resurrection. Her combination of comfort-seeking escapism, hovering fear, and lack of basic skills was crippling her. We gave her practical instruction about prayer, especially encouraging her to address her anger with God by admitting to him where she felt he had let her down in her various forms of suffering. The same kind of humble honesty was also needed in her marriage since she needed to learn to confess her sins to Nate and to forgive him for his sins toward her, as together they learned to communicate graciously.

Julie also needed recommitment and practical training in homemaking and life management. She found it difficult to get up in the morning, make breakfast, and get the children going. She wrestled with eating junk food, neglected regular exercise, and struggled with carving out time to read her Bible and pray. Once again Lauren and Jan were indispensable as they provided hands-on help and mobilized other godly women to help Julie, all with her permission and gratitude. For instance, Lauren spent an entire morning with Julie at her home. After reading to the children and asking them to play quietly and only interrupt if it was really important, Lauren talked with Julie about the why and how of Bible reading and prayer, helped her set up a plan to read through Ephesians in small sections (three to six verses at a time), and encouraged Julie to battle her distracted mind by recording a daily prayer of thanksgiving to God based on the passage she read that day.

Lauren also helped Julie establish a daily schedule with the kids. They also marked out regular bedtimes for the children, allowing ample time for Bible reading and personal care both before the kids awoke and after Nate left for work. Because Sunday mornings were hectic for Julie and filled with family conflict, Lauren explained the value of preparing for Sunday morning on Saturday night. This included washing and ironing Sunday clothes for each family member, preparing breakfast in advance (e.g., muffins or a breakfast casserole), giving the children their baths, and going to bed on time so that everyone could be well rested in the morning.

Lauren also encouraged Julie to wean all of the children from sleeping in their parents' bed. This adjustment would require moving the bedtime ritual from Nate and Julie's bed to each child's bed as well as reclaiming the parents' bedroom as a private room instead of a family playroom.

Finally, Lauren helped Julie recognize the anger and manipulation she directed towards her children when she was tired or experiencing pain—"I can never have time to myself!" or "Didn't I tell you mommy has a headache?" While Nate himself had already said some of the things Lauren and other women were now saying, hearing them from other women made Julie more receptive. Julie seemed genuinely humbled by the attention and instruction she was receiving, and though she continued to lack consistency, homemaking and mothering went more smoothly when she applied what she was learning.

Once again, though, it seemed to be two steps back for every one step forward. As summer approached, the marital issues reheated. Julie wanted out: "We need a separation." Nate and Julie fought about everything: Julie's parenting, Julie's homemaking,

Julie's medical care (gynecological problems), Julie's addictions (alcohol, spending), and Nate's leadership. Julie complained, "I'm afraid of Nate more than God. One nurse said that I'm in an emotionally abusive relationship." To our counseling team Julie's words sounded revengeful.

In our times together Julie confessed that God seemed far away and that her anger against both God and Nate were creating that distance. Julie admitted her guilt as a Christian, a wife, and a mother but still seemed to be avoiding full responsibility. One of our counseling team spoke up: "Julie, you seem to have decided that Nate is the cause of all your stress. Nate may add to your stress, but Nate is not to blame. Julie, you need to battle evil instead of battling Nate. Stop blaming Nate; go to God to ask for his help and receive his grace and mercy."

We continued regular counseling with Nate and Julie through the summer but saw little growth. We discussed Julie's lack of parental discipline over her children and her constant conflicts with Nate. Yet our focus on their marital dynamics was undercut by Julie's minimal commitment to complete the practical homework assignments designed to help her establish new patterns of thinking and interacting. By the time fall arrived (which marked one full year of counseling), the marriage showed no significant improvement while Julie's addictions to alcohol, cigarettes, and prescription drugs had increased. With the support of the church's elders, Nate and our counseling team agreed that Julie needed to detoxify at an in-patient facility. Julie objected but eventually acquiesced. We found a recommended site in another state where she was admitted for 30 days. Our phone communication was limited during this time, but we were able to maintain minimal contact.

The Crisis Stage Continues: More Addictions and an Adulterous Relationship

The in-patient facility achieved its detoxifying goal: Julie emerged chemically clean of alcohol, and her psychiatrist even cut back on her psychiatric medications. But another serious problem had arisen during her month in rehab: Julie had been surrounded by a new set of relationships with non-Christian male and female patients who had influenced her negatively. The devastating news came while Julie was still in her 30-day program: she had committed adultery with one of the male patients. Overcome with guilt, she had called Nate from the facility to confess her unfaithfulness, and Nate soon informed us. I immediately called Julie, mentioned what Nate had told me, and tried to call her to repentant faith in Christ in the limited time we were allowed to talk.

The week Julie was discharged, we met with her and Nate several times. She explained what led to her adultery: "I felt camaraderie with several patients. This guy and I hit it off. I don't know why I slept with him. He made me feel special, and I liked it too much." It was difficult to tell if she was truly repentant. On the one hand she said: "I don't feel proud. I want to see our marriage work, and I want our family to work. It felt right at the time, but I know it wasn't right." Yet there were strains of justification and no evidence of Spirit-wrought repentance: "I found someone who accepted me, who loved me for who I am. He pursued me, and I received his love and attention." Moreover, her commitment to her marriage was lower than ever: "I'd get out of the marriage if I could, and I've wanted to for a long time. But I care about the kids. And I'm afraid I won't make it on my own. I know God doesn't want divorce, but I feel like I'm in a cage. I had the thought that after rehab I could be a better mom, but I can't." Julie was even considering a return to the town where the rehab center was located, keeping the connection alive through phone conversations with one of the unbelieving women she had met in the program.

It had become apparent to everyone but Julie that she had deep heart issues that needed radical attention. The core problems were not chronic pain, psychiatric medications, marriage and parenting failures, substance abuse, or even infidelity. At root Julie remained consumed with herself as she pursued happiness on her own terms. Self-will dominated her life, manifesting itself in both rebellion and unbelief. There was rebellion against God and his ways—the independent spirit depicted in Luke 19:14: "But his subjects hated him and sent a delegation after him, saying, 'We don't want this man to rule over us!'" Yet there was also a deep measure of unbelief and fear. Julie felt hopeless, helpless, miserable, and condemned, though she never recanted her faith in Jesus. While theologians debate whether sin ultimately springs from rebellion or unbelief, we saw both root sins staring us in the face.

Our intervention again included explicit instruction about the forgiving and empowering grace that Jesus promises to all who repent, believe, and follow him. Naturally, it also included firm, passionate pleadings from every one of our counseling team members, urging our sister Julie to turn back to God (we included specific steps for what such repentance would look like). Lauren and Jan even offered to meet with Julie privately for spiritual and hands-on help, but in the face of our manifold pleas and our offers of assistance, Julie never cried out to God for mercy and grace.

Our next two weekly sessions multiplied our summons for repentance. We turned to Joel 2:1–11, where God's people had incurred his judgment through their disobedience, bringing on themselves a divinely orchestrated invasion of locusts. But in 2:12–13, the prophet shines a bright ray of hope: "Even now—this is the LORD's declaration—turn to Me with all your heart, with fasting, weeping, and mourning. Tear your hearts, not just your clothes, and return to the LORD your God. For he is gracious and compassionate, slow to anger, rich in faithful love, and he relents from sending disaster." Joel called God's people to a thorough, heart-driven repentance—with inward sincerity, not outward hypocrisy—yet his call was rooted in God's gracious character. Israel's repentance would not *make* God gracious and compassionate. Rather, God is *first* compassionate, and on this basis he invites us to repent. Joel alluded to God's famous self-revelation to Moses in Exod 34:6–7. It is God's gracious character and his promise of mercy that lay the foundation for his invitation to his people to return to him. His grace also provides the assurance that Israel would be received should she embrace his kind invitation and choose to return. Julie needed to hear the prophet Joel as I reiterated his kind and serious summons:

> Julie, you have turned away from the God who loves you, the God who loves you so much that he sent his own Son to die for you. Your life and marriage and family are reaping the consequences of your self-centered pursuits, and God your Savior is grieved. But he offers you this hope: Because he is the God of all grace and compassion, he will receive you, Julie, if you turn back to him with all your heart. Not just with some remorse and some new resolutions but with a heart that acknowledges your helplessness, hopelessness, rebellion, self-centeredness, and unbelief. And we all love you and are here to help you.

I wish I could tell you that this counsel and plea turned Julie's heart. But it did not. Instead, things were about to worsen yet again.

The Crisis Stage Accelerates: Addiction, Rehab, Adultery . . . and Flight

Within a week Julie had taken another downward turn. Nate called to say that she had resumed her regular drinking and smoking, had left him and the children, and had moved in with a man she had met at a bar. She had also met with an attorney to discuss her plan for a legal separation followed by divorce. Not surprisingly, she did not want to meet with us.

We met several times with Nate alone, reminding him of God's promises for his life and giving him practical counsel on what to do and what not to do. In our times together, in conjunction with the elders, our counseling team developed a six-point crisis intervention plan.

Step one was to reach out to Julie. We decided who among the counseling team, church leaders, and small-group members would phone Julie (and when) to seek her out and engage her in discussion. We wanted Julie to be overwhelmed by the magnitude and consequences of her sin, the sincerity and breadth of our love, and the active pursuit of God's grace—but not by an uncoordinated free-for-all approach which might confuse her with competing voices and crush her with unrelenting pressure.

Step two was to keep the church leaders updated on the situation in case it became necessary to move farther down the path of restorative church discipline. Obviously, the process of confronting Julie about her sin had already begun, and we wanted to be sure our church leaders were involved in our intensifying efforts to reclaim her.[10]

Step three was to continue ministering spiritually to Nate through ongoing counsel, encouragement, and accountability. We wanted to help him pursue Christ in the midst of such a difficult situation. Together we discussed his identity in Christ, his ability to forgive Julie from the heart, and how he should treat Julie, especially when she visited the children. We agreed that given her drunkenness, instability, and irresponsibility, Nate should not allow her to take the children out of his home unless she pursued legal action (which she did not). We encouraged Nate to be civil and loving when Julie visited, to express his love and commitment to her and their marriage, to invite her to repent and recommit to the marriage, and to allow her time alone with the children while he went upstairs.

Step four involved advising Nate on legal steps (in case Julie initiated proceedings), child-care decisions, financial matters, church ministry commitments, and his response to inquiring church members. As he bore up under the pressure of complex details, swirling emotions, and weighty decisions, we needed to

---

[10] The NT clearly teaches the necessity of church discipline for the purity of the church, the validity of her testimony, and the spiritual health of her members; see Matt 18:15–20; 1 Cor 5:1–13; 2 Cor 2:5–11; Gal 6:1–2. These passages lay out clear principles and practices for gracious, loving, and firm church discipline which aims at restoration. However, while Matt 18:15–20 outlines the intensifying steps Christians and church leaders should take with wayward brothers and sisters, the length of time between each step depends on the unique dynamics of each situation. Paul explained how to deal with several different types of unhealthy church members, but his overarching principle is *patience with all* (1 Thess 5:14).

be faithful to provide him with the kind of external objectivity that we all need when facing overwhelming circumstances.

Step five focused on practical assistance for Nate. Todd and Jan discreetly shared with their small group the big picture of Nate and Julie's situation. Since these faithful small-group leaders had been involved from the beginning, they were able to share about the situation carefully and compassionately and then mobilize their small group to assist Nate with meals, child care, and occasional housecleaning so that he could continue his full-time employment.

Step six involved counseling Nate and Julie's three young children on how they should view the situation and respond to their mother. We sat down with the children and tried to explain to them in simple and gentle terms that their mom was living somewhere else right now; that she still loved them; that she was not following Jesus and obeying God right now; that they should pray for her; and that they should love her, respect her, and obey her when she visited.

Seemingly unconcerned about the devastation and confusion she was causing her family, Julie continued her prodigal ways over the next three months, including sexual involvement with one or two other men. During this time we continued to reach out to her and minister to Nate.

In God's providence there was a small breakthrough when Julie's new boyfriend kicked her out of his house, replacing her with another woman. Our counseling team (in conjunction with church leaders) introduced her to a mature Christian woman in the community who took Julie into her home, established and enforced strict rules concerning Julie's behavior, and sought to talk with her about the Lord.

As Julie began to sober up both physically and spiritually, she grew willing to meet with us again. We reemphasized God's grace and promises, reiterated her need to repent, explained what repentance would look like, and once again discussed her commitments to the Lord and to Nate. During this period we also helped Nate develop a set of reasonable conditions for Julie's return to their home. In order to return, Julie needed to make a firm commitment to break completely her sinful relationships with other men, to abstain from alcohol and smoking (except for a nicotine patch under medical advisement), to resume individual and marital counseling with a recommitment to completing her homework, and to embrace daily accountability with specific mature women that we had designated to help her. Julie also needed to commit to learn and apply godly parenting principles, homemaking skills, and time-management practices with the help of several older women who would mentor and assist her. Finally, she also needed to be honest with Nate and to support his efforts to follow Jesus in his own life and to lead both her and the children. After much discussion Julie agreed to these terms. After months of wayward rebellion, she finally moved back in with her husband and family.

The Restoration Stage Arrives: Julie Finally Begins to Repent and Change

If one defines counseling as a conversation between one person who is earnestly seeking wisdom and another person who is feeding welcomed insights to a listening ear, then I had done little "counseling" with Julie. While she dutifully came to each session (prior to her flight of rebellion), her behavior made clear that she did not really want our help. She made little effort to follow my counsel and carry out the instructions we gave her, nor was she forthcoming about the depth of her difficulties. Eventually she fled into a pattern of sinful living. So in one sense Julie was not—strictly speaking—a counselee.

Church-based counseling is not consigned to the kind of finger-tapping approach that simply waits for the counselee to "come around." Christ's agenda for his people is much broader than that. Though much biblical counseling is reactive, we are not mainly to be responders but pursuers, like Jesus. Though Julie herself was not really pursuing change, our efforts to help her were not in vain for at least two reasons.

First, the sessions in my office were building a relationship between Julie and me, along with our counseling team. The time we spent together showed Julie our commitment to her. Even our admonitions and pleas were seen (as she later admitted) as acts of love, evidences to her that we truly cared despite her stubbornness. Our willingness to meet with Nate and Julie time after time in the face of paltry growth and growing opposition showed her God's love embodied in her brothers and sisters. I'm afraid that in a professional, fee-based, nonchurch counseling setting, either Julie or the counselor would have ended counseling long before our final stage when restoration began to blossom.

Second, our church-based counseling went far beyond conversations in scheduled office sessions. As a team we were able to serve Nate and Julie practically and have conversations in more personal settings. Lauren, Jan, and two servant-hearted ladies from Julie's small group were especially active in helping Julie, her husband, and their children through home visits, at-home companionship, cleaning, meals, and much more. Church-based counseling can and should go far beyond the weekly 50 minutes of talk therapy that so often qualifies as "counseling." In our situation it was the body of Christ counseling Julie—patiently loving her in word, action, and presence, holding forth the hope of the gospel, and calling her to a meaningful commitment to Jesus and to her husband, children, and church. Despite the sporadic nature and apparent fruitlessness of the actual counseling sessions, God had been at work.

With her return to Nate and her family, we found in Julie a new desire to follow the Lord. In this sense she now became a true counselee. The prodigal daughter had returned. In many ways the work of individual and marital counseling was now just beginning. I found myself reviewing some of the same biblical teaching I had offered her earlier as well as reassigning some of the same practical assignments she had already been given. This time, though, the results were different.

Our team continued to address a variety of major issues in our remaining months of counseling, some of which differed from the issues we initially identified.

Fighting Old Addictions

While Julie stopped drinking, she continued to wrestle with desires to drink, smoke, and abuse prescription pain medications. Her previous injuries and surgery produced chronic bouts with pain, and she was still dogged by the desire to drown the pressures of life not only with legitimate relief but illegitimate "feel-good" means of escaping hardship. Her willingness to submit to accountability from her husband and friends was a vital behavioral fence. However, it was mainly the call to trust and obey God in the midst of pain coupled with the promise of a perfect body in the future that helped her guard her heart and endure by faith. Julie began to see how Jesus could indeed set her free (John 8:31–36) and how God's Spirit could truly strengthen her as she faced the strong temptations to revert to addictive behavior. She was beginning to appropriate the truth of 1 Cor 10:13: "No temptation has overtaken you except what is common to humanity. God is faithful and he will not allow you to be tempted beyond what you are able, but with the temptation he will also provide a way of escape, so that you are able to bear it."

Strengthening the Marriage

Although Julie and her diverse problems have been the focus of this chapter, both Julie *and* Nate needed serious help to stabilize and strengthen their marriage. Most of all, they needed to learn to bear with, minister to, be gracious with, and forgive each other (Phil 2:1–5; Mark 10:45; Eph 4:29–5:2). Our team was so encouraged when Julie said, "I love Nate more than when we married." A paradigm-creating passage that we unpacked and explored in several sessions was Col 3:12–17: In light of what God has done for us in choosing us, making us his own, loving us, and forgiving us (vv. 12–13), we should love our spouse with gospel-reflecting graces (vv. 12–14) and do all of our duties with God as our ultimate audience (v. 17). Because God has loved us, forgiven us, and humbled himself to serve us, we can love, forgive, and show humility toward our spouses. I helped Julie and Nate understand the triangular relationship of Christian marriage with God at the apex and their individual relationships with him and with each other completing the triangle. We also discussed Jay Adams's pamphlet, *What Do You Do When Your Marriage Goes Sour?*[11] which helped them see that biblical love is more a matter of service and commitment than merely a romantic feeling.

Restoring Sexual Intimacy

For Julie and Nate, sexual difficulties had existed long before we met for counseling, but their sexual relationship had virtually ceased during this nineteen-month saga. The challenge in their recommitted marriage included many of the factors that typically contribute to sexual problems—selfishness, resentment, ungodly communication—but was exacerbated by their joint consciousness of Julie's infidelity. At times Julie experienced flashbacks of being with other men and would push Nate away, leading to recycled feelings of guilt over both her past actions and her present memories.

Further, earlier in the counseling process, we had encountered yet another surprise. During the months when Julie was living with the man she had met at the bar, Nate had confessed his own infidelity during a one-night stand early in their marriage. Although we had addressed Julie's multiple adulteries in an initial way earlier on, we took Nate's confession as a providential opportunity to deal thoroughly with their joint sins in this area.[12] God in his grace brought about mutual confession, repentance, and forgiveness.

Weaning Off Psychiatric Medications

Before and during our lengthy counseling process, Julie had been taking a host of psychotropic drugs. Throughout counseling she had expressed a desire to come off of these drugs, and Nate had agreed. I reminded Julie on several occasions that other

---

[11] Jay E. Adams, *What Do You Do When Your Marriage Goes Sour?* (Phillipsburg, NJ: P&R, 1975).

[12] The substance of my approach can now be found in my *Restoring Your Broken Marriage: Healing After Adultery* (Greensboro, NC: New Growth Press, 2009). I also used Ken Sande's excellent book *Peacemaking for Families* to aid in the confession, repentance, and forgiveness process.

concerns were more pressing than the issue of her medications, assuring her that when the time was right, she would need to seek the oversight of a physician to wean her off of the medications. Now, in her season of restoration, she desired even more strongly to reduce her medications. Her prescribing doctors cooperated with her desire as she displayed more stability.

Yet there were still obstacles to overcome. Nate strongly desired that his wife be free of psychiatric medications, believing that a growing Christian should be able to handle life without them. But Julie was more ambivalent. On the one hand she agreed with Nate and felt guilty about needing her medications. On the other hand she feared what life would be like without them; depression was a terrifying prospect for her. On several occasions Nate's desire led Julie to suddenly decrease or discontinue her doctor's prescription without professional consultation. These rash decisions never ended well for Julie.

On one of these occasions, Julie slid into an out-of-control mania that could not be overcome even by hours of biblical talk. All of our efforts to talk her down—face-to-face or by phone—were fruitless. On one occasion, from 12:45–1:30 in the morning we sat by the phone as I repeatedly sought (to no avail) to center her mind on Ps 121:1–2: "I lift my eyes toward the mountains. Where will my help come from? My help comes from the LORD, the Maker of heaven and earth." Thankfully, this episode was short-lived, and Julie was soon stabilized with the help of her prescribed medication. Despite these types of difficulties, over time Julie was able to reduce significantly her dependence on psychiactric medication through a controlled, physician-monitored step-down process.

Developing Parenting Skills

Marriage and parenting problems frequently merge in counseling, and Nate and Julie's parenting differences were amplifying their conflicts. Four major recurring issues were simmering as they tried to parent their children together.

First, Julie was reluctant to discipline the kids. She admitted that she hated to hear her children cry or scream when she told them no. Her oversensitive capitulation also led her to butt in and overrule Nate even when he tried to parent the children with appropriate discipline. Here we helped Julie address her many fears by showing the biblical connection between love and discipline and explaining how a loving and controlled spanking was an appropriate and effective means of training her children. Along with sharing relevant passages of Scripture, we asked her to read Ginger Plowman's insightful book, *Don't Make Me Count to Three*.[13]

Second, Nate and Julie disagreed about whether their children should sleep in bed with them. Julie was permissive, but Nate thought it needed to stop. Deep down Julie agreed, realizing that this issue was connected to her hatred of denying the children whatever they desired. As we discussed their disagreement in a controlled environment, Julie confessed her laxity and acknowledged its negative effects on the family. Together we worked out a reasonable plan to discontinue the habit.

Third, Nate and Julie disagreed on schooling options. In particular, they differed on the issue of homeschooling. Educating our children is a significant matter freighted with a heavy weight of responsibility and bound up with strong (and often divergent) opinions, so we knew it was essential to spend substantial time discussing this issue. Nate preferred that Julie homeschool their children and even did some hands-on teaching as they tried it. When Julie was unsuccessful, they wisely discontinued the step. This compromise turned out to be a major step in Nate's life as he released one of his strong desires in order to serve the interests of his wife.

Finally, Nate and Julie disagreed about whether they should have more children. Nate wanted more, but Julie felt they should be finished. While this was clearly their decision, I encouraged Nate to let go of his agenda until Julie's personal problems and their marriage problems improved. Even then I encouraged him to

---

[13] Ginger Plowman, *Don't Make Me Count to Three: A Mom's Look at Heart-Oriented Discipline* (Wapwallopen, PA: Shepherd Press, 2004).

wait until Julie shared his desire for a fourth child. Nate agreed, and his humble acquiescence to Julie's desire signaled another degree of change in his life as he grew in his love and service toward his wife.

Stabilizing Family Finances

Another area of pressure and conflict was Julie's spending. At times her handling of finances was out of control, and she was often unwilling to stay within a budget. We helped Nate and Julie develop financial wisdom and budgeting practices by partnering with a church member trained with a biblically based financial counseling organization. Julie's previous habit of running to the doctor's office or emergency room and paying for prescriptions had taken its toll on their already-tight finances. To Nate's frustration he was the one who frequently felt the weight of this debt. But as Julie learned to handle her personal struggles better and as their marital love and communication grew, they were able to reduce her expenditures and partner together on a spending plan.

Developing Homemaking Skills

Our formal counseling advice along with hands-on help from several godly women in the church helped Julie continue to develop her homemaking skills. It was encouraging to see how effective the body of Christ could be in such a practical area like nurturing a warm and efficient home environment. Women from both the counseling ministry and Julie's small group volunteered to help. Improvements were small, but Lauren and Jan noticed steady progress.

Julie's life was not perfect, but she was improving in many areas. With God's help she had quit drinking and was enjoying significant victory over her increasingly irregular temptations. Under the care of a physician, Julie had also quit taking her psychiatric medication, and she was grateful to Jesus for his grace, which enabled her to respond to her trials without turning to prescription drugs. Nate and Julie's marriage continued to grow as well. They were learning to navigate conflict, experiencing increased sexual intimacy, and maintaining their forgiveness for their previous sins against each other. Their children were becoming a renewed source of joy instead of a source of conflict as Nate and Julie grew in their ability to (jointly) apply loving, firm, and consistent discipline. They were also developing a healthy rhythm of income and spending which greatly reduced their conflict in this high-anxiety area of life. Seeing so many angles of good progress, we mutually agreed to discontinue formal counseling even though we continued to have ongoing conversations and check-up sessions. Their small group, which had offered such strong support and consistent help through their crisis stages, continued to be a source of fellowship and encouragement.

Conclusion: Lessons from a Hard Case

This case taught me a number of lessons, especially illustrating and confirming the value of both biblical and church-based counseling. First, in hard cases like these, psychiatric medications are not the answer; however, they may be useful for a limited time and limited purpose. Biblical counseling provides answers that psychiatric medications cannot. At best, medication can stabilize a person's mind and mood for a season, but it cannot change the person. At the same time I was reminded of my need to communicate clearly with the counselee about her medications and to advise her and her husband on how to communicate with their doctors.

Second, in hard cases like these, secular counseling is not the answer. While Julie never pursued secular talk therapy on a weekly basis, she did receive some professional secular advice during her visits to her various psychiatrists. Her 30 days of rehab were also filled with individual and group therapy. But none of these efforts went deep enough to expose the self-centered, fearful, guilty, stubborn heart at the root of Julie's struggles. And they never went high enough to connect her with her Redeemer, the one in whom she ultimately found forgiveness, hope, and the power for progressive change.

Third, in hard cases like these, even biblical counseling—if narrowly defined as mere biblical talk therapy—is not enough. Biblical counseling must not only be church based; it must also be church driven and church saturated. One of the critiques often leveled against biblical counseling is that we can leave observers thinking that all you need for successful counseling is a godly counselor, a Bible, the Holy Spirit, and a willing counselee. All biblical counseling that is faithful to the Scriptures will recognize the vital role played by the church in the life of a Christian counselee (see Romans 12; 1 Corinthians 12–14; Eph 4:1–16; 1 Thess 4:9–10; 5:12–15; Heb 3:12–14). People entangled in severe sins tend to isolate themselves for a variety of reasons. They are in love with their sin, ashamed of their sin, too proud to let others know, too self-sufficient to let others in, lack a true desire to change, believe they can beat their problems on their own, or don't want to inconvenience their friends with their long-term problems that defy simple solutions. Julie herself was marked by some of these tendencies. As our counseling team walked with her over the long haul and our small group leaders discreetly mobilized her fellow small-group members, Julie experienced Christ's love through us, his church.

Fourth, in hard cases like these, situational dynamics and counseling angles can change drastically. What began as a straightforward marital case morphed into intense counseling with one spouse, at least for a majority of the time. My initial plan was to counsel Nate and Julie on their marriage, but soon it became apparent that we needed to focus more on Julie. While Nate was not faultless and needed to change and while their relationship certainly needed help, we had to make some in-flight adjustments and center our attention on Julie.

Fifth, in hard cases like these, change is a long-term process. No eight-to-twelve-week counseling period—or even an eight-to-twelve-month counseling period—was long enough for Julie. Many factors prevented this from being a short-term case: her entrenched "Christian" legalism, her prior bad church experiences, her varied and chronic medical problems, her dependence on pain medications, her lack of extended family support, her husband's high standards and critical spirit, the pressures of mothering several small children, her dishonesty about the depth of her difficulties, and her months-long flight from her Christian community—not to mention the everyday hindrances emanating from the world, the flesh, and the Devil.

Sixth, in hard cases like these, biblical counseling ultimately relies on the power of God's Spirit working through individual and corporate means of grace. This is true in any life situation no matter how simple or complex, brief or prolonged. But the hard cases reveal a more pronounced need—a desperation—for the powerful grace of God to act with precision. As I reflect on my relationship with Nate and Julie, I realize that I did a good job but not a great job. At times I should have intervened more quickly; early on I missed the depth of Julie's problems; I could have probed more deeply into Julie's life and history; I misunderstood her psychiatric medications and how the doctors were trying to treat her; I underestimated the strength of her addictions; and I failed to adapt my own counseling strategy with Julie quickly enough. While I had used many of the same counseling methods successfully for many years, in Julie's case they didn't seem to "take." Through this hard case God was not only gracious in changing Julie but was equally gracious in growing me into a more competent counselor.

I am grateful to God for Julie. She became my sister and my friend. From my sideline coaching box, she showed me how God was at work. She modeled a dim but persevering faith in the face of numerous obstacles, including her own entangling sins. One of my counseling professors often wished upon his students that at every point in our ministry we would have at least one hard case—a stubborn, slow-to-change person—to serve as a perpetual reminder that sin is deep, change is hard, growth is progressive, love requires patience, and God alone transforms people in his time and in his way. With Julie, my professor's prayer for me was answered.

CHAPTER 11

"JENNIFER" and an Apparent Hard Case

John Babler

WHAT MAKES A COUNSELING CASE *hard*? Is it the presence of bizarre behavior that makes the average person raise his brow? Is it the presence of an unusual difficulty that the individual counselor has never heard about? Is it a fairly "normal" problem with many layers that requires much time to sort through? When does counseling cross the line from easy to hard? Any of the factors listed here (and many more) could make counseling difficult. Generally speaking, counseling is hard when counselors sense they are in over their heads with no idea how to help, when the counseling process is going to take a long time, or when a counselee is resistant to change.

I want to tell you the story of a fairly straightforward counseling case. Most wise Christians could be helpful with this kind of case if they took the time to listen well and fully understand what was actually taking place in the mind and heart of the person involved. Many wise Christians, however, would never take the time because the case begins in the emergency room.

Background of the Case

I received the phone call early on a Monday morning. Jennifer, the wife of one of our students, was in the emergency room at a local hospital. The initial report was that she had been acting strangely for several weeks and her husband, Jim, noticed that she did not go to bed at all on Sunday night. When Jim awakened on Monday morning, he noticed that she seemed "distant" and "distracted." After completing his Bible study, he noticed that Jennifer was crying in a corner. When he touched her shoulder, Jennifer jumped and told him she was scared that someone was coming to get her and take her away. She said she had been hearing voices all night telling her this message. She continued to cry uncontrollably for over an hour. Jim decided to take her to the emergency room. I was asked to come to provide support and counsel.

When I arrived, I found Jennifer sitting on a gurney; a friend sat in a chair across from her. It was obvious that Jennifer had been crying, but by the time I arrived, she was calmly talking. I introduced myself to Jennifer and her friend, Elaine. They were both glad I had come. After Elaine explained that Jim had to go to work and could not remain at the hospital, she excused herself so Jennifer and I could talk more privately. Jennifer apologized for "causing trouble" and explained that since arriving at the hospital they had seen several people and that blood had been drawn to run a variety of tests. She also said that a social worker had asked her to sign a release for a psychiatric evaluation. She was not sure if she wanted a psychiatric evaluation and wanted to talk to me about it.

She said she had been having a difficult time sleeping for over a week. For about three weeks she had struggled with paranoia and believed she was in danger. She grew to fear those around her, including her new husband, and found herself unable to complete even the simplest of tasks. Jennifer experienced constant difficulty sleeping and told me she had not slept more than an hour a night for the last two weeks. She became seriously concerned and had only shared the details with her mom.

She searched the Internet in an effort to diagnose herself and concluded that she likely had several mental disorders. Her family had a history of mental disorders and experienced interactions with the state's mental health system. She knew something was clearly wrong, but she feared getting involved in the mental health system. I told Jennifer that I believed the Bible had answers for her, and I would be happy to counsel her and her husband if she was open to the opportunity. A physician soon came and told her that she had a urinary tract infection requiring an antibiotic. He would prescribe a sleep aid for her as well. He asked if she had come to a decision regarding the psychiatric evaluation. In the end she did not want it. Jennifer told me she would like to see me for counseling soon. Elaine returned, offering to take Jennifer home and help her get her prescriptions filled. Jennifer went home, called her husband and mom, and went to sleep. We scheduled a meeting for the next day.

Case Process

The process of gaining information about a counselee is always ongoing. Usually, after a first session the counselor can come to some initial conclusions about what needs to be addressed and how the path forward might look. In the case of Jim and Jennifer, the first session was a bit longer than most and yet yielded more questions than insight. When I met with Jennifer the next morning, she said she had slept for about 12 hours and was feeling a little better. Jim was not able to take time off away from his job. I began to obtain some basic information. I asked her to tell me her personal Christian testimony. She described a commitment to Christ that began when she was 13, a history of regular church involvement, and a call to ministry that came about the time she met Jim. When I asked her to describe her recent relationship with the Lord, she acknowledged that in the midst of all that had been going on in her life she had not spent much time reading Scripture or praying. She said God seemed distant from her.

She told me her parents were married and that she had two younger brothers. Two of her aunts had been diagnosed with clinical depression. During the session Jennifer received a phone call from her mother. Her father was on a flight to see her and would arrive at noon. Her mom had told her that she and her dad had discussed her situation and wanted to make sure that she was receiving good care. They were hoping I could meet with them that afternoon. I asked whether she could contact her husband Jim to see if he would be available to join the meeting. He was not able to leave work early but offered to talk with me by phone on one of his breaks.

Jennifer described her family as close and loving. They did most everything together, and her parents were involved in her life. Jennifer was 21 years old. She graduated from high school one year early and entered an accelerated college program studying journalism and psychology. She had met Jim about 10 months earlier at a church function. Their relationship developed quickly, and Jim proposed to her in June. He had received a call to ministry and was planning to enroll at Southwestern Baptist Theological Seminary. Since she would graduate in December, they decided to marry on the Saturday after her graduation. Her parents liked Jim and were supportive of the marriage. She described a stressful and busy fall semester as she prepared for a wedding, finished school, and planned a honeymoon. During this time she quit exercising, did not eat well, did not have time for personal devotions, and became discouraged.

While this case continued to have unexpected twists and turns, I was able to begin ministering Scripture to Jennifer. I began by expressing compassion to her and stating that as difficult as things were I believed God's Word had the answers to the problems she and Jim were facing. I told her that her life was in chaos and out of order. She agreed. I asked her what she thought was the most important thing in the Christian life. She answered that it was important to care for others. I asked her to open her Bible to Matt 22:36–40 and to read the verses aloud:

> "Teacher, which command in the law is the greatest?" [Jesus] said to him, "'Love the Lord your God with all your heart, with all your soul, and with all your mind.' This is the greatest and most important command. The second is like it: 'Love your neighbor as yourself.' All the Law and the Prophets depend on these two commands."

We discussed that the most important thing for Christians is to love God with all of our hearts, souls, and minds. If God is not in first place, then our lives are indeed out of order, and some form of chaos is the natural result. I asked if she thought disobeying the command to love God with all of her heart, soul, and mind was a sin. She responded that she understood that it was a sin and desired to repent and get her life back in order. I said that in the rebuilding of any building the foundation must be solid. I helped Jennifer see that in order to deal effectively with the chaos in her life, she needed to purpose to love God with all of her heart, soul, and mind. Jennifer needed to know that her biggest problem was her heart—not simply the circumstances which might have caused her instability and lack of focus. Engaging this heart issue did not involve some tortuous process of introspection but rather repentant faith toward her Savior.

I challenged her to consider what it means to love God truly. Her response centered on going to church and reading the Bible. I suggested that to love God it is important to spend time with him, similar to spending time with those whom we love in order to develop our relationships with them. A regular daily Bible reading and prayer time is a way to deepen a relationship with God even as we learn from him and share our deepest concerns and needs with him. In addition to that regular time of study whereby we are exposed to the whole counsel of God, we should also be involved in more in-depth study of the Word as well as regular worship and study with other Christians. I encouraged Jennifer to begin thinking of her time with God as part of an ongoing relationship, not as a task or a series of tasks that must be completed. A regular quiet time can often become a mere task to accomplish as we begin each day. All too frequently worship can become rote as well. I told Jennifer that the first order of business was to restore and deepen her relationship to God.

Practically, I suggested two resources that might be helpful for her. The first was a Bible reading plan developed by Robert Murray M'Cheyne, which, over the course of a year, allows a person to read through the New Testament and Psalms twice and the

Old Testament once. Second, I wanted her to read the book of Ephesians. I described to her how the first three chapters speak to our identity in Christ, and the latter three chapters speak of the Christian life. I asked her to read the first three chapters of Ephesians three times during the next week, to note at least five verses that personally impacted her, and to bring these with her to discuss at our next meeting. I also asked her to begin praying each day and record specific requests to God on a prayer list. Plans were made to meet with her dad, and Jim would be calling during his break from work. Jennifer was teachable and open to counsel. There was no mention of her paranoia, and she remarked at least twice how much difference a little sleep made.

When Jim called me, he apologized for not being more involved and mentioned that they needed his income to make ends meet. I asked for his perspective of what was going on with Jennifer. It quickly became apparent that Jim was overwhelmed and confused. He echoed what Jennifer had said about the challenges of their courtship, but he said that they had both been looking forward to the wedding, the honeymoon, and just being married. He told me that his parents were Christians and supportive of their marriage. Since the wedding, they had given them space to develop their life together. He said Jennifer's family seemed almost the opposite. During their courtship there had been minimal but positive contact with them. After the wedding it seemed to Jim as if they were constantly with them. Her parents helped them move to Fort Worth and stayed with them a few days. During that time Jennifer's dad was quick to offer suggestions, even commands, to both Jim and Jennifer. Jim said that since the first day of the honeymoon nothing seemed to be under control. I learned that Jennifer became sick on the second day of their honeymoon and remained sick until two days after they returned home. Life was somewhat normal for the first two weeks in Fort Worth. He immediately started work and school. Approximately two weeks later she began to have problems sleeping. This was about three weeks before she ended up in the emergency room. Jim agreed to meet later in the evening to continue our discussion and expressed willingness to meet with Jennifer and her father if it would be beneficial.

I met with Jennifer and her dad for a few minutes in the afternoon. Wayne, Jennifer's father, was a pleasant man and immediately stated that he wanted to make sure everything was all right with his daughter. When he and his wife had heard about Jennifer's visit to the emergency room, they quickly decided to travel to see her. He said that he had considered the events of the past few days and realized that both Jennifer and Jim had challenges both before and after their wedding. He specifically mentioned the importance of "leaving and cleaving." Wayne felt that he and Jennifer's mom might have unintentionally made the leaving hard for Jennifer. He said he would be happy to stay if he could be of any help but was prepared to return home tonight if that would be best. Jennifer had a relieved look on her face and expressed thanks to him. Wayne talked about Jennifer's two aunts who had been diagnosed with clinical depression and said Jennifer was not currently acting like they had acted.

Normally I prefer to counsel couples together. In this case, however, I had already seen Jennifer alone. I decided to meet with Jim alone as well. My plan was to meet with them together beginning the following week. During my meeting with Jim that evening, he confirmed many of the same details Jennifer shared earlier. Jim recounted to me a solid conversion to Christ and an ongoing walk with God through repentant faith and consistent Scripture reading and prayer. Jim acknowledged that he would like to lead Jennifer in family devotions, but with all the challenges he had withdrawn based on his fear of how she might react. When I inquired about their church membership, he stated they were still working to find a church home. I assigned to him the same M'Cheyne reading plan of the Bible. I asked him to read it as well so they would be exposed to the same passages each day and also asked him to lead Jennifer in a brief discussion about at least one of the verses read each day. Another assignment was for him to consider prayerfully the instruction to husbands in Eph 5:25–33 and to list any areas where he needed to improve. We concluded our meeting with a discussion about the church as a body (Rom 12:4–8; 1 Cor 12:12–31) and how he and Jennifer in their situation needed the support, encouragement, and exhortation inherent with being members of a local church. I encouraged them to join a local church as soon as possible.

Sessions with Jennifer and Jim began with two labor-intensive days. As I prepared for our meeting, I planned to focus on strengthening the foundation of loving God before moving to loving others. When they arrived for their first evening appointment, they both appeared more comfortable than when I encountered them previously. Jennifer admitted that she still remained anxious about things in their life together, but she was sleeping well. She no longer heard voices and did not feel as paranoid. However, she still wondered whether something was seriously wrong with her psychologically. She continued to search the Internet to review symptoms of certain mental illnesses. While she concluded that her symptoms were not as severe anymore, she was still afraid that at least one of the diagnoses applied to her.

I asked her about her homework. She had almost completed the Bible reading plan for the week, and she also completed the assignment in Ephesians. She was encouraged by Eph 1:3: "Praise the God and Father of our Lord Jesus Christ, who has blessed us in Christ with every spiritual blessing in the heavens." She also mentioned Eph 2:1–5 as a particular encouragement to her. These verses reminded her that God had loved her even when she was dead in her sins. She said she did not profit as much from the M'Cheyne reading, but she had done it five or six days. I reminded her that God calls us to love him and that spending time in his Word was a way to spend time with him. She agreed to purpose in her heart to read Scripture and pray every day.

I asked Jim to share about his homework next. He was convicted by his time doing the homework—especially reading the Eph 5:25–26 passage about husbands loving their wives as Christ loved the church. He realized that the Bible had not been a central part of his relationship with Jennifer since they had married and that he had not loved her in this way. He began to see that he had been impatient and frustrated with her before their wedding and had withdrawn from her to some extent, thinking things would improve after the wedding. After Jennifer got sick on the honeymoon, Jim grew more distant and withdrawn. While Jim was speaking, Jennifer moved to the edge of her chair and was nodding her head in agreement. She stated that if Jim had been more loving during this time it would have been easier for her to move beyond her struggles. I asked them to open their Bibles and read Matt 7:1–5:

> Do not judge, so that you won't be judged. For with the judgment you use, you will be judged, and with the measure you use, it will be measured to you. Why do you look at the speck in your brother's eye but don't notice the log in your own eye? Or how can you say to your brother, "Let me take the speck out of your eye," and look, there's a log in your eye? Hypocrite! First take the log out of your eye, and then you will see clearly to take the speck out of your brother's eye.

After reading these verses, they admitted they had blamed each other for the problems in their marriage. After this breakthrough I drew them back to Eph 5:22–32 and asked each of them to explain, in their own words, the meaning of the text. Jim replied that he was to love his wife as Christ loved the church. Jennifer replied that she was to submit to her husband and respect him. I shared with them that they each had a lifetime of work in front of them, joyfully learning how to do what God called them to do individually without being distracted by what the other one was or was not doing. We discussed that all humans are self-centered and possess deceitful hearts (Jer 17:9). When we encounter problems in our relationships, the first tendency is always to blame others rather then look to our own hearts to see the sin present there. In light of Matt 7:5, they knew each must work to rid their hearts of their own sins (taking the log out of their own eye) rather than looking to the other as the source of their pain. Jim needed to focus on loving his wife as Christ loved the church and Jennifer on how she was to submit to and respect her husband.

Before concluding, I asked that they continue the M'Cheyne reading and their joint discussion during the upcoming week. Jim said he had led in a daily discussion of one of the verses from the reading, and Jennifer expressed her enjoyment of this. They also announced that they had decided on a church to join next Sunday. I asked them both to read Ephesians 4–6 three times during the week and write down at least five things that challenged them. I also asked them to plan at least one date night.

When Jim and Jennifer came to the next session, they seemed much happier and even held hands during the meeting. Jennifer had returned to a normal sleep pattern, and her physician had given her a clean bill of health. They spent time with each other and began walking together each evening. Regular Bible reading was beginning to work its way into their minds and hearts. Jennifer said she was beginning to see the M'Cheyne reading more relationally. She truly wanted to read and was blessed by the time with God, even when she was tired. In terms of "leaving and cleaving," they concluded that Jennifer's closeness to her parents caused some unexpected problems between them. She began their marriage sharing concerns with her parents; now she turned to Jim for counsel and support instead. They summed things up by saying that for the first time since the first two months of their relationship they were focusing on and enjoying each other and that God was prominent in their relationship.

We spent a few minutes rejoicing in the changes that had occurred since we started meeting. I asked Jim to lead us in a prayer of thanksgiving and praise. In light of the progress, I then asked what were the most significant challenges or concerns they still had with their marriage. Jennifer struggled with thoughts of how bad things had recently been and still wondered if she had a serious mental problem. While she no longer feared that she had one of the diagnoses that she had previously researched, she still felt discouraged when thoughts entered her mind regarding her past experiences and the obvious patterns of thinking that led to her recent emergency room visit. I asked Jennifer to read 2 Cor 10:3–5:

> For though we live in the body, we do not wage war in an unspiritual way, since the weapons of our warfare are not worldly, but are powerful through God for the demolition of strongholds. We demolish arguments and every high-minded thing that is raised up against the knowledge of God, taking every thought captive to obey Christ.

As we considered this passage, I emphasized that contrary to what we often think we are not powerless over our thoughts. By the Holy Spirit's power, we can take them captive to the obedience of Christ. I also pointed out that taking thoughts captive is done in the context of spiritual warfare. Jennifer asked what it would look like to take thoughts captive. I asked her to read Eph 4:22–24: "You took off your former way of life, the old self that is corrupted by deceitful desires; you are being renewed in the spirit of your minds; you put on the new self, the one created according to God's likeness in righteousness and purity of the truth." The biblical process of change is not presented as simply ceasing something. Rather, it is a process of "putting off" the old and "putting on" the new—being renewed in the spirit of your mind. I asked Jennifer if she could think of how these verses could help her in taking her thoughts captive. She answered that when thoughts occurred that did not line up with God's Word, she could immediately pray and ask God to help her arrest those thoughts and set her mind on Scripture or some truth that would honor God.

They decided it would be good for Jennifer to volunteer with a particular ministry as well as join a women's Bible study that had just begun at their new church home. I wanted to help them better fulfill the second greatest commandment of loving their neighbor. I suggested that they were each other's closest neighbor, and displays of neighborly love should begin at home. As we explored the truth about real love, we considered 1 Cor 13:4–8:

> Love is patient, love is kind. Love does not envy, is not boastful, is not conceited, does not act improperly, is

> not selfish, is not provoked, and does not keep a record of wrongs. Love finds no joy in unrighteousness but rejoices in the truth. It bears all things, believes all things, hopes all things, endures all things. Love never ends.

Over the coming week they both were to look for at least three different opportunities to serve each other as a way of demonstrating love.

In light of Jennifer's sickness during their honeymoon and the challenges thereafter, sexual intimacy had been nonexistent. As they focused on these problem areas and ways to love and serve each other, God had been working to deepen their sex life as well. Over time Jim realized that his tendency in the marriage was impatience with Jennifer as she worked though various problems in her own heart and mind. This was his greatest challenge as he reflected on 1 Corinthians 13. Jennifer struggled with keeping a record of wrongs. She mentioned that once she recognized this pattern, she began to see that when Jim or someone else sinned against her, she would withdraw and become sullen. During these discouraging times, she struggled with thoughts about something being seriously wrong with her. Since she had begun to take her thoughts captive, she had also discerned other thoughts that needed to be addressed as well.

I reminded them that the church was a body and that they needed not only to find their places and use their gifts, but they could call on the body to assist them as well. I suggested that they both pray that God would lead Jim to a godly man who could disciple and encourage him and that he would lead Jennifer to a godly woman who would do the same.

Concluding Reflections

Six months after counseling, Jim and Jennifer were still doing well. Jim was excelling at seminary, and Jennifer was enjoying volunteering at the pregnancy center. They were active in a local church, and God had provided Jennifer relationships with older women who were able to help her in many ways. Initially, I considered this a hard counseling case due to the presentation, the extent of the problems, and the initial challenges of the persons involved. Many counselors might have focused on the paranoia and the voices Jennifer heard in her mind. The error in such a focus, once Jennifer was given a clean bill of health, would have been to perpetuate the selfish focus of her heart. My approach exhibited a focus on God and his Word.

The case of Jennifer and Jim reveals that sometimes bizarre and serious behavior can be a product of a combination of stressors, bad decisions, sleep deprivation, significant changes in life, and the ever-present challenge of spiritual warfare for the Christian. Planning a wedding, finishing a challenging college degree, graduation, a wedding, an illness, a major move, and sleep deprivation would impact anyone. Once the emergency symptoms were dealt with, counseling proceeded in a way that any wise and growing Christian should be equipped to navigate. This case serves as an example of why biblical counselors should not be intimidated by challenging situations. A combination of the hope that comes through God's Word, the Holy Spirit, and the body of Christ can be the beginning of healing, growth, and a new commitment to marriage. Jennifer and Jim were initially discouraged with little hope and not sure what to do, but God brought healing and wholeness to them.

Concluding Reflections

Heath Lambert and Stuart Scott

THIS BOOK CENTERS ON THE sufficiency of Scripture. The editors and contributors all believe that the Bible is comprehensively sufficient to deal with any problem that requires counseling. Additionally, we believe that both the descriptions and prescriptions of human problems found in God's Word are far superior to anything that secular psychology has to offer. Only God understands the problems of humanity at the deepest level—and how to fix them. Furthermore, we believe this truth reveals how desperately the church needs to recover a vision of ministry that employs the Scriptures in one-on-one ministry to those who are plagued by all of the diverse difficulties that can be experienced in this life.

Although this book is about the sufficiency of the Bible, the Christian community, and Christ himself, it is not *merely* about sufficiency. This is also a book about people. As the stories they tell indicate, every contributor to this volume is a counselor. They have devoted their lives to spending time with individuals and walking with them in order to see God change his people by the gospel of grace. None of us views the sufficiency of Scripture as an abstract doctrine. Rather, sufficiency has everything to do with whether we as ministers of Christ possess a firm hope that we can offer to those who are sinking into despair. Sufficiency has everything to do with whether we have clear guidance to offer those who are confused and disoriented by life in a fallen world. Sufficiency has everything to do with whether we can actually help those weighed down by their enslaving sins. Biblical counselors are not armchair theologians but pastoral theologians—active ministers of the gospel of Jesus Christ. They desire to connect hurting and troubled people to the timelessly relevant truths of Scripture and be used by the Holy Spirit as he graciously changes his people. This is a book about sufficiency, but it is also about loving people well as Jesus commands.

As pastors who spend time with other ministers, and as professors who teach biblical counseling to current and future pastors, we are convinced that two kinds of people neglect to use the Scriptures in counseling. First, there are those who do not understand the doctrine of the sufficiency of Scripture. Many do not understand that the content of Scripture directly addresses the manifold problems we all face in this life—no matter how extreme. This is true despite the fact that the Bible uses different language and categories to identify these problems. In many ways the purpose of this book is to correct those who have a mistaken view of sufficiency.

Second, there are conservative evangelicals who "believe the Bible" but do not want to spend the time necessary to help people with serious and specific problems. The work is just too hard. It seems too demanding truly to understand a complex, secularly defined problem in light of the Scriptures. It is too tiring to sit with a person week-in and week-out in the difficult, slow work of heart change. It is too challenging to discern what to say to a person who describes a problem the minister has never even thought about, much less struggled with. It is too much of a strain to walk the fine line between encouragement and exhortation with those who are either sinning in response to their suffering or suffering because of their sin.

There really are two kinds of people who avoid counseling. The first kind of person does not understand, and the second kind of person does not care.

Does it sound harsh to say that those who are reticent about doing the hard work of loving people through counseling simply might not care? Consider what the apostle Paul said in Gal 6:1–2, 9–10:

> Brothers if someone is caught in any wrongdoing, you who are spiritual should restore such a person with a gentle spirit, watching out for yourselves so you also won't be tempted. Carry one another's burdens; in this way you will fulfill the law of Christ. . . . So we must not get tired of doing good, for we will reap at the proper time if we don't give up. Therefore, as we have opportunity, we must work for the good of all, especially for those who belong to the household of faith.

The word *counseling* never appears in this text, but the passage is all about counseling as it is understood in contemporary culture. Paul described two basic categories of counselees. On the one hand are those who have sinned and have been "caught in wrongdoing." On the other hand are those who are suffering and are weighed down with "burdens."[1] For these two kinds of counselees, Paul described two basic ministry approaches. Gentle restoration is prescribed for those guilty of wrongdoing, and help in carrying the burdens is stipulated for those suffering under the weight of their struggles. Notice also that the activities of restoring and burden-bearing are not optional. Instead, the fulfillment of the law of Christ is at stake.[2] If we are to be faithful servants of

---

[1] "Burdens" here may refer to the weight that comes from the baggage of the wrongdoings mentioned earlier, but the word more likely refers to all kinds of struggles and sufferings experienced in this fallen world. See Ronald Y. K. Fung, *The Epistle to the Galatians*, New International Commentary on the New Testament (Grand Rapids: Eerdmans, 1988), 287.

[2] We join many commentators in seeing the law of Christ as a foil in Paul's argument against the Judaizers who were mandating that converted Gentiles still obey the Mosaic law. We also think it is helpful to see this as a possible reference to Jesus' new commandment which he originally gave in the upper room: "I give you a new commandment: Love one another. Just as I have loved you, you must

our master Christ—if we truly desire to obey his loving law—all Christians must engage their brothers and sisters in such ministry.

Many different responses typically come to mind when people hear these exhortations to love their fellow believers through counseling. "I'm not gifted for that kind of ministry." "I'm too busy, and I need to delegate the counseling load to others around me." "I'm too scared to try to help that kind of person." "I'll just preach to the congregation, and that should be good enough." Such excuses can sound wise, humble, or strategic. They often are well intentioned, but they fail to engage the fact that God commands all Christians to join in the interpersonal ministry of the Word.[3] To see this one only needs to carefully read the Gospels, which show what the life and ministry of Jesus was like in ministry to people. He preached publicly (a few sermons are recorded), and he ministered personally to people in the context of conversation (much more is recorded on this aspect). He taught and modeled that it's not the primacy of preaching but instead the primacy of God and his Word in both sectors—public and personal—that every church should practice. If one continues to read in the rest of the New Testament, one quickly finds Paul following Christ's example of ministering God's Word publicly, from house to house and from person to person (Acts 20:20; Col 1:28–29). Why do so many today think they are following Christ's example when they only preach and won't minister personally to their people? Do they think they are busier than Christ or Paul? Do they think perhaps they can improve on Christ's and Paul's model of discipleship?

We both have pastored at churches (small and large), and it amazes us to see men who say they are pastors of the church but do only one aspect of pastoring. They believe they have a special calling to preach, but the Scriptures do not teach that anywhere. Instead, Scripture teaches the role of a pastor is to equip others for

---

also love one another" (John 13:34). See J. B. Lightfoot, *Notes on the Epistles of St. Paul* (1895; repr., Grand Rapids: Zondervan, 1980), 216; F. F. Bruce, *Paul: Apostle of the Heart Set Free* (Grand Rapids: Eerdmans, 1977), 187.

[3] Though there are some, who for reasons of calling and vocation do more personal ministry of the Word than others, all are called to be involved in some way.

the work of ministry (Eph 4:11ff). So the pastor must be ready to minister the Word of God publicly in preaching and also personally in counseling.

Neglecting such a significant aspect of the pastoral ministry would be like one of us going to his wife and saying, "Honey, I can only provide for you. If you want someone to talk to or need other help, I have a name of someone who would be pleased to meet with you. It might even cost you some money." We both think we might end up single if we tried that with our wives. Yet how many in ministry are doing that very thing in their churches? We believe the Scripture is clear that pastors who don't want to get involved with their sheep (at the level of counseling and discipleship) really aren't faithfully doing the full work of the pastor.

For those who are passionate about spreading the vision for Bible-based counseling ministry, we must continue fighting on two fronts. We must make the case that the Bible is indeed sufficient for all counseling needs. However, we must simultaneously urge all Christians toward the battlefield of love—the task of walking with broken people in the work of counseling. Understanding Scripture is only half the battle. The other half is acknowledging and recommitting to the fact that true and lasting change in people's lives depends on radical, sacrificial love experienced from each person's local body of believers. The stories in this book make clear that either one of these values without the other would never have led to substantial and lasting change. Offering only the precepts of Scripture while withholding practical help is empty religion; offering only practical help while tossing out a few life tips is superficial and shortsighted.

The purpose of this book is vigorously to highlight the resources in Scripture. We are also compelled to drive home the high calling and sacrificial commitment to love people. Consider 1 Thessalonians.

In one passage Paul described three kinds of people who need help: "We exhort you brothers: warn those who are irresponsible, comfort the discouraged, help the weak, be patient with everyone" (1 Thess 5:14). Unruly Christians need admonishment and rebuke;

discouraged people need comfort and encouragement; and weak people need help and assistance. What is fascinating about the stories in this book is that most of the counselees fit into all three categories. The stories here were "hard cases" not only because the problems often sounded scary but because ministering wisely to them required a complex and savvy approach. It required wearing several different hats.

What does all of this have to teach us about loving people through counseling ministry? Counseling the hard cases of the world requires an awareness of how the Bible richly informs us on all the many different counselees it is possible to encounter: the unruly, fainthearted, and weak. The essential element 1 Thessalonians requires for counseling each one, however, is *patience*. Every person and every situation require patience. Whether the person is unruly, discouraged, or needing practical help, patience is a requirement to truly help. This means that God frowns on ministry done out of frustration. This has absolutely everything to do with showing love in counseling ministry because patience is a defining element of love in the Bible (1 Cor 13:4). Therefore, if we claim to be loving ministers of the Word, we must minister to people in a patient way whether they are high-handed sinners, strained saints, or weakened sufferers.

The people in this book definitely required patience in the midst of their difficulties. The counselors who ministered to them were busy and had other good things that they could have been doing. In spite of that, they took the time necessary to walk with these people down the long road of encountering hope, joy, and Christ in the midst of their difficulties. They were patient.

This is exactly what love does. Love is patient and kind, and it considers the interests of others above oneself (Phil 2:3–4). All of the understanding in the world about what the Bible teaches would not have come to life for the people in this book were it not for the generous, wise, careful, and sacrificial love of Spirit-indwelt individuals who each embraced the divine "interruption," laid down other important things in their lives, and ran to help their fellow Christians. After making such a statement, it is also helpful to observe that when we are seeking to minister to others in need, it actually is a mistake to think that the counselee is the only one in need. Actually, all of God's people in the counseling room are in need of growing in their faith in Christ. The Holy Spirit does not take a sabbatical on the counselor's sanctification while he or she is ministering to others. Faithful counselors should regularly say after counseling, "Wow, I needed to hear what they said" or "I needed to hear what Scripture said." So it may be that those who ask for help are in greater need (like the difficult cases in this book), but let us never forget that the counselor is also in need of growing during the counseling sessions. We are all in need of God's grace and his gospel truths as we run together in the race set before us, looking at our Savior Jesus Christ (Heb 12:1–2).

There really are two kinds of people who avoid counseling. The first kind of person does not understand the Bible, and the second does not care about people the way Jesus exemplifies and commands. We hope that hearing the stories in this book encourages you to grow in both areas—in the wisdom of God's Word and in the care for God's people. May God empower the body of Christ to speak to one another in wise and loving ways and thereby grow up into our head, who is Jesus Christ the Lord.

Contributors

John Babler, Ph.D.

John serves as the assistant professor of counseling at Southwestern Baptist Theological Seminary in Fort Worth, Texas. He is also a chaplain with both the Edgecliff Village Fire Department and Raceway Ministries.

Kevin Carson, D.Min.

Kevin serves as a professor in biblical counseling at Baptist Bible College, Springfield, Missouri. He is also the senior pastor of Sonrise Baptist Church. Kevin is a council member of the Biblical Counseling Coalition.

Laura Hendrickson, M.D.

Laura Hendrickson, trained as a medical doctor and a board-certified psychiatrist, presently ministers as a biblical counselor, author, speaker, and consultant through Gospel Balm Ministries. She is the author of *Finding Your Child's Way on the Autism Spectrum: Discovering Unique Strengths;* coauthor of *Will Medicine Stop the Pain; Finding God's Healing for Anxiety, Depression, and Other Challenging Emotions*; and *When Good Kids Make Bad Choices: Help and Hope for Hurting Parents.* Laura is a council member of the Biblical Counseling Coalition.

Garrett Higbee, Psy.D.

Garrett is the executive director of Harvest Bible Chapel's Biblical Soul Care Ministries in Chicago, Illinois. He is also the founder and president of Twelve Stones Ministries in Brown County, Indiana. Dr. Higbee was trained as a clinical psychologist with a specialty in family counseling. Garrett is a board member of the Biblical Counseling Coalition.

Robert Jones, D.Min.

Bob serves as a biblical counseling professor at Southeastern Baptist Theological Seminary in Wake Forest, North Carolina. He is a certified conciliator, adjunct instructor, and church intervention team leader/trainer with Peacemaker Ministries. He is also the author of *Uprooting Anger.* Bob is a council member of the Biblical Counseling Coalition.

Heath Lambert, Ph.D.

Heath Lambert serves as the assistant professor of biblical counseling at The Southern Baptist Theological Seminary in Louisville, Kentucky, and at their undergraduate institution, Boyce College. He also serves as the pastor of biblical living at Crossing Church overseeing their counseling and marriage ministries. Heath is the author of *The Biblical Counseling Movement After Adams*. He is a council member of the Biblical Counseling Coalition.

Martha Peace, RN, BSN

Martha serves as a biblical counselor at Faith Bible Church Counseling Ministry, in Sharpsburg, Georgia. She is the author of *The Excellent Wife; Becoming a Titus 2 Woman*; *Damsels in Distress*; and coauthored *Tying the Knot Tighter* and *The Faithful Parent*.

Stuart Scott, D.Min.

Stuart serves as an associate professor of biblical counseling at The Southern Baptist Theological Seminary. He is the author of *The Exemplary Husband*, and coauthor of *The Faithful Parent.* He is a council member of the Biblical Counseling Coalition.

Steve Viars, D.Min.

Steve Viars serves as the senior pastor at Faith Baptist Church and biblical counselor at Faith Biblical Counseling Ministries in Lafayette, Indiana. He is the author of *Putting Your Past in Its Place*. He is a board member of the Biblical Counseling Coalition.

Dan Wickert, M.D.

Dan is a practicing physician (OB/GYN) in Lafayette, Indiana. He also serves as a biblical counselor at Faith Baptist Counseling Ministry.

Name Index

Scripture Index